SHARKS

WS
WHITE STAR PUBLISHERS

Texts
Angelo Mojetta

Editorial production
Valeria Manferto De Fabianis
Laura Accomazzo

Graphic Design
Patrizia Balocco Lovisetti
Clara Zanotti
Anna Galliani

Drawings
Monica Falcone
Elisabetta Ferrero

Translation
A.B.A., Milan

CONTENTS

© 1997, 2004 White Star s.p.a.
Via Candido Sassone, 22-24
13100 Vercelli, Italy.
www.whitestar.it

Revised Edition in 2004

ISBN-13: 978-88-540-0128-2

Reprints:
 2 3 4 5 6   11 10 09 08 07

Printed in China

THE BIRTH OF A LEGEND

D

E

Floating in the water at sunset, when the sea bed beneath begins to grow hazy, or at midday in the open sea, where the rays of the sun are swallowed up in the bottomless depths of the ocean, it's hard not to feel a vague sense of unease which makes you sharpen your eyes and produces a slight surge of adrenaline that puts all your senses on the alert. Suddenly, the many legends which recount that the sea is inhabited by dangerous unknown creatures, constantly lying in wait, emerge from your land-dweller's sub-conscious. None of them is real enough to constitute a threat, but the shark is, and it's sharks that we have in mind, even if we don't always admit it.

There's a common saying that the only place where sharks are not encountered is on dry land, yet that is where we have to look for them in order to reconstruct their history and discover the secret of their success. People often wonder how they became one of the best-known inhabitants of the sea. The most common version in the western world is the Biblical account: "And God said, Let the waters bring forth abundantly the moving creatures that hath life… And God created great whales, and every living creature that moveth, which the waters brought forth abundantly, after their kind…" Specific references to sharks are made in other accounts, recounted by populations perhaps more familiar with the sea. For example, the inhabitants of the Bismarck Archipelago tell of two brothers, To Kabinana and To Karvuvu, who created all things. To Karvuvu was less careful than his brother, and in addition to useful things, he also created sharks. What he wanted was a companion to help him catch fish, but his creation escaped, and since then has roamed the seas, devouring fish and man alike.

F

A - This is how Swedish historian and cartographer Olaus Magnus imagined sharks and sea monsters in his Historia de gentibus septentrionalibus (1555).

B - This 1870 engraving, published in a zoology treatise, shows a shark attacking a shipwrecked sailor. The scene is quite realistic, and shows that the animal's dangerous reputation was already well established.

C - According to an early 20th-century French newspaper, this print portrays the perilous escape of a number of convicts from the infamous Devil's Island, French Guiana.

D, E - In his Cosmographia Universalis (1550), Sebastian Munster described the monstrous creatures that made navigation dangerous. Some of them (e.g. those marked K, N and S) may have derived from exaggerated descriptions of sharks.

F - In Brehms, one of the best-known zoology treatises of the 19th century, sharks were presented as bloodthirsty creatures always ready to devour shipwrecked sailors.

A

B

A - A sea serpent
attacks a whale. This
scene was witnessed
by Captain Drenan,
skipper of the Pauline.
According to some
experts, the legends of
the sea snake may
have originated from
sightings of the whale
shark.

C - This engraving is
one of the oldest
illustrations of the jaws
and teeth of the great
white shark; it was part
of a study conducted
by Danish geologist
and anatomist Niels
Stensen on a great
white shark captured
off Leghorn in 1666.

B - In this attractive
engraving with its
chiaroscuro effects,
Gustave Doré imagined
the dawn of the world
and the creatures that
populated its waters.

Over 550 million years ago, life was
already well established in the waters
of the planet where it originated.
If we had a time machine and could
program a dive in the warm, shallow
seas of the Cambrian period we would
find a world which, according to
palaeontologists' reconstructions,
featured a wealth of fascinating
contrasts. Sea scorpions nearly 3
metres long, great jellyfish and
primitive cephalopods would swim
over sea beds covered with sponges
and corals or odd shells, similar to
the present bivalves but unrelated to
them. We would see long stretches
of unusual conical formations
belonging to archaeocyathids,
sponge-like creatures which, like
modern corals, were able to build
reefs, providing refuge for annelids,
holothurians, ostracods, and trilobites
with their three-sectioned shells.
The waters would be teeming with life
forms and organisms quite different
from those we are used to.
Strange as it may seem, they were all
experiments conducted by Evolution,
each one engaged in conquering and
exploiting its own ecological niche.
But none of them could be compared
with a fish, let alone a shark.
At the end of the Cambrian period,
half a billion years ago, there was a
mass extinction – one of the great
catastrophes with which Nature
puts her creatures to the test.
After only 80 million years' dominion
over the sea beds, the

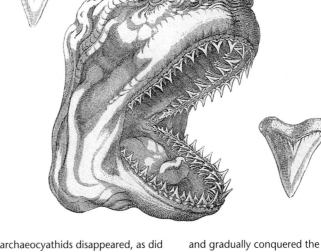

C

archaeocyathids disappeared, as did
some molluscs and trilobites.
The areas left free were divided
up between the survivors which
multiplied rapidly, developing new
shapes and abilities. Brachiopods
and molluscs became the prevalent
creatures in the shallow waters of
aquatic environments which occupied
much of the present-day continental
land masses.
The free waters were the place where
cephalopods developed and fought
one another. Originally a simple
conchiferous mollusc with septa and
siphons enabling them to balance in
the water (the oldest of all known
forms), they became larger and larger,

and gradually conquered the
underwater world. The Nautiloids of
the Ordovician (a period that lasted
65 million years), the ancestors of the
modern pearly Nautilus of the Indo-
pacific, swam in a vertical position
and developed larger and larger
shells. The Nautiloids needed calcium
for their cell metabolism but
it was over-abundant in the sea,
so they disposed of the excess by
converting it into straight or conical
shells which could grow to 10 metres
long. This size was mainly due to
the increased volume of the inner
chambers designed to
counterbalance the weight of the
limestone deposits, a necessary

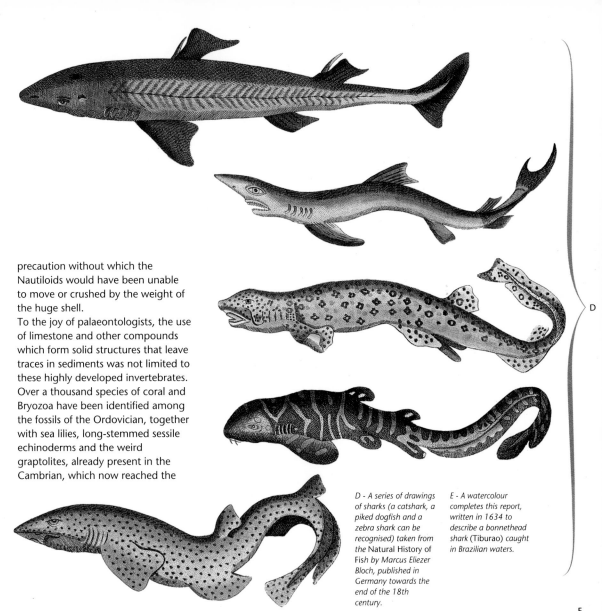

precaution without which the Nautiloids would have been unable to move or crushed by the weight of the huge shell.

To the joy of palaeontologists, the use of limestone and other compounds which form solid structures that leave traces in sediments was not limited to these highly developed invertebrates. Over a thousand species of coral and Bryozoa have been identified among the fossils of the Ordovician, together with sea lilies, long-stemmed sessile echinoderms and the weird graptolites, already present in the Cambrian, which now reached the

D - A series of drawings of sharks (a catshark, a piked dogfish and a zebra shark can be recognised) taken from the Natural History of Fish *by Marcus Eliezer Bloch, published in Germany towards the end of the 18th century.*

E - A watercolour completes this report, written in 1634 to describe a bonnethead shark (Tiburao) caught in Brazilian waters.

peak of their development so that they constitute the major index fossils of the period. Graptolites were colonial planktonic organisms; the colonies consisting of small overlapping annular segments that branched at more or less regular intervals, developing small chitinous cups in which the individual creatures were lodged.

These were the dominant elements, at least those found most frequently. However, in the older strata bordering on those dating from the Cambrian, and almost certainly even earlier, incomplete fossils have been found which must have belonged to primitive vertebrates.

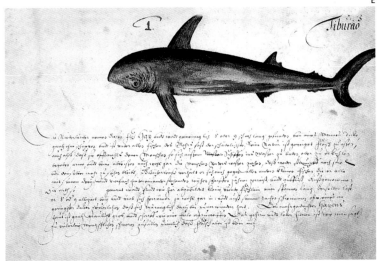

THE FIRST FISH

The true forebears of the vertebrates, including man, are still concealed in the realm of theory, but they are probably to be found in the group of filter-feeding invertebrates that includes life forms similar to the ascidians.

The latter apparently have nothing in common with the vertebrates, but this is only true of the adults, as their larvae present some extraordinary similarities with common tadpoles. The *Urochordata*, *Cephalochordata* and *Vertebrata*, the three sub-phyla into which the *Chordata* are divided, are situated at the top of the evolutionary scale. Their common denominators, at least in the embryonic forms, are three characteristics found in no other animal: a hollow dorsal nerve cord, a set of gill slits and a notochord. The presence of these features suggests that despite their different appearance, the primitive Chordates were closely related to the vertebrates, and constituted an essential stage in their evolution. However, not all experts agree with the theory that ascidians are the most direct ancestor of fish. According to some researchers, this honour goes to the far more evolved amphioxus, an extraordinary Cephalochordate that still survives, and in some areas (such as China) is so abundant that it is used for food. This organism, on which thousands of studies have been conducted, seems to have preceded the ascidians, which are believed to have separated from it, choosing a less active life.

The clays and schists of Burgess (Canada), which is famous among palaeontologists because some of the oldest known fossils were found there, still retain traces of organisms resembling the present amphioxus. The sequence of the changes that led to the diversification of forms is unknown, but at some stage, one of the evolutionary lines which were experimenting with new ways of life, each independently of the other, must have developed a degree of specialisation in swimming which significantly differentiated it from

other animal groups. The most plausible theory is that it was a filter-feeding organism, originally consisting of a few segments, which developed a primitive notochord that was rigid but flexible, surrounded by muscles arranged in an orderly sequence. The muscles must have been able to contract in a co-ordinated manner and impart lateral flexions to the notochord which pushed forward the new creature by a more effective method of locomotion – swimming. It later developed a protective outer shell and an axial skeleton consisting of jointed vertebra with lateral projections that provided better support for the increasingly developed muscle masses.

Traces of those which, at least because of their habits, can be described as fish, are now to be found in marine deposit rocks, but there is evidence to suggest that they were transported to the sea from freshwater environments after their deaths. This can be deduced from a comparison between the concentrations of mineral salts dissolved in the blood of marine and freshwater fish. Despite the obvious differences between the two types of habitat, the amount of salts is very similar in both cases, and closer to that found on average in freshwater environments.

This means that saltwater fish had to solve some complex physiological problems associated with the need to maintain their fluids in osmotic balance with the surrounding marine environment, which contained a wealth of dissolved substances. However, evolution teaches that problems like this are always solved in time in one way or another, even drastically if necessary, by the extinction of the species.

The first fish did not have to overcome this obstacle, as they originated in fresh water or the slightly salt water found at river estuaries. The lucky discovery of armoured bony plates in which the imprint of the soft parts they protected was visible has enabled the morphology and anatomy of these very ancient vertebrates to

This diagram shows the evolution of the vertebrates that colonised and lived in the fresh waters of the earth, starting from the Silurian. They included some shark genera such as *Ctenacanthus* and *Xenacanthus*. (The drawing is complementary to the illustration on p. 12).

Silurian (A):
1. Anaspida
2. Tremataspida
3. Cyathaspida

Lower Devonian (B):
4. Cephalaspida
5. Acanthodii
6. Palaeoniscida
7. Pteraspida
8. Placoderms

Upper Devonian (C):
9. Psammosteida
10. Acanthodii
11. Lungfish
12. Rhipidistia
13. Placoderms
14. Arthrodira
15. Ctenacanthus (shark)

Upper Carboniferous (D):
16. Amphibia: Lepospondyli
17. Amphibia: Labyrinthondontia
18. Lungfish
19. Palaeoniscida
20. Rhipidistia
21. Xenacanthus (shark)

Lower Permian (E):
22. Lungfish
23. Reptilia: Embolomeri
24. Nectridea
25. Acanthodii
26. Palaeoniscida

Upper Permian (F):
27. Lungfish
28. Reptilia: Embolomeri
29. Nectridea
30. Palaeoniscida
31. Acanthodii

Middle Triassic (G):
32. Reptilia: Thecodontia
33. Amphibia: Labyrinthodontia
34. Turtle (Triassochelys)
35. Amphibia: Plagiosauria
36. Holostei

Upper Triassic (H):
37. Reptilia: Thecodontia
38. Amphibia: Labyrinthodontia
39. Turtle (Triassochelys)
40. Amphibia: Plagiosauria
41. Holostei

Jurassic (I):
42. Holostei
43. Crocodile
44/45. Teleosteans
46. Salamander
47. Turtle

Cretaceous (J):
48. Teleosteans
49. Salamander
50. Crocodile
51. Turtle
52. Holostei
53. Amphibia: Anura

Eocene (K):
54. Salamander
55. Turtle
56/57. Teleosteans
58. Amphibia: Anura
59. Crocodile

Oligocene/Miocene (L):
60. Turtle
61. Salamander
62/63. Teleosteans
64. Crocodile
65. Amphibia: Anura

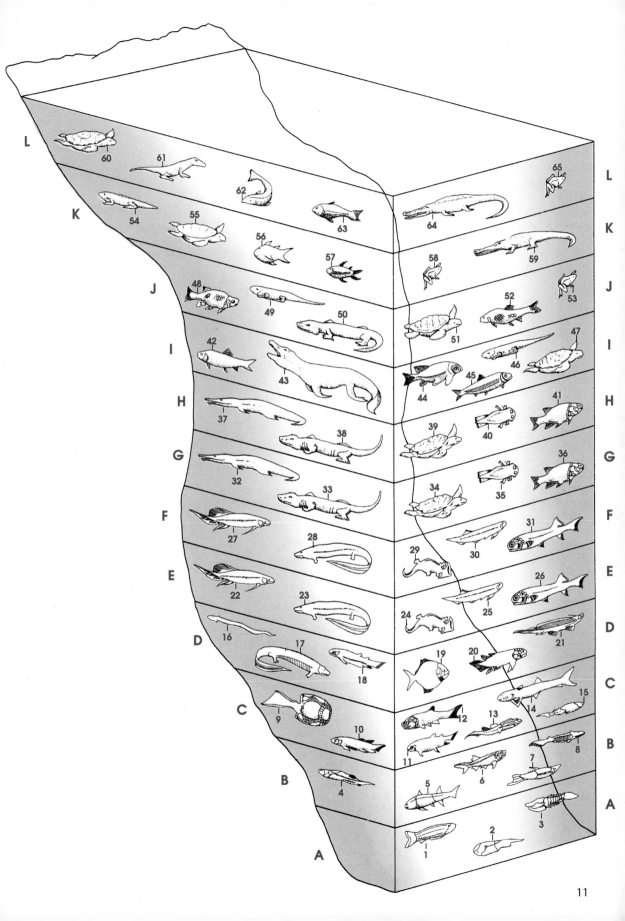

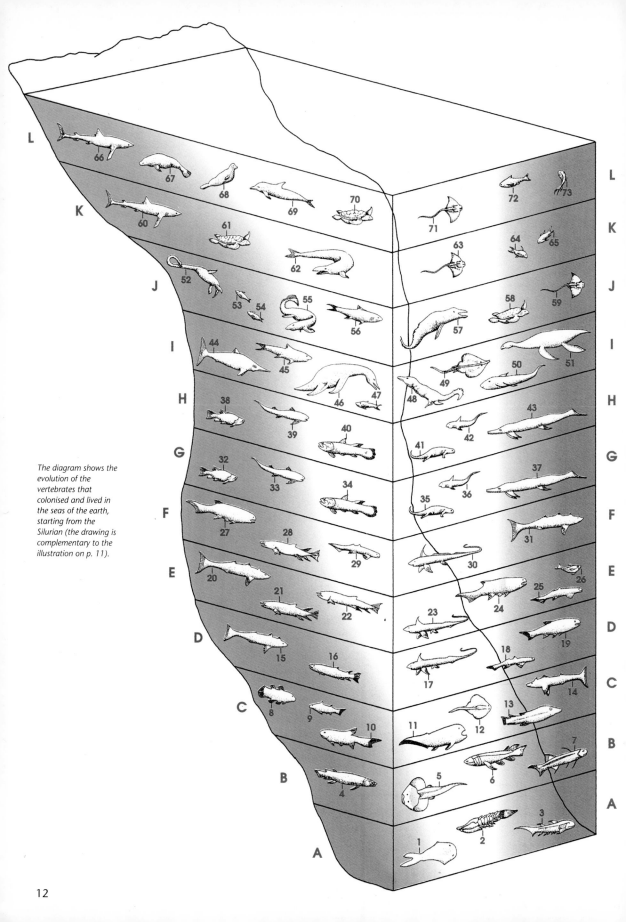

The diagram shows the evolution of the vertebrates that colonised and lived in the seas of the earth, starting from the Silurian (the drawing is complementary to the illustration on p. 11).

Silurian (A):
1. Thelodonti
2. Cyathaspida
3. Acanthodii

Lower Devonian (B):
4. Lungfish
5. Placoderms
6. Rhipidistia
7. Acanthodii

Upper Devonian (C):
8. Coelacanthidae
9. Acanthodii
10. Palaeoniscida
11. Arthrodira
12. Placoderms
13. Lungfish
14. Cladoselache
   (shark)

Upper Carboniferous (D):
15. Cladoselache
   (shark)
16. Coelacanthidae
17. Holocephali
18. Cladodontidae
   (shark)
19. Acanthodii

Lower Permian (E):
20. Cladoselache
   (shark)
21/22. Coelacanthidae
23. Holocephali
24. Acanthodii
25. Cladodontidae
   (shark)
26. Holocephali

Upper Permian (F):
27. Acanthodii
28. Coelacanthidae
29. Cladodontidae
   (shark)
30. Holocephali
31. Cladoselache

Middle Triassic (G):
32. Holostei
33. Cladodontidae
   (shark)
34. Coelacanthidae
35. Reptilia: Placodontia
36. Holocephali
37. Ichthyosaurus

Upper Triassic (H):
38. Holostei
39. Cladodontidae
   (shark)
40. Coelacanthidae
41. Reptilia:
   Placodontia
42. Holocephali
43. Ichthyosaurus

Jurassic (I):
44. Teleosteans
45. Ichthyosaurus
46. Plesiosaurus
47. Teleosteans
48. Crocodile
49. Rajiformes
50. Holocephali
51. Plesiosaurus

Cretaceous (J):
52. Plesiosaurus
53/54. Teleosteans
55. Plesiosaurus
56. Shark
57. Mosasaurus
58. Turtle
59. Rajiformes

Eocene (K):
60. Shark
61. Turtle
62. Basilosaurus
63. Rajiformes
64/65. Teleosteans

Oligocene/Miocene (L):
66. Shark
67. Dugong
68. Seal
69. Dolphin
70. Rajiformes
72/73. Teleosteans

be reconstructed; they had a small, round, immobile mouth which suggests that they were mainly filter feeders. Because of their particular mouth these "proto-fish" have been attributed to the superclass *Agnatha*, and because of their bony plates to the class of the Ostracoderms, a name derived from Greek, like many others used in science, which means "with a skin-like shell".

Although the Ostracoderms had a mouth, this part of the anatomy did not feature the typical division into upper and lower jaw. In this respect they resembled the *Agnatha* which have survived to the present day, namely lampreys and hagfish. Some of them have retained the placid habits of filter-feeding creatures, while others have turned into fearful parasites that fasten onto other fish with their sucker-like mouths, equipped with horny denticles which rasp the victim's flesh. The first fairly complete fossils of Ostracoderms, which are divided into the two sub-phyla *Pteraspidomorphi* and *Cephalaspidomorphi*, are those of species that lived in the Ordovician such as *Astrapis desiderata*, whose name seems to indicate the anxiety with which researchers had waited to fill one of the gaps in their knowledge. These were fish-like aquatic animals with unpaired fins (dorsal, caudal and anal) that were well differentiated and maintained their balance in the water while they swam.

Ostracoderms were 20-30 cm long on average, but specimens over one metre long have been found, especially among the *Pteraspidomorphi*, which comprise numerous species grouped into over 150 genera. The wide bony plates typical of these ancient *Agnatha* were inserted into the skin of the head and the front of the trunk, while the rest of the body and the tail were covered with dermal scales. Apart from the dermal skeleton, an interior bony skeleton has also been identified in most Ostracoderms. They lived on the sea bed, where they could easily rest on their flat underbellies.

Here they foraged among the sediments in search of the tiny organisms they fed on, filtering them through well-developed gills which fulfilled the dual function of feeding and breathing.

The Ostracoderms developed at the beginning of the Devonian, known as the era of fish; they dominated the waters and escaped from the gigantic arthropods of the period, which sometimes resembled water scorpions with awesome claws, with the aid of their armour and their more agile movement. The final blow to their existence, which continued until the end of the Palaeozoic, was struck by an extraordinary innovation that was to prove crucial to the subsequent evolution of all the vertebrates: the mobile mouth.

The novelty lay in the transformation of the third branchial arch, which lost the task of supporting the gills and was modified to support the mouth. With the aid of their articulated jaws these new fish, known as Gnathostomata (having a jawed mouth) could follow and kill their prey more efficiently; this meant that they no longer had to follow a monotonous diet mainly consisting of tiny organisms buried in the mud, and eliminated the need to stay close to the sea bed.

At the peak of their evolution, the Placoderms had already exploited the new shape of the cranial bone and adapted their jaws to every type of diet; their jaw system is known as autostylic jaw-suspension, because the upper jaw articulated directly with the neurocranium. Some, like *Dunkleosteus*, had sharp teeth to pierce and lacerate their prey; others, like *Bothriolepis*, had flat teeth resembling grindstones to crush the armour or shells of their prey. The appearance of the mobile mouth can be compared to the discovery of tools by man and, like that discovery, was to revolutionise nature.

Like the Ostracoderms, the new fish had bony plates which clearly shows their origin, although this was probably not one of the most perfected evolutionary forms.

Reconstruction of their shapes demonstrates that the first Placoderms were squat and heavy, at a time when the armoured *Agnatha* had already evolved towards agile, elegant shapes.

The new fish, equipped with paired fins (the pectoral and ventral fins) and armour of varying degrees of development, which in some cases was reduced to thin scales or even non-existent, demonstrated greater mastery of swimming.

As a result of these characteristics, the number of Placoderms rapidly increased, and they were differentiated into various evolutionary branches, the major ones being the *Arthrodira* and

Antiarchi. The former were strongly-armoured active predators with two articulated shields; a front shield to protect the head and pharyngeal region, and one on the trunk. The latter, also armoured, were typical benthic (deep-sea) fish, distinguished by their inferior mouth, narrower jaws and jointed pectoral fins, and had a pair of accessory sacs believed to act as lungs. At first they lived in all fresh waters, then in brackish water; eventually, as they grew larger and larger (up to 3 metres long), they conquered the marine environment, causing the disappearance of all other fish. Other experts believe that the stages leading to the appearance of the

sharks should be interpreted differently, starting not with the Placoderms but with the *Acanthodii*, which they consider to be the first fish to have developed jaws, over 400 million years ago. Because of their shape, these fish have been described as thorny sharks, but in fact they are unrelated to true sharks, spiny or otherwise.

They are so called because of the strong spines at the front of all the fins except the tailfin, which was asymmetrical like that of the sharks. The paired fins of modern fish probably originated with the *Acanthodii*. In some of them, the pectoral and ventral appendages are just one of the various spiny appendages, with a more or less developed fleshy membrane, which ran all the way along the trunk. Later, these appendages may have disappeared, except for a front pair and a rear pair destined to become the paired fins we know today.

The body of the *Acanthodii* was covered with diamond-shaped bony scales, similar to the ganoid type still possessed by the last representatives of the Lepisosteiformes, primitive bony fish of Northern and Central America. Whether or not they constitute a branch of the Ostracoderms, the *Acanthodii* were their contemporaries, and were equally doomed to extinction, though at a different time.

The Placoderms had disappeared almost entirely by the end of the Devonian era (350 million years ago), except for a genus that survived to the end of the Carboniferous period (65 million years later), whereas the

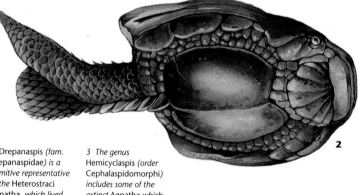

1 The Ostracoderms are the oldest known vertebrates, and were the first fish to colonise the waters. They developed in fresh water, and had no upper or lower jaw (Agnatha class). The head and trunk were covered with large bony plates, while the rest of the body was covered with smaller dermal scales.

2 Drepanaspis (fam. Drepanaspidae) is a primitive representative of the Heterostraci Agnatha, which lived from the Silurian to the Devonian. This genus had a typical flattened shape with a very wide frontal region where the head and gills were located, with the mouth situated right at the front.

3 The genus Hemicyclaspis (order Cephalaspidomorphi) includes some of the extinct Agnatha which were part of the Ostracoderm group of armoured fish. Like the extant Agnatha, they did not have articulated jaws. They had a single naris and numerous gill slits.

Acanthodii are believed to have survived to the end of the Permian era (230 million years ago). With a process very similar to that involved in the development of the Placoderms, the new evolutionary lines of fish began to appear in the waters of that far distant past; millions of years later they were to inhabit all the waters of the planet, and one of their most perfected branches, the *Crossopterygii* (lobefins), actually lived on dry land. While the primitive *Agnatha* were about to be driven

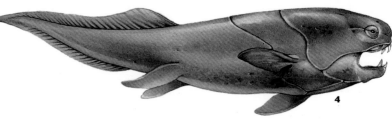

4 *The* Dinichthys, *the great predators of the Devonian, were members of the Placoderms, a primitive group of jawed fish* with robust bony plates on the head and on the front of the body that formed an articulated pair of defensive shields.

to extinction by the Placoderms, some Placoderms had already set off on a diverging evolutionary route, and were destined not only to achieve rapid success, but to survive to the present day. It should be borne in mind that these developments took place with overlapping time scales, although it somewhat complicates understanding of the stages of evolution and the appearance of the various orders and families, which often took place during the same period. The oldest class which, at least at the beginning, perhaps maintained the greatest resemblance to its ancestors, was differentiated mainly by the loss of the outer armour and the possession of an internal skeleton consisting only of cartilage. The Chondrichthyes or cartilaginous fish had appeared, and with them the fish that this volume is all about: the shark.

5 *The genus* Climatius *is a member of the Acanthodii, a group of primitive fish that lived in both salt water and fresh water from the Devonian to the Permian periods. These fish, which had bony* elements in the inner skeleton and therefore resembled the present-day Osteichthyes, are also called spiny sharks because of the robust spines that reinforced the fins, and the upward-pointing tail.

6 *The* Sarcopterygii, *here represented by* Osteolepis, *were fish with typically fleshy paired fins which had an internal skeletal support. They were* particularly common in fresh water in the Mid and Upper Devonian periods (375-345 million years ago), and the first terrestrial vertebrates originated from them.

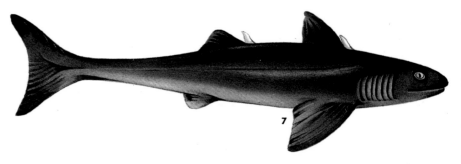

7 *The members of the* Cladoselache *genus (family Cladoselachidae) which lived in the Upper Devonian era are* considered the ancestors of the sharks. They had two dorsal fins with robust spines, and no anal fin.

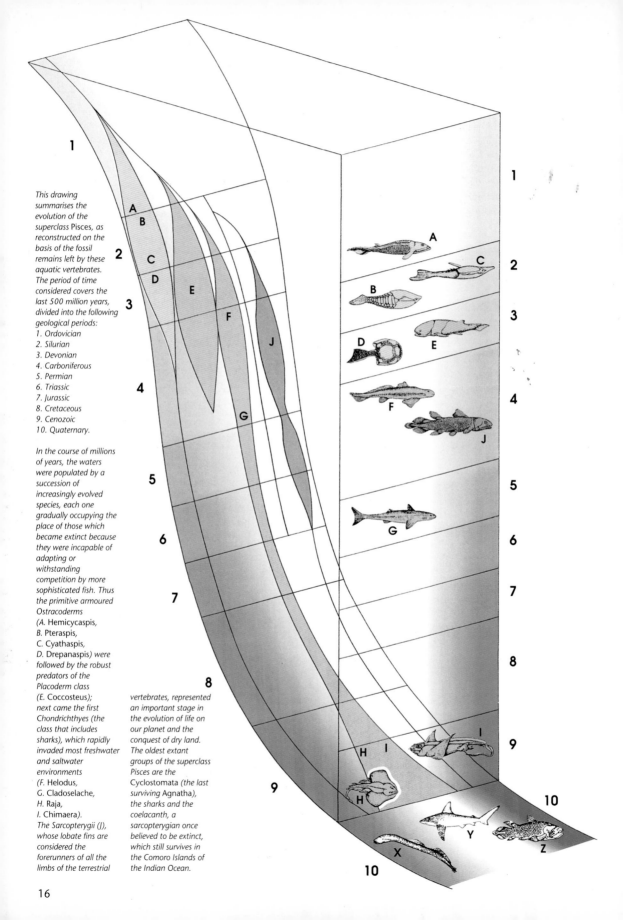

This drawing summarises the evolution of the superclass Pisces, as reconstructed on the basis of the fossil remains left by these aquatic vertebrates. The period of time considered covers the last 500 million years, divided into the following geological periods:
1. Ordovician
2. Silurian
3. Devonian
4. Carboniferous
5. Permian
6. Triassic
7. Jurassic
8. Cretaceous
9. Cenozoic
10. Quaternary.

In the course of millions of years, the waters were populated by a succession of increasingly evolved species, each one gradually occupying the place of those which became extinct because they were incapable of adapting or withstanding competition by more sophisticated fish. Thus the primitive armoured Ostracoderms
(A. Hemicycaspis,
B. Pteraspis,
C. Cyathaspis,
D. Drepanaspis) were followed by the robust predators of the Placoderm class
(E. Coccosteus); next came the first Chondrichthyes (the class that includes sharks), which rapidly invaded most freshwater and saltwater environments
(F. Helodus,
G. Cladoselache,
H. Raja,
I. Chimaera).
The Sarcopterygii (J), whose lobate fins are considered the forerunners of all the limbs of the terrestrial vertebrates, represented an important stage in the evolution of life on our planet and the conquest of dry land. The oldest extant groups of the superclass Pisces are the Cyclostomata (the last surviving Agnatha), the sharks and the coelacanth, a sarcopterygian once believed to be extinct, which still survives in the Comoro Islands of the Indian Ocean.

16

THE SHARKS OF THE PAST

A and B - Sharks' teeth are the most important fossils used to reconstruct the evolution of marine fauna and discover the major biozones of the past. As a result of their composition, which makes them almost immune to attack by external agents, the teeth are perfectly preserved in fossiliferous rocks. However, identification of isolated sharks'

The evolutionary line from which the present sharks and rays (known to zoologists as elasmobranchii) and other cartilaginous fish such as the chimaeras (Holocephali) are believed to have originated, rapidly conquered the seas of the Devonian period. The word "rapidly" is obviously relative, as we refer to a geological time scale measured in millions of years. Their conquest of the seas of the past was by no means easy, as they had to compete with the Placoderms and defeat the

constituted a great step forward and an advantage in aquatic life, it has the disadvantage of disintegrating rapidly under the effect of atmospheric agents, so that well-preserved fossils are seldom found. Most of the sharks of the past are therefore described on the basis of small scattered remains, such as teeth, spines and dermal denticles. The latter, which derive from disintegration of the rough sharkskin, are perhaps the most abundant residues, but in view of their tiny size they are only used by micropalaeontologists.

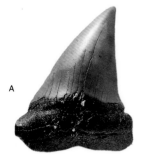
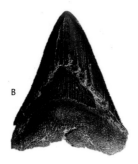

A   B

C

teeth is hampered by the different morphology characteristic of the animal's teeth (heterodont dentition). Among the most easily recognised are the triangular teeth of the Carcharodons, which were believed to be dragons' tongues or petrified thunderbolts in ancient times.

C - Whole sharks' jaws are rarely found. The jawbones are very fragile and liable to deteriorate in time, unlike the teeth, which can be used by an expert palaeontologist as the raw material to reconstruct parts like this jaw of a fossil Carcharodon.

D - The sharp teeth of the sand-tiger shark have been studied in detail since the first half of the 19th century, when systematic research into fossil sharks began.

voracious *Arthrodira*, which until then had had no enemies. During the Secondary Era the class had to share the waters with a myriad of other groups, including the bony fish, the holosteans (a special class of highly calcified fish) and, above all, the great sea reptiles (plesiosaurs and ichthyosaurs), against which even the most powerfully armed sharks were almost powerless. In fact, fossil finds demonstrate that most groups of proto-sharks had become extinct by the end of the Palaeozoic era (245 million years ago) together with the holosteans, and that the number of their species fell sharply as a result. The appearance of the present groups of sharks is believed to date from the Jurassic and Cretaceous periods (245-65 million years ago). They cannot be said to have changed much on average over the past 150 million years, with the result that a hypothetical evolution counter would see the shark hand almost stationary on zero. Their history also appears to be independent of that of other fish; it ends with them, and no further forms evolved from their evolutionary line. At least for the time being, the shark can be considered as a successfully concluded experiment. While the cartilaginous skeleton

D

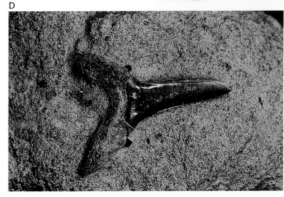

The first shark fossils are represented by a few teeth and spines, found in stratifications of the Devonian period (370 million years ago). This is perhaps not enough to determine the general appearance of the fish which, according to some experts, still resembled the Placoderms, but sufficient to establish the sequence of some stages in the evolutionary scale of the elasmobranchii.

The first teeth, in particular, consisted of a basal disc plate surmounted by a central conical cusp with two or more smaller tips at the side. This structural model is called cladodont, and all the sharks with similar teeth are called Cladodonts. The mouth was the terminal or slightly sub-terminal type. The upper jaw was rigidly fixed to the brain-case, and could only perform very limited movements. The lower jaw, supported by the cartilages of the second branchial arch, was also fixed at the rear. This kind of structure, considered to be a

primitive type, is now called amphistylic.

Some of the most important Cladodonts in the reconstruction of the history of sharks were those of the *Cladoselache* genus, typical inhabitants of the seas of the late Devonian period. To the delight of future palaeontologists, some of them on their deaths happened to land on sea beds covered with soft mud, lying under placid water, where they were partly buried and rapidly covered by new sediments. In the millions of years that followed, the mud grew compact and was pushed upwards in the form of great slabs of black schist, like those now commonly found around Lake Erie in the Great Lakes region of North America. Some well-preserved *Cladoselache* skeletons found here towards the end of the 19th century allowed the identification of a series of characteristics that suggested that this creature was not the ancestor of all sharks, as had until then been

supposed, but was preceded by unknown forms.

It had a tapered body (estimated to have been up to 2 metres long) with long narrow jaws and a tail which apparently had equal lobes, but was actually heterocercal in view of the conformation of the end of the spinal column. The strong tailfin, which had lateral keels similar to those of modern pelagic sharks, probably generated enough speed to enable the *Cladoselache* to catch the small fish on which it fed, swallowing them almost whole. On its back there were two dorsal fins with a strong anterior spine. The pectoral fins were fairly wide and triangular and, like the smaller ventral fins, supported by an interior cartilage structure. There were five gills, as is the general rule with sharks, and the rather large eyes, situated in the antero-superior position, were surrounded by a ring of small plates. This particular structure may have been associated with the need to convey light to the

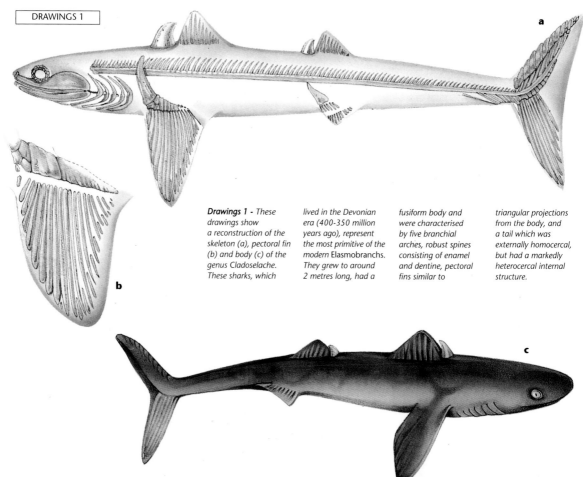

DRAWINGS 1

Drawings 1 - These drawings show a reconstruction of the skeleton (a), pectoral fin (b) and body (c) of the genus Cladoselache. These sharks, which lived in the Devonian era (400-350 million years ago), represent the most primitive of the modern Elasmobranchs. They grew to around 2 metres long, had a fusiform body and were characterised by five branchial arches, robust spines consisting of enamel and dentine, pectoral fins similar to triangular projections from the body, and a tail which was externally homocercal, but had a markedly heterocercal internal structure.

eyes when the fish went hunting in the deeper and darker waters, or with the need to protect these delicate organs against the damage that a prey such as an armoured fish could inflict on them when it struggled after being caught.

These sharks became extinct in the Mississippian period, at about the time when other members of the Cladodont family (the genus *Cladodus*, which includes various species of uncertain affinity) and Symmoriidae family (*Denaea* and *Symmorium*) disappeared; the common denominators of this last family were a single dorsal fin and no spine, but they differed in general appearance and in the form of the skeleton of the pectoral fins, which corresponded to different swimming abilities.

The *Stethacanthus*, a shark around one-metre-long, resembled the latter, and is worth mentioning because of a curious anatomical characteristic. In the position occupied by the first dorsal fin in other sharks, it had an appendage edged with a dense row of denticles, which was repeated on the top of the head.

Some experts believe that these denticulated areas were a means of defence, and suggest that this shark had such strong dorsal muscles that it could bend its head and back towards one another until they touched.

The two denticulated surfaces would thus be brought together to resemble the open mouth of a predatory shark, terrifying any aggressor.

In view of the position of the

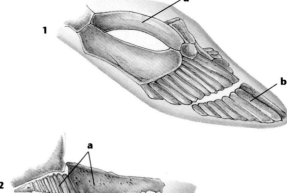

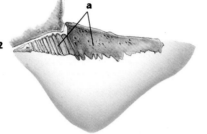

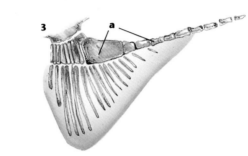

Drawings 2 - *These drawings show the skeletal parts of the pectoral fins of four species of primitive shark. In* Tristychius arcuatus *(1) there are two large basal bones (a) which recall the radius and ulna of the Amphibia; these bones are articulated with the pectoral girdle, while the radial bones (b) extend to the tip of the fin, making it more rigid.*
The fin of Symmorium reniforme *(2) is simpler; a set of small basal bones is followed by a more developed bone (the metapterygium).*
In Cladodus neilsoni *(3), the basal bones (a) are very elongated, which probably made the fin highly mobile.*
In Denaea fournieri *(4), the basal bones (a) are reduced to two elements articulated with the pectoral girdle and well-developed radial bones (b).*

denticles, others suggest, perhaps more plausibly, that their function was similar to that of the suckers of the remoras, and that the *Stethacanthus* could cling onto larger sharks or other fish with its denticles to hitch a ride. Other fish similar to the *Stethacanthus* (which was so characteristic that the Stethacanthidae family is named after it) were the *Damocles* and *Falcatus* sharks, which lived from the Devonian to the Pennsylvanian periods.

A highly specialised order, the *Xenacanthiformes*, developed at about the same time; it colonised the fresh waters of the whole world, living in rivers and shallow lakes. These sharks, of which various genera have been described (*Xenacanthus*, *Orthacanthus*, *Triodus* and *Tamiobatis*) lived for over

Drawing 3 -
Stethacanthus *was a shark around one metre long, which had a set of close-set denticles on the first dorsal fin and the head. Some experts* believe that these denticles acted as a defensive weapon, while others compare their function to that of the suckers of the remoras.

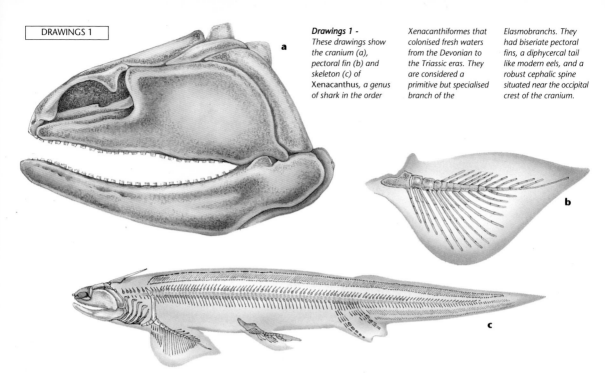

Drawings 1 -
These drawings show the cranium (a), pectoral fin (b) and skeleton (c) of Xenacanthus, a genus of shark in the order

Xenacanthiformes that colonised fresh waters from the Devonian to the Triassic eras. They are considered a primitive but specialised branch of the

Elasmobranchs. They had biseriate pectoral fins, a diphycercal tail like modern eels, and a robust cephalic spine situated near the occipital crest of the cranium.

200 million years, especially in Australia, where they became extinct in the Triassic period. They had pleuracanthid dentition, namely teeth with three cusps (two lateral ones and a smaller central one) and a flat base with a button-like projection which was articulated with the next tooth. The tapering body unusually had two anal fins, and especially a long cephalic spine preceding the dorsal fin, which extended along most of the back. The tail was diphycercal (pointed).

The fossils found have enabled the two genera *Xenacanthus* and *Orthacanthus* to be distinguished easily. In the former, the spine had a flat section and a row of denticles on the sides. In the latter the spine had a rounded section and a double row of lateral denticles. Although they were specialised, they retained the type of cranium typical of the Cladodonts, with amphistylic jaw-suspension.

The next stage of evolution, which definitely brings us to the modern sharks or *Euselachii*, according to the latest classifications, was represented by the Ctenacanthiformes, very few remains of which have been found apart from the two strong spines

situated in front of the dorsal spines, easily recognisable by experts because of their longitudinal grooves and osteodentin ornamentation. The two spines differed in terms of orientation; the front spine was steeply inclined, while the almost vertical rear spine preceded a fin supported by a basal plate and a number of rays, a structure which anticipated the fins of the future sharks. The Ctenacanthiformes lived in the waters off the east coast of

America and the North European continent, especially during the Carboniferous era, as demonstrated by the remains of a specimen attributed to the genus *Goodrichthys* found in Scotland; it was just under 2.5 metres long, and represented a palaeontological jigsaw scattered between more than 200 pieces of rock. Its closest relations were the smaller *Ctenacanthus costellatus* (approximately 1.5 m long) and *Tristychius arcuatus*. On the basis of

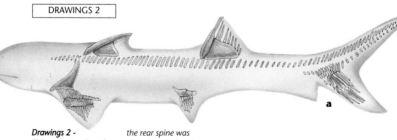

Drawings 2 -
This reconstruction of the known parts of the skeleton of Ctenacanthus (a) shows the probable shape of this genus of shark, which was very common in the Lower Carboniferous. Like many others, the Ctenacanthidae had spiny dorsal fins; the front spine was steeply inclined and rested on a single basal bone, while

the rear spine was almost vertical and followed by a number of radial bones.

These drawings show the pectoral fins of two different species of Ctenacanthus: C. costellatus (b) and C. clarki (c).

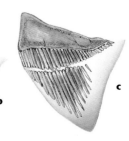

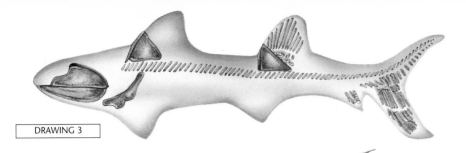

DRAWING 3

DRAWING 4

palaeontologists' reconstructions, the latter was a highly specialised ctenacanthid, equipped with two identical smooth dorsal spines, and a tailfin which resembled those of modern sharks. Its teeth were flattened and practically devoid of cusps, which made them suitable for a diet consisting mainly of benthic creatures such as molluscs, crabs

DRAWING 5

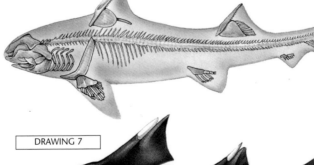

DRAWING 6

Drawing 3 - The genus Goodrichthys comprises sharks that could grow to 2.5 metres, a length that makes them some of the largest fish of the Palaeozoic era. They presented many similarities with the Ctenacanthidae, such as spines on the two dorsal fins, an anal fin situated well towards the rear of the body, and an almost symmetrical tailfin.

and the like. It also had a kind of operculum to protect the gills, a structure totally unknown in the world of sharks. Another curious creature was *Bandringa rayi* whose skeleton, probably that of an immature young creature, indicates that it was a freshwater shark with a very long snout, a tail with a very large upper lobe, and poorly-developed dorsal spines.

The next stage of evolution was represented by the Hybodontiformes (comprising the genera *Acrodus, Asteracanthus, Hybodus, Lissodus, Polyacrodus, Ptychodus* and *Tribodus*), which appeared in the late Devonian era (approximately 320 million years ago) and colonised both oceans and freshwater environments, where they become the dominant sharks in the Mesozoic era, between the Triassic and the Jurassic periods. They constituted a halfway stage between the Cladoselachiformes and modern sharks, of which they are considered a group of "sister species".

Although the amphistylic jaw-suspension structure was retained, the jaws became more mobile and elastic and the length of the mouth was reduced, making the fish more efficient in catching its prey.

The paired fins became more tapered and mobile, improving propulsion in the water. The males possessed perfectly functioning claspers which demonstrate that internal fertilisation was now an accomplished fact, and

DRAWING 7

had spiny formations near the eyes which are believed to have served to hold the female still during mating. The teeth were of two kinds: sharp at the front and molar-shaped or rounded at the back. This has been interpreted as an adaptation to a diet that included molluscs and crustaceans as well as fish.

The arrangement of the fins recalls that of many modern sharks. The two dorsal fins were supported by a strong spine, and there was a single anal fin in front of the tailfin which became

Drawing 4 - The genus Tristychius, which was very common in the Mississippian (Carboniferous) era, was characterised by two smooth, arched, robust spines and a tailfin with an underdeveloped bottom lobe.

Drawing 5 - This drawing shows an example (possibly an immature young specimen) of the highly specialised Ctenacanthiformes Bandringa rayi with a well-developed top lobe.

Drawings 6 and 7 - These drawings show the skeleton and possible appearance of the fossil sharks from the genus Hybodus. These predatory sharks, which lived from the Triassic to the end of the Cretaceous period, are considered to be among the most typical representatives of the Ibodontiformes, and perhaps the most direct ancestors of modern sharks. Their paired fins were particularly well developed, and supported by highly flexible rays.

typically heterocercal in the more evolved species because of the greater development of the upper lobe.

The Hybodontiformes varied greatly in size. As well as sharks just over 15 cm long (*Carinacanthus sp.*) or 50 cm at the most (*Lissodus sp.*, *Lonchidion sp.*) there were others over 2.5 metres long such as Hybodus, a predatory shark that lived from the Triassic era to the end of the Cretaceous period, and is considered to be one of the most typical members of the order.

A - Many Chondrichthyes with a flattened shape were covered at the time of death with silt which perfectly preserved their details, as in the case of this male, recognisable by its claspers.

B - When conditions are very favourable the delicate cartilage of sharks is perfectly preserved, enabling experts to reconstruct anatomical details like the structure of the spinal column or the fins.

A

B

THE MODERN PERIOD

The evolution from hybodonts to modern sharks, the remains of which are found with greatest frequency from around 100 million years ago, involved a series of anatomical transformations which mainly related to the diet and swimming style of the elasmobranchii. The jaw-suspension was transformed from amphistylic to hyostylic, an axial skeleton appeared with calcified vertebra supporting distinct haemal and neural arches, and the bones of the pelvic girdle fused ventrally. The hybodonts disappeared during the Cretaceous era, which ended 65 million years ago, when most of the present sharks had already become well established, following a pattern which is common in the world of nature; the competition between two groups led to the disappearance of the less evolved one.

Another crucial factor in this change was the simultaneous spread of the versatile teleosts, destined to become the main source of nutrition for the new Elasmobranchii.

The stages that led to the predominance of the "modern" shark model are not yet fully understood, and the sea beds of the past, transformed into rock, still conceal many of the missing links needed to reconstruct the evolution of sharks. However, three families still exist (Chlamydoselachidae, Heterodontidae and Hexanchidae) which retain such primitive characteristics that they are considered possible examples of how sharks evolved.

The Chlamydoselachidae are

represented by *Chlamydoselachus anguineus*, caught for the first time in Japanese waters in the second half of the 19th century (1869-1871) by Austrian researcher Ludwig Doderlein. Although Doderlein was given credit for this first catch, owing to a series of unfortunate circumstances he was unable to report the existence of the new species, which was officially described in 1884. The appearance of this shark, typical of deep waters, is precisely what would be expected of a fossil shark: an elongated body, a snake-like head with an aggressive expression, a terminal mouth equipped with three-pointed teeth that relentlessly grasp its prey, and six pairs of gill slits with wide undulating edges forming a kind of lacework which gives the species its common name of "frill shark". The term "fossil shark" is not even an exaggeration,

C

C - This photo shows an exceptional skeleton of a 2.2 metres long fossil shark (Orthacanthus senckenbergianus) found in Germany in 1982. Despite the distortion caused by deformation of the rocks that protected it for tens of millions of years, this specimen is recognisable as a male.

D - An Ibodontid shark dating back to approximately 300 million years ago. This is one of the oldest fossil sharks, and enables experts to study how sharks have evolved to the present day.

D

as similar teeth belonging to the related species *Chlamydoselachus lawleyi* have been found in the Tuscan hills, in geological strata of the Pliocene and the Eocene epochs. The anatomical characteristics of the modern frill shark place it at a backward stage of development. Its jaws, at least in functional terms, are the amphistylic type, and therefore primitive. Its teeth resemble those of the extinct Xenacanthids. The six branchial arches are an unusual characteristic, but destined to reappear several times in the history of

sharks. The lateral line organ is almost wholly external. In the *Chlamydoselachus* the notochord, practically absent in present-day sharks, is constituted by a series of cartilage segments, and extends from the cranium to the tip of the tail. Only life in an environment like the depths of the ocean between 200 and 1,200 metres down, where variations in ecological parameters are limited, has enabled these sharks to survive and maintain their characteristics unchanged for over 50 million years. The Hexanchidae (cow sharks), which

appeared towards the middle of the Jurassic period, share some characteristics with *Chlamydoselachus*, and are thus included in the same order. They are sharks with a massive body, some six-gilled (*Hexanchus sp.*) and some seven-gilled (*Heptranchias sp.*, *Notorhynchus sp.*), with varying jaw structures – amphistylic in *Hexanchus* and hyostylic in *Heptranchias*. Some cranial bones (e.g. the palatoquadrate) are similar to those of the cladodonts and the first hybodonts. The notochord presents some calcified rings, but is continuous

23

on the whole.

The Heterodontidae (horn sharks) are considered a branch of the Hybodontidae of the Jurassic era. The sharks in this family have dorsal fins with strong anterior spines, and their teeth are considered to be the hybodontid type, though considerably modified. The palatoquadrate continues towards the snout, and the jaws are functionally the amphistylic type. A comparison of the characteristics listed above demonstrates that all these sharks can be considered to feature a mosaic of characteristics belonging to most of the known types of elasmobranchii. Cladodonts, hybodonts, intermediate and modern sharks all present affinities with these families which, having survived for 150 million years due to their special biology, as if their evolutionary mechanisms were frozen, are considered by many as proof of the testing and selection of increasingly suitable characteristics, which have led to the modern sharks. The oldest known is *Paleospinax*, a genus which lived in the seas that covered the southern parts of Great Britain during the Lower Jurassic era (180 million years ago). It represents the first example of a shark with hyostylic jaws (which were highly mobile because the upper jaw was not attached to the cranium, thus producing a protractile bite), and calcified vertebra. On the basis of these characteristics, it is destined to occupy the uppermost position in the family tree of modern sharks for some time to come, although it has not yet been decided which are its most direct descendants. Some consider that they are dogfish, while others opt for horn sharks or sand-tiger sharks. Others, taking a middle road, suggest that the descendants of *Paleospinax* include both dogfish and sand-sharks.

Modern cartilaginous fish, which include members of the genera *Odontaspis, Alopias, Galeocerdo, Carcharodon, Scyliorhinus, Galeorhynus, Carcharinus, Lamna, Isurus, Negaprion, Squalus* and *Isistius*, are probably very similar to those that

lived in the seas 50 million years ago. A comparison between fossils and living specimens demonstrates that some species have slowly evolved, giving rise to "chronological" sub-species which often differ only in terms of size, while others have remained identical. Finally, fossil fauna demonstrate that affinities exist with present-day sharks involving other scientific disciplines, such as biogeography and ecology, which allow the past distribution of the various groups to be reconstructed, thereby contributing to our understanding of evolutionary developments in many basins. The Mediterranean is emblematic in this respect; the fact that it was

inhabited by fossil sharks seems to confirm the theory that life in that sea recommenced after the Messinian crisis when the Atlantic once again crossed the Gibraltar threshold, taking part of its flora and fauna with it. In the later chapters we will examine in detail the anatomy and biology of sharks and the characteristics which enable orders and families to be distinguished. Now, at the end of the long journey which has enabled us to discover the origin of sharks, it may be useful to summarise the main

characteristics that make these extraordinary creatures unique and similar to one another:
1) the jaws are of the hyostylic suspension type, and protractile
2) the notochord is replaced by calcified parts
3) the neural and haemal arches are in close contact along the entire spinal column
4) the pectoral and pelvic girdles consist of ventrally fused bones
5) the scales are placoid, with a single tip.

C

A, B - One of the oldest known modern sharks, Paleospinax, lived approximately 180 million years ago. The fossil has enabled experts to study its vertebra, teeth and scales, and some very modern characteristics have been found in this genus.

C - In a very delicate operation, a cast has been made from stone containing imprints of the muscles, gills and skeleton of a Cladoselache that lived some 400 million years ago. This species was smaller than the present-day catsharks.

This plate compares the major predators of present-day oceans with Carcharodon megalodon (1). The killer whale (Orcinus orca) (2), the great white shark (Carcharodon carcharias) (3), the tiger shark (Galeocerdo cuvieri) (4), the bull shark (Carcharhinus leucas) (5) and the sperm whale (Physeter catodon) (6) are shown alongside the extinct predator.

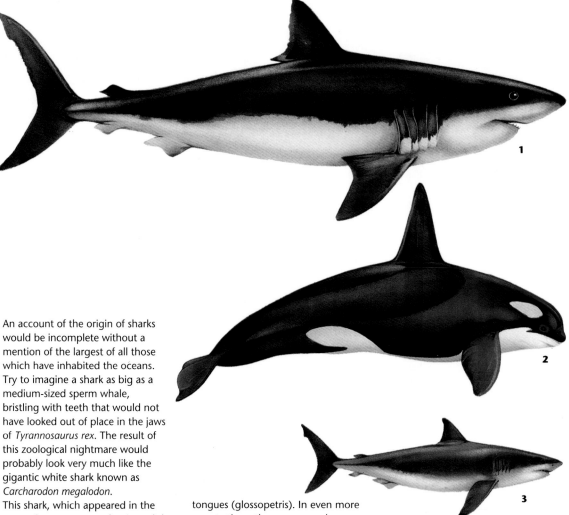

An account of the origin of sharks would be incomplete without a mention of the largest of all those which have inhabited the oceans. Try to imagine a shark as big as a medium-sized sperm whale, bristling with teeth that would not have looked out of place in the jaws of *Tyrannosaurus rex*. The result of this zoological nightmare would probably look very much like the gigantic white shark known as *Carcharodon megalodon*.

This shark, which appeared in the upper Cretaceous era, dominated the temperate seas of the world practically unchallenged; it was most widespread between 25 and 10 million years ago. Sadly, as is common in the world of sharks, even this giant left no trace apart from its teeth, which have been found practically everywhere – in America, Australia, Europe and Africa. Sharks' teeth have been known since ancient times, and were believed, at least among the ancient Greeks and Romans and until the Renaissance, to be the remains of thunderbolts, dragons' teeth or giant serpents'

tongues (glossopetris). In even more remote times they may even have been considered a gift of the gods and employed as arrowheads or cutting tools; this use continues to the present day, as demonstrated by the objects made with sharp sharks' teeth in the islands of the Pacific. Having gradually developed from the Eocene to the Oligocene eras, this species became widespread in the Miocene, and disappeared at the beginning of the Pliocene. As some exceptionally large *Carcharodon* teeth have been found at a depth of 4,000 metres on the ocean floor of the South Pacific, researchers believe that some

A - A set of fossil teeth of Carcharodon megalodon. *These teeth, which are quite numerous at some sites, can present varying degrees of preservation.*

B - The colouring depends on the minerals associated with the fossiliferous rock.

A

B

specimens may have survived until recent times (24,000-11,000 years ago), when man had already appeared on the face of the earth. Even if this was the case, the extinction of the gigantic sharks would not have been noticed by our ancestors, to whom they never constituted a threat.

By studying the teeth, an attempt has also been made to establish if and how these sharks evolved and became differentiated from a common ancestor. The best-known expert on fossil white shark teeth, Swiss researcher Jean-Louis Rodolphe Agassiz, considered that numerous species of *Carcharodon* could be identified, and he gave them different names, based on the shape of the teeth: *megalodon, rectidens, sulcidens,*

angustidens, semiserratus, lanceolatus, heterodus, leptodon and *subserratus,* not to mention *subauriculatus, productus, polygyrus, auriculatus, turgidus, toliapicus, megalotis, disauris* and *Escheri.* This wide range of names clearly demonstrates the researcher's desire to understand the origin of these sharks. Another theory about the evolution of the *Carcharodons,* formulated more recently, divides then into two new genera: *Paleocarcharodon* and *Procarcharodon.* The former, which had highly compressed teeth with irregular serrations, is believed to have given rise to the modern white shark. The latter, which had wide but not very compressed teeth with regular serrations, and lateral denticles which have disappeared

in the more recent species, is believed to have led to other species, now extinct. However, this subdivision is not universally accepted, although comparison of the teeth does show that the lateral cusps gradually disappeared as the sharks of the Eocene era evolved into those of the Miocene period.

In the past 10 years the argument about the origin and evolution of the great sharks, which had never entirely died down, has flared up again on the basis of some interesting theories which could revolutionise the *Carcharodon* family tree. Detailed analysis conducted on numerous teeth of *Isurus hastalis,* a fossil mako shark very common in the Cenozoic era, which reached its maximum average size in the Miocene era,

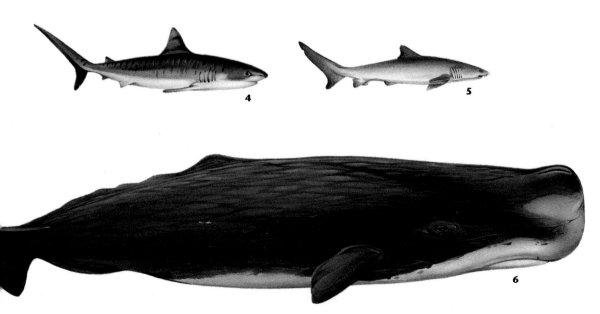

4

5

6

seems to indicate the existence of an almost continuous succession of forms which led gradually to the teeth of the present white sharks. This would mean that the modern *C. carcharias* (great white shark) is descended from the claspers of the *Isurus* sharks, not those of *C. megalodon*. It has been suggested that the latter should be included in a different genus, *Carcharocles* (synonymous with *Procarcharodon*), used in the past to identify a group of extinct sharks which lived in the Mid-Eocene period. However, the issue is still far from being settled. Fossil deposits continue to provide abundant material attributable without a shadow of doubt to extinct mackerel sharks, which were very similar to the white sharks but differed from them in terms of serration, shape or other details, sometimes minimal, destined to arouse doubts rather than provide answers. Until palaeontologists are able to give a definite answer, it is perhaps best to leave *Carcharodon megalodon* to live in the seas of the past, at least in those

1, 2 - A reconstruction of the cranium and jaws of the extinct Carcharodon megalodon *(1) and its direct descendent the great white shark* (Carcharodon carcharias) *(2). The* Megalodon *presents more robust, thickset bones designed to support the enormous weight of its teeth (the largest of which could exceed 13 cm long) and the muscles designed to open and close its jaws.*

A

1

2

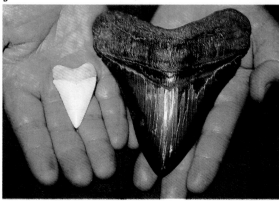

B

A - Fossil teeth of the mega-toothed giant white shark (Carcharodon megalodon) *have enabled palaeontologists to reconstruct its jaws. Recent studies indicate that many of the reconstructions displayed in museums in the past were too large, and their potential size has been reduced from 15-18 m to 12-13 m.*

B - A comparison between the teeth of the extant white shark and its fossil ancestor shows the probable difference in the size of the creatures; it is widely believed that Carcharodon megalodon *was the largest predator that has ever lived on our planet.*

C

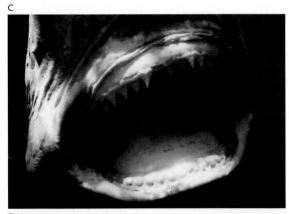

C - The last stage of an attack, when the shark has its mouth wide open and teeth ready to close on its prey, is considered one of the most outstanding manifestations of natural aggression.

D. The successor of the giant white shark (Carcharodon megalodon) is the great white shark, found in all temperate seas, where it occupies the summit of the food pyramids. The great white shark supplanted megalodon because it is better adapted in terms of diet and physiology.

D

described in books. Regardless of the numerous theories, it is known beyond reasonable doubt that teeth which grew to a total length (enamel + crown) of 15 centimetres could only belong to sharks over 12 metres long with tailfins over 4 metres high, dorsal fins nearly 2 metres long, and a weight of 12-14 tons. Although these are astonishing measurements, they are considered perfectly plausible, unlike the gigantic ones which, in the past, amazed visitors to numerous museums, such as the American Museum of Natural History in New York. Here, at the beginning of the century (1909), a pair of *megalodon* jaws were reconstructed from teeth found in a number of sites, which were sufficient to complete both dental arches. When the work was finished, the jaw thus obtained was 2.74 metres wide and 1.83 metres high. This extraordinary size was highlighted by the photo taken at the inauguration, which shows all those who worked on

the reconstruction framed by the encircling teeth. On the basis of mathematical ratios between jaw size and total size of sharks, it was deduced that the hypothetical specimen with a mouth of that size could have been 24 metres long. In fact, later studies, greater knowledge of the meristic ratios of the present white shark and finds of teeth belonging to a single specimen have led to a reduction in the measurements and the construction of more accurate models such as the one exhibited at the Smithsonian Institution since 1985, which is a third smaller than the previous reconstruction. What caused these sharks (whatever their origin and whatever they are called) to grow to such a size is unknown. Perhaps the reason lies in their extraordinary level of perfection and adaptation to their environment together with the multiplication and

diversification of marine mammals which, as demonstrated by fossil evidence of attacks on cetaceans, provided an abundant supply of food for these carnivores, situated at the top of the marine food chain. Why they disappeared is another question which has not yet been satisfactorily answered. Their fate may have been similar to that believed to have befallen the Tyrannosaurus, supplanted by more agile predators which intercepted its food supplies before it was able to reach them. Those who cannot accept the idea that the *megalodon* "shrank" as it became more difficult to procure sufficient amounts of food might prefer to imagine that it was replaced by the present white shark, more efficient and better adapted to the overall biological conditions of the modern oceans, in which it remains one of the dominant and most interesting species, perhaps the last for which man occasionally represents merely a prey.

THE ENIGMA OF THE SHARK

Many people almost automatically associate the word "shark" with the idea of a huge aquatic creature with a mouth bristling full of sharp teeth, ready to seize and tear apart its prey. With the aid of films, documentaries, and a long series of accounts dating from time immemorial, it is easy to recognize in this description a great white shark, a porbeagle or a tiger shark; however, even with the most fervid imagination, it is very unlikely to be a catshark, a zebra shark or a nurse shark, still less a goblin shark or a megamouth, all species which are nevertheless classed as "sharks."

In view of this highly diversified world, the term "shark" as commonly understood seems more useful in linguistic research than in the precise descriptions of a naturalist. There's no better way of finding out what a shark really is and how every part of it seems to be designed and constructed for a single purpose than to analyze its morphology and anatomy and consider its habits. Only in this way, by examining its parts, is it possible to

understand, for example, why the liver is not only important for digesting food but also plays a crucial part in controlling the buoyancy of the fish, and how its rough scales are structurally connected with its teeth and, surprisingly, with its locomotion.

AN IDEAL SHAPE

One way of evaluating the success of a zoological group is to establish how widely distributed its members are. According to this parameter, the "shark project" has definitely succeeded. Less numerous than other classes in terms of species (just over 350 grouped in 30 families), they are found everywhere: in fresh and brackish waters, in warm tropical seas, temperate seas, and polar seas, near the surface and thousands of feet down, near the coasts and far out to sea.

This extensive distribution, the result of the long evolutionary history described in the previous chapter, is mainly manifested in the perfect match between each species and its ecological niche, i.e., what ecologists consider to be an animal's "vocation." The concept is perfectly obvious; it would be ridiculous to think that you could find a creature

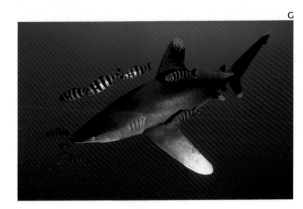

G - The oceanic whitetip shark (Carcharhinus longimanus) is one of the species most frequently found in tropical oceans; it is easily recognizable by its well-developed pectoral fins.

Drawings 1, 2, 3, and 4 - The elegant silhouette of a typical requiem shark (1, 2) shows the arrangement of the fins, gills, mouth, nares, and spiracles and the anatomical characteristics of the ventral fins which enable the female (4) to be distinguished from the male (3); the fins of the males extend to form the copulatory organs or claspers.

F - The blue shark (Prionace glauca) is typical of pelagic waters, as demonstrated by its shape and coloring.

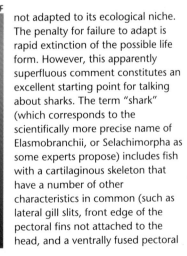

not adapted to its ecological niche. The penalty for failure to adapt is rapid extinction of the possible life form. However, this apparently superfluous comment constitutes an excellent starting point for talking about sharks. The term "shark" (which corresponds to the scientifically more precise name of Elasmobranchii, or Selachimorpha as some experts propose) includes fish with a cartilaginous skeleton that have a number of other characteristics in common (such as lateral gill slits, front edge of the pectoral fins not attached to the head, and a ventrally fused pectoral

girdle). However, contrary to common belief, sharks are by no means all the same–quite the opposite. If you consider them as a whole, you may be surprised that there is not one typical shape, but a number of ideal shapes which, when examined one by one, enable all the intermediate stages between the more streamlined forms of the pelagic sharks and the squat, but still elegant shapes of the benthic sharks to be identified.

FAST SHARKS AND "LAZY" SHARKS

The shape of an animal designed to move quickly through the water must be as streamlined as possible, in order to offer the least possible resistance to the fluid in which it lives and swims. However, although resistance can be easily tested, it is by no means a unitary phenomenon. In fact, there are two kinds of resistance (skin resistance and form drag), each of which requires different solutions. Skin resistance is minimized in the case of very slender objects whose longitudinal axis is parallel to the direction of movement. Conversely, the more the objects in question approach an ideal spherical shape (the sphere being the solid possessing the most favorable surface-to-volume ratio), the more form drag is reduced.

When the possible ideal shapes between these two extremes (exemplified by a needle and a football) were analyzed in a wind tunnel, the conclusion was reached that the bodies offering least resistance, including those of certain fish (the origins of this discovery date from 1800) have an elongated drop

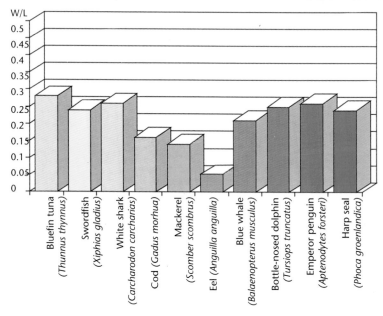

The ratio between the width (W) and length (L) of the body is a parameter used to analyze the hydrodynamicity of aquatic organisms.

As will be seen, the values reached by the great white shark are only exceeded by those of the bluefin tuna, considered the best of the pelagic swimmers.

shape, in which the largest diameter is situated about one-third of the way along, while the remaining two-thirds of the body tends to taper toward the rear.

On the basis of these findings, some researchers have endeavored to relate the maximum height of the body of a great white shark to its length. This ratio was found to be 0.26, higher than the corresponding values for the swordfish and dolphin, and a little lower than that of the tuna fish, considered the ideal model of streamlined shape. The eel, on the other hand, has a height-to-length ratio of 0.05, the least favorable imaginable, despite its proverbial agility. This suggests (and the facts bear out the theory) that the white shark may have some features in common with the chassis of many racing cars and has all it takes to be considered the prototype of the fast sharks. It is therefore no accident that all members of the Lamnidae family are similar, and that numerous members of the Carcharhinidae family share many of the external characteristics of the white shark *Carcharodon carcharias*.

A further, more detailed examination of the body of a white shark also demonstrates that if a series of incisions perpendicular to the length are made, the form of the cross-sections obtained tends to change. In cross section, the front part of the body looks like a flattened ellipse, while the middle part is almost circular, and the rear is very similar to the front section, but on a smaller scale.

C

C - A blue shark swims elegantly with rhythmic oscillations of its tail fin; the faster and narrower the oscillation the higher the speed.

D - A requiem shark bends its body so that the force accumulated in this way can be transmitted to the surrounding masses of water, enabling it to move forward.

E - Nurse sharks, which have adapted to life in direct contact with the seabed, have wide, flattened bodies and long, highly flexible tails.

D

E

Once again, these differences are no accident, but are associated with the movement of sharks.

If you observe one of them from above while it is swimming undisturbed, you will see that the various parts of the body perform different movements. The central part, corresponding roughly to the part with the largest diameter, remains almost immobile, in practice becoming the center of gravity of all the forces involved in the forward movement, while the front and rear parts present lateral oscillations inversely proportional to the diameter of the part in question. It is usually the

This drawing shows how the body of a shark has a variable cross section, depending on the point considered. Toward the front, the cross section (1) appears subcircular and slightly flattened dorso-ventrally. This gives the shark more buoyancy when swimming. The central part (2) of the body has a more laterally compressed cross section, in order to counteract horizontal drift more effectively. The tail section (3) has a more hydrodynamic shape suited to the width of the movements it performs.

33

Drawings 1 - If a typical shark is observed from above, its body will be seen to move by means of rhythmic horizontal oscillations, which are more accentuated at the front and back. These oscillations create concave surfaces which exert a thrust on the surrounding masses of water. The trunk is the least mobile part of the body, especially in the area where the pectoral fins are attached to it, while the rear section and tail oscillate widely to push the animal forward. The narrower and more elongated the shark's body and the less pelagic its habits, the more accentuated the propulsive waves.

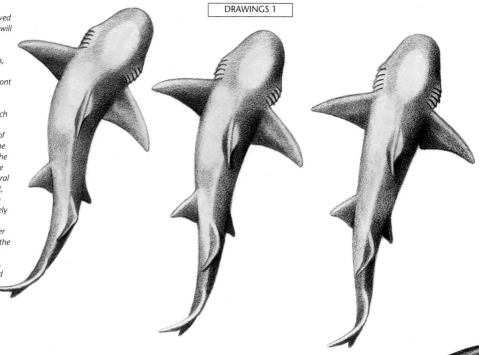

A

A - This photo of a gray shark shows how the body of these fish is bent laterally by the action of the antagonist muscles distributed along its flanks.

DRAWINGS 2

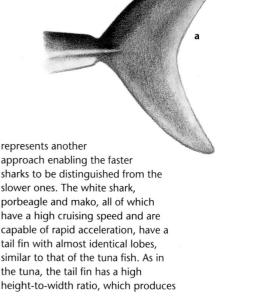

a

Drawings 2 - The shape of the tail fins of the tuna fish (b) and of the sharks belonging to the Lamnidae family-mackerel sharks, including the great white shark (a) and the mako shark (c)-constitute a typical example of adaptive convergence. Like tuna fish, mackerel sharks are very fast creatures; they swim by optimizing the energy produced by their muscle masses, which is almost entirely transmitted to the large, sickle-shaped tail. The tall tail fins exert part of their thrust on masses of water undisturbed by the vortexes produced by the forward movement of the body.

caudal part which presents the greatest oscillations; their width varies not only from species to species, but also within the same species, depending on the situation. Its propulsive function is aided by a small diameter, designed to reduce resistance to lateral movements.

In some species, however, the forces unleashed by the tail are so powerful that they would damage it if it were not equipped with ancillary reinforcement structures. In the Lamnidae, for example, the caudal peduncle is stiffened and strengthened by lateral keels which also have a streamlining function, accelerating and directing water to the middle of the fin in order to increase its thrust.

Comparison of their tail fins

represents another approach enabling the faster sharks to be distinguished from the slower ones. The white shark, porbeagle and mako, all of which have a high cruising speed and are capable of rapid acceleration, have a tail fin with almost identical lobes, similar to that of the tuna fish. As in the tuna, the tail fin has a high height-to-width ratio, which produces very efficient thrust, even with limited lateral movements. Although they feed on planktonic organisms, the whale shark and basking shark have similar tails, very different from those of the benthic sharks (which include dogfish and nurse sharks). Their long migrations and mainly pelagic life have probably led these species to

B

C

b

c

B - The tall, symmetrical tail of this whale shark (Rhiniodon typus) is considered a typical adaptation to pelagic life. This species performs long ocean migrations within its distribution area, which extends to the tropical bands of all oceans.

C - A tail with an elongated top lobe that is much more developed than the bottom lobe is one of the most typical features of sharks which spend much of their time in contact with the seabed, like this zebra shark (Stegostoma fasciatum).

develop shapes similar to those of the predatory sharks, which are necessarily more active. Despite the title of this section, there are no lazy sharks. Even what are known as sleeper sharks (*Somniosus sp.*) are not really lazy; many experts agree that the lack of attacks by these sharks, which prefer cold waters and are capable of attacking and devouring large seals without difficulty, is mainly due to the low likelihood of their encountering human beings. However, if a nurse shark or carpet shark is observed and its shape compared with that of a gray reef

shark swimming in the vicinity, there will appear to be some differences. And so there are, but laziness is not one of them. This is just an old wives' tale, mainly due to lack of knowledge of the biology of the various species. In most cases, their apparent laziness is nothing more than adaptation to life on the seabed, with circadian rhythms which mainly give priority to nocturnal activity, accompanied by a series of perfect anatomical solutions. Consequently, these are not lazy sharks, but very special, specialized sharks.

D - A Carcharhinus brachyurus, *known as copper shark, swims close to the coral reef. Just under 10 ft (3 m)*

long, it is a shark of temperate waters which is quite common in the Pacific and the Atlantic.

FINS AND PROPULSION

DRAWINGS 1

Sharks' fins, whether unpaired (dorsal, anal, and caudal) or paired (pectoral and ventral) each have their own function; they are used for propulsion, to maintain position, to slow down, or to curve. The fins, considered a choice morsel by some Asian populations, can be described in anatomical terms as large body folds supported by an internal skeleton. The skeleton is formed by cartilage arranged in parallel rows, which can be divided into two main parts: one closer to the body, consisting of large basal cartilages, and one further away (distal cartilages). Fibrous dermal rays (ceratotrichs), which form the framework of the largest part of the fin nearest the edge, are connected to the distal cartilages. In this way, each fin acquires the strength and elasticity

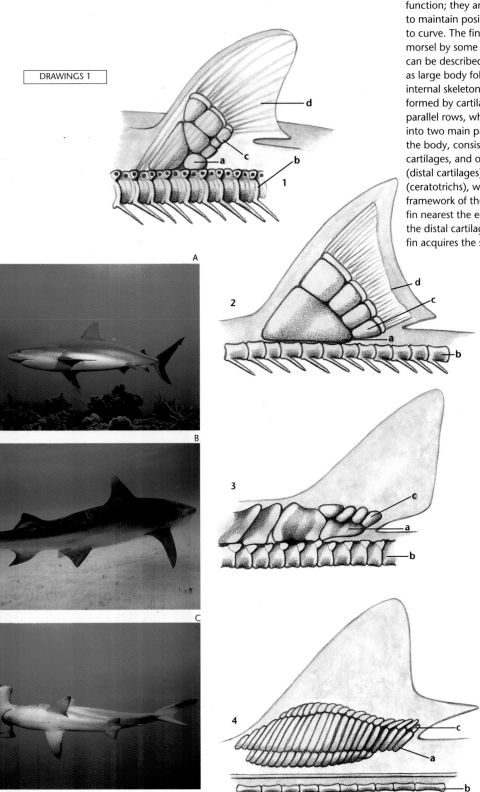

Drawings 1 - *Sharks' fins are body folds supported by an inner skeleton. This skeleton consists of robust basal cartilages (a) at varying distances from the spinal column (b), and radial cartilages (c) connected to fibrous rays (d) (keratotriches), which stiffen the most expanded part of the fin. This drawing shows the dorsal fins of four sharks:*
1) Heterodontidae;
2) Scyliorhinidae;
3) Squatinidae;
4) Triakidae.

A - The streamlined silhouette of a Caribbean reef shark (Carcharhinus perezi) shows the arrangement of the various fins.

B - A female tiger shark, recognizable by the absence of claspers, swims close to the seabed, controlling attitude with her fins.

C - This ventral photo of a hammerhead shark (Sphyrna lewini) shows the arrangement of the paired fins (pectoral and ventral) and the asymmetrical shape of the tail fin from an unusual angle.

Drawings 2 -
The lifestyle of sharks
can be deduced to
some extent from the
position of the dorsal
fins. The closer together
and further back they
are situated, the more
marked the
benthonic
habits of
the species. This
drawing compares a
pelagic species (the
requiem shark) (a) with
a nekto-benthonic
species (the nurse
shark) (c) and a species
typically adapted to
bottom-dwelling life
(the angelshark) (b).

Drawings 3 - The
drawings shows the
three main types of fin
involved in the shark's
movement control:
pectoral fins (a); tail fin
(b); dorsal fin (c).

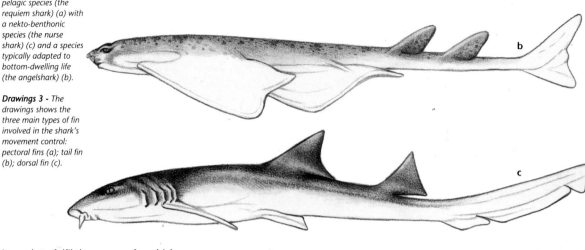

it needs to fulfil the purpose for which
it is designed.

DRAWINGS 3

Most sharks have two dorsal fins,
which may be trapezoidal or rounded.
Their position depends on the habits
of the individual species; they are
situated further back in the less active
sharks which spend much of their
time in direct contact with the ocean
floor. Both the dorsal fins and the anal
fin have the important function of
helping the shark keep on course and
counterbalancing the lateral thrust
exerted by the tail, thus preventing
the shark from oscillating excessively
along its longitudinal axis while
swimming. The ventral fins, which
are joined by an internal cartilaginous
lamina that forms the pelvic girdle

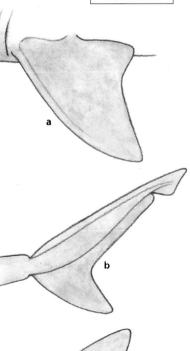

D - A gray shark,
photographed just
before lashing out
with its tail.

E - A blue shark
silhouetted against the
pale surface of the
California waters. The
long, mobile pectoral
fins of this species are
highly efficient in
guaranteeing rapid
direction control.

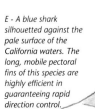

A

B

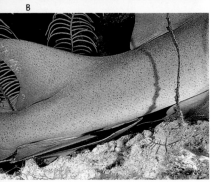

C

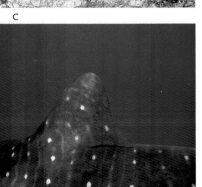

C - The first dorsal fin of
the whale shark can
have an area of several
square yards.

D - The dorsal fins of
the Port Jackson sharks
are preceded by a
robust spine, deriving
from the transformation
of a placoid scale.

E - A detail of the first
dorsal fin of a Port
Jackson shark
(Heterodontus
portusjacksoni).

F - The dorsal fin of a
young Heterodontus
francisci off the Pacific
coast of California.

DRAWINGS 1

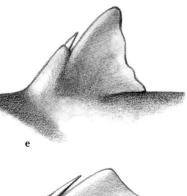

a

b

c

d

e

f

D

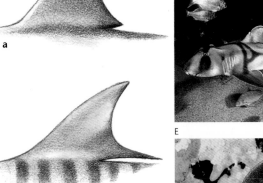

E

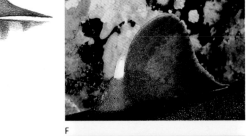

F

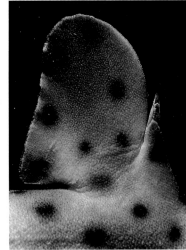

Drawings 1 -
These drawings show
some of the forms
taken by sharks' dorsal
fins:
a) Carcharhinus sp.;
b) Galeocerdo cuvier;
c) Carcharhinus sp.;
d) Stegostoma
   fasciatum;
e) Heterodontus sp.;
f) Squalus sp.
In some cases their
appearance is sufficient
for the order or family
to be identified without
difficulty.

A - The tall, triangular
first dorsal fin of the
great white shark is the
traditional symbol of
these predators, whose
alleged ferocity has
given rise to numerous
stories and beliefs since
ancient times.

B - The dorsal fins of
the nurse shark are
attached toward the
rear of the body,
well behind the
pectoral fins and
almost opposite the
ventral and anal fins.

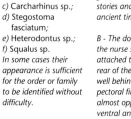

a

b

G

Drawings 2 -
Although it is widely believed that a fin emerging from the water is an unmistakable sign that a shark is present, this is not always true. Manta rays (a), marlins (c), and dolphins (d) can all appear with fins or parts of their bodies resembling the dorsal fin of a shark (b) emerging above the surface.

and are transformed into genital organs (claspers) in the males by the addition of skeletal elements, may have a similar function.

While the dorsal fin is infallibly destined to attract our attention as a typical, but not always true, sign of the presence of a shark, it is the tail fin that propels it along, as mentioned in the previous paragraph. The tail fins of certain sharks, usually ignored, can be just as awesome as their teeth. Finding yourself face to face with the long fin of a thresher shark or totally surrounded by the arch formed by the tail fin lobes of a great white shark can make a big difference to your ideas about who really rules the roost, at least in the oceans.

c

d

H

G - A shark's dorsal fin emerging from the water is the best-known sign of the presence of these creatures.

H - The tiger shark can venture into very shallow water, so that its dorsal fin projects considerably.

39

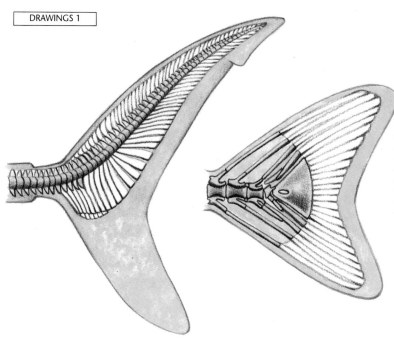

Drawings 1 -
The tail fins of sharks (left) have a different shape from those of bony fish (right). In sharks, the last part of the spinal column curves upward, with the result that the top lobe is more developed (epicercal heterocercal tail fin). In bony fish, the terminal part of the spinal column is supported by fanned-out rays, and therefore has a symmetrical shape (homocercal fin).

A, B - The tail of the whale shark is roughly symmetrical, a fairly characteristic feature of the larger pelagic sharks.

C - The asymmetrical development of the tail fin of most sharks is due to the upward curve of the tip of the spinal column.

D - The tail fin of the Port Jackson shark has a tall dorsal lobe which is more developed than the bottom lobe.

A

B

In numerous species the tail fin is typically asymmetrical (heterocercal), a shape which reaches its extreme in the thresher sharks. This irregular appearance is due to the conformation of the shark's spinal column, which tends to bend upward at the end, turning into a support for the upper lobe. On average the latter is more developed, and often ends in a triangular apical part with a notch on the underside. The lower edge, perhaps the most important in determining the overall shape of the tail, can present different degrees of development. It may remain almost invisible, as in the case of the nurse shark and the zebra or leopard shark (*Stegostoma varium*), which can thus swim unhampered even close to the seabed, or grow to resemble the upper lobe, thus transforming the tail from hetero-cercal to crescent-shaped, as in the porbeagle.

More detailed analysis of the internal anatomy of the tail fin has led to the discovery that the asymmetry of the lobes is reflected in the muscle masses and the energy they apply to the tendons connected to the expanded part of the fin, which generates much of the force exerted on the surrounding mass of water. The tendons of the lower lobe have a smaller diameter. At the point where the caudal peduncle and the actual fin meet there are often crescent-shaped transverse dimples called precaudal pits, which probably have a streamlining function.

The structure and shape of the tail are crucial to understanding some aspects of the movement of sharks. If you observe one from behind as it swims slowly along, you will see that the thrust generated by the upper and lower lobes differs. Because of the particular structure of the tail, the upper part is more powerful. As a result, while it moves the shark forward, it also pushes it inexorably downward. Fortunately, each stroke of the tail fin is accompanied by a different behavior of the lobes which reduces this negative thrust and helps rebalance the situation, thus transmitting much of the propulsive force to the animal's center of gravity.

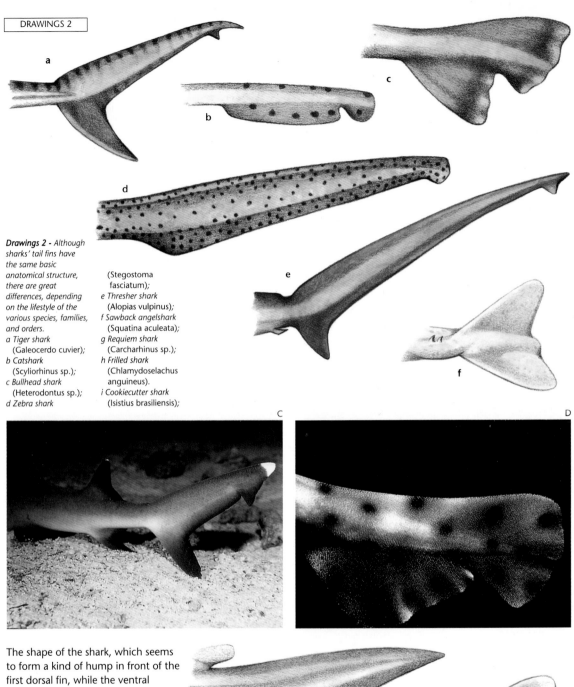

a

b

c

d

e

f

Drawings 2 - *Although sharks' tail fins have the same basic anatomical structure, there are great differences, depending on the lifestyle of the various species, families, and orders.*
a Tiger shark (Galeocerdo cuvier);
b Catshark (Scyliorhinus sp.);
c Bullhead shark (Heterodontus sp.);
d Zebra shark (Stegostoma fasciatum);
e Thresher shark (Alopias vulpinus);
f Sawback angelshark (Squatina aculeata);
g Requiem shark (Carcharhinus sp.);
h Frilled shark (Chlamydoselachus anguineus).
i Cookiecutter shark (Isistius brasiliensis);

C

D

The shape of the shark, which seems to form a kind of hump in front of the first dorsal fin, while the ventral section is flat, counteracts the downward thrust. During swimming this shape causes a faster flow of water along the back, and consequently generates a force that operates in an upward direction. The flattened cross-section of the snout also has a direct influence on swimming, not only facilitating lateral movements, but also increasing upward thrust.

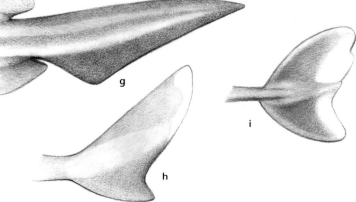

g

h

i

An extreme example of this adaptation is provided by hammerhead sharks like *Eusphyra blochii*, the width of whose head is equal to about half its body length. In practice, the head is transformed into a wing able to support and aid changes of direction.

The pectoral fins are very important in this context, and their shape indicates the habits of the shark, though to a lesser extent than other characteristics. The long pectoral fins after which *Carcharhinus longimanus* is named, and those of the smaller porbeagle, indicate that they are creatures which prefer life in the open sea. The pectoral fins of the white shark are

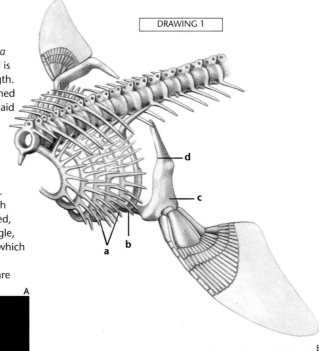

DRAWING 1

A

B

smaller, sickle-shaped, and rigid, despite its greater size. Once again, this is not a mistake, but an adaptation resulting from the greater propulsive force of the species. The large, wide pectoral fins of the Squatiniformes or angel sharks, which like to stay half-buried in sand and mud for long periods, are typical of a benthic shark. As regards their operating mechanism, this pair of fins, joined by a rigid cartilage (the pectoral girdle) located near the center of gravity of the shark, behaves exactly like a pair of aircraft wings or the skids of a hydroplane, supplying the necessary lift to the moving body.

If their inclination is slightly varied with the powerful muscles that act like tie-bars on the internal cartilages, the shark can more easily and efficiently regulate its horizontal position, move upward or downward, or turn.

C

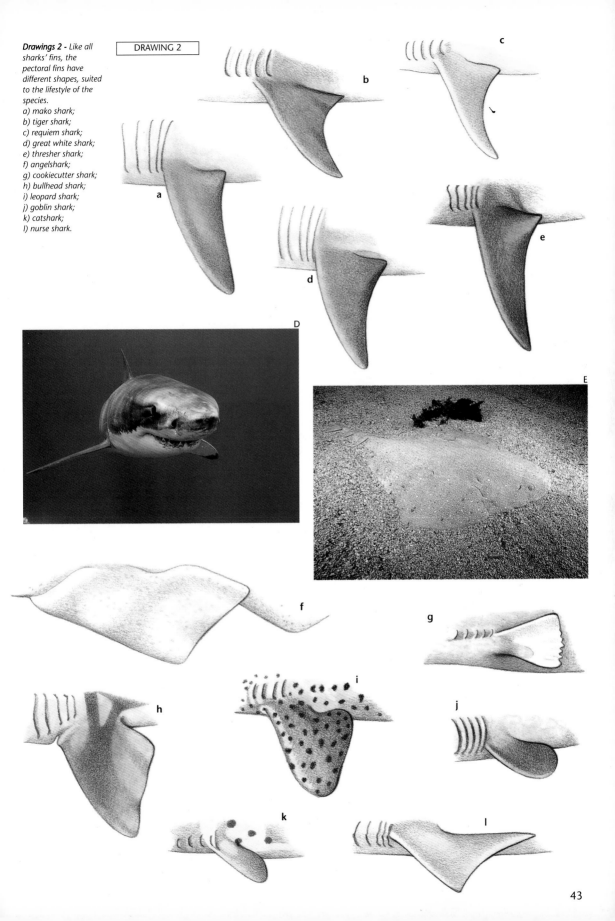

Drawings 2 - *Like all sharks' fins, the pectoral fins have different shapes, suited to the lifestyle of the species.*
a) mako shark;
b) tiger shark;
c) requiem shark;
d) great white shark;
e) thresher shark;
f) angelshark;
g) cookiecutter shark;
h) bullhead shark;
i) leopard shark;
j) goblin shark;
k) catshark;
l) nurse shark.

DRAWING 2

Drawings 1, 2, and 3 -
Sharks' fins are generally less mobile than those of other fish, but they, too, have balancing and direction control functions. The dorsal fins, which are often tall and wide, prevent the shark's body from oscillating excessively around its longitudinal axis (1), acting like the keel of a boat. The pectoral fins form an angle with the body which counteracts the downward thrust exerted on the fish by the greater strength of the top lobe of the tail fin, which is well developed in most sharks -heterocercal tail- (2). However, the pectoral fins can vary their angle and operate independently of one another, acting in the same way as diving and directional rudders. This enables the shark to move upward or downward and reverse its direction (3).

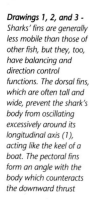

1

C - *This front view of a great white shark shows the domed shape of the front of the body, the arrangement of the pectoral fins, and the central position of the tail fin, whose short but powerful oscillations impart rapid acceleration to the whole of the shark's robust body mass.*

A

A - *This group of gray reef sharks (Carcharhinus amblyrhynchos) seems to be demonstrating all the shark's swimming positions and the effect of its fins on movement control.*

B - *The well-developed pectoral fins of the blue shark (Prionace glauca) provide the creature with the necessary lift, which enables it to swim forward without sinking to the bottom.*

B

Their function is gruesomely highlighted by some cruel shark fishing techniques designed solely to obtain the fins. After being caught and deprived of their pectoral and dorsal fins, the sharks are thrown back into the water still alive, where they sink hopelessly to the bottom, deprived of their buoyancy and direction-finding apparatus.

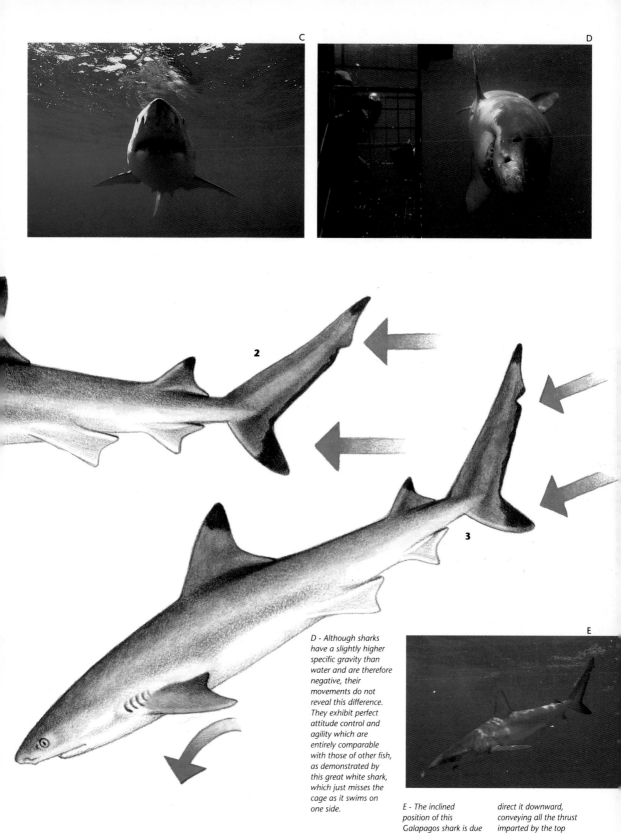

C

D

2

3

E

D - Although sharks have a slightly higher specific gravity than water and are therefore negative, their movements do not reveal this difference. They exhibit perfect attitude control and agility which are entirely comparable with those of other fish, as demonstrated by this great white shark, which just misses the cage as it swims on one side.

E - The inclined position of this Galapagos shark is due to the movement of the pectoral fins which direct it downward, conveying all the thrust imparted by the top lobe of the tail fin in that direction.

SKIN

When you handle a shark, one of the senses most stimulated is the sense of touch because of the unusual texture of its skin. If you stroke it from tail to head, it usually feels rough because of the special scales, called placoid scales. This characteristic is reflected in the common names of many species, such as the velvet dogfish (*Scymnodon squamulosus*), angular roughfish (*Oxynotus centrina*), prickly dogfish (*Oxynotus bruniensis*), roughskin spurdog (*Squalus asper*), and prickly shark (*Echinorhinus cookei*). In the recent past this rough skin was dried, tanned, and transformed into shagreen, which was used, depending on the type concerned, as an abrasive or a strong upholstery fabric sold under the tradename of Galuchat. This use dates back from time immemorial and is found in a large number of civilizations. The craftsmen of ancient Greece used shagreen to polish wooden objects, while Japanese swordsmiths used sharkskin (same) to cover the hilt (tsuka) and scabbard (saya), as did the ancient Persians. If the placoid scales (also known as denticles) are examined in detail, they will be seen to consist of a basal plate embedded in the dermis and a spine, oriented toward the tail, sticking out of the skin. The shape of the spine differs according to species, with keels, grooves, and cusps. The basal plate, which consists of bony tissue similar to the dentine of teeth, is attached to the dermis by connective tissue fibers. The

A - Like all sharks, nurse sharks (fam. Ginglymostomatidae) have a rough body covered with finely pointed enamel-coated placoid scales.

B - The placoid scales of nurse sharks vary to some extent from species to species. Nebrius have grooves which run the whole length of the scale, while in Ginglymostoma the grooves are much shorter.

C - The placoid scales of horn sharks are particularly well developed and robust. They gradually become larger and stronger as the shark grows and tends to spend more time on rocky parts of the seabed.

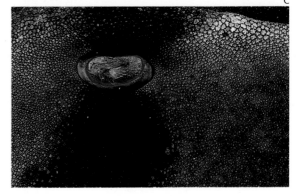

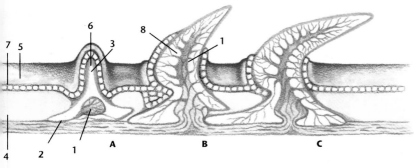

spine, often supported by a caudal peduncle, is also made of dentine, but is covered with enamel, a hard, strongly mineralized substance. When scales fall (and a shark can lose nearly 20,000 a year), newly-formed scales replace them, becoming larger and larger as the shark grows, and sometimes acquiring a different, unpleasant appearance. The strong, sharp spines connected to the dorsal fins of many sharks (such as the spiny dogfish *Squalus acanthias* and other Squalidae) are also placoid scales. These particular scales, which are sometimes poisonous, have lost the large basal plate but developed a large spiny process. A layer of

Drawing 1 *shows the formation of the placoid scales that cover sharkskin, giving it its typical rough appearance. The formation of a scale (A), consisting of a basal* *plate and a cusp, begins in the dermis (4) with the formation of a dermal papilla (1). The basal plate (2) and the spine (3), which is pushed into the* *epidermis (5), originate from the dermal papilla. The growing spine (B, C) is surrounded by the basal layer of the epidermis (7), which produces the enamel* *covering (6). The dermal papilla then expands to form the inner part of the spine, which consists of pulp rich in blood vessels (8) and dentine.*

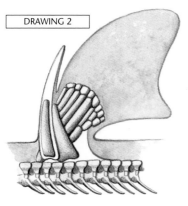

Drawing 2 -
The robust spines preceding the dorsal fins of bullhead and dogfish sharks are none other than overdeveloped placoid scales.

pigment lies between the enamel (which does not cover the rear part) and the dentine of the spine, which therefore has a dark color. The variety of the scales goes far beyond these macroscopic differences and can even be seen in different parts of the body of a single animal; the entire epidermis is actually a mosaic of scales. For example, in the nurse shark and the Port Jackson shark the denticles on the snout are rounded, those on the back are elongated, those on the flanks have keels, and the ventral denticles are shield-shaped with ribbing.

A comparison between several species indicates that the denticles on the flanks can be classed under three basic types: lanceolate with a single

lamina (e.g., *Mustelus canis*), three-pointed (e.g., *Hexanchus griseus*), and having five or more laminae (e.g., *Carcharhinus obscurus*). Oddly enough, the scales of sharks that live in cold or deep water are sharper than those of warm water dwellers; the reason for this difference is as yet unknown. Like all the anatomical structures which go to make up a shark, the wide variety of the placoid scales serves specific purposes in addition to the more general purpose of covering the animal and providing a partial barrier against the outside environment. One of the main purposes of placoid scales is defense, although this theory is not universally accepted, as sharks are mainly preyed on by other sharks.

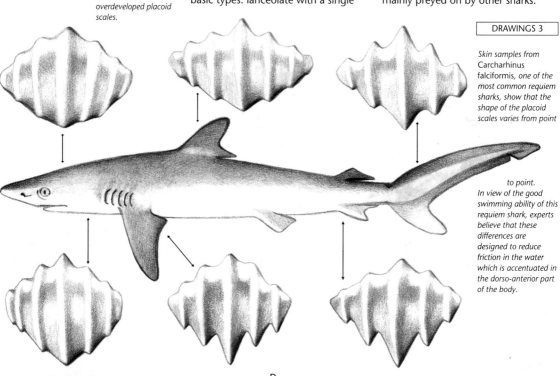

Skin samples from Carcharhinus falciformis, *one of the most common requiem sharks, show that the shape of the placoid scales varies from point to point. In view of the good swimming ability of this requiem shark, experts believe that these differences are designed to reduce friction in the water which is accentuated in the dorso-anterior part of the body.*

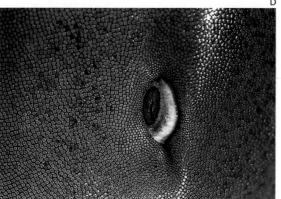

D

D - The scales of sexually mature female nurse sharks are wider and stronger than those of the males, as they have to withstand the violent bites inflicted by the males during mating.

In some species, however, the denticles are so abrasive that the entire skin constitutes a weapon capable of inflicting such deep and painful wounds as to discourage potential aggressors. In *Cephaloscyllium sufflans*, known as the balloon shark, the numerous lanceolate denticles represent an excellent example of adaptive convergence. As in the case of porcupine fish, the spines stand on end when the shark swells up by swallowing water, turning into hooks that block the fish in the fissure where it has taken refuge.

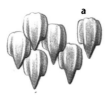

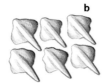

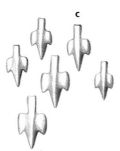

Drawing 1A, 1B -
The placoid scales, like the teeth, differ from species to species, and reflect the lifestyle of the shark. They may have a general covering (Mustelus asterias (a), Scyliorhinus stellaris (f), Squalus acanthias (e); *a friction-reducing function* (Prionace glauca (c), Isurus oxyrinchus (b); *or a defensive function* Squatina squatina (d), Oxynotus centrina (g).

Drawing 2 - In many species the male (left) and female (right) have differently shaped placoid scales. These scales can thus make an important contribution to the study of sharks, even on the basis of a few skin fragments. Galeocerdo cuvier (a); Sphyrna lewini (b); Mustelus canis (c); Carcharhinus falciformis (d).

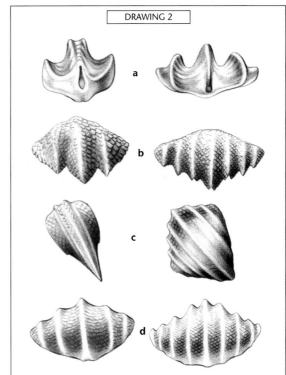

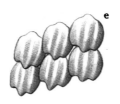

A

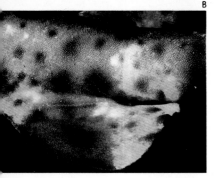

B

A - The head of the catshark is covered with very fine but strong scales, which protect the delicate sense organs on its snout.

B - The rough skin of the shark was used in many ways in the past. Strong hide was obtained from some species, while others provided an upholstery material (shagreen) used to protect objects and make them nonslip.

Another possible defensive function is protection against cuts and grazes. This is clearly found in the benthic sharks that live on rocky seabeds or near coral reefs. Young horn sharks, which prefer muddy seabeds, have less strong scales than the adults, which prefer coral-covered seabeds. Like the angel sharks, which are adapted to catching their prey while lurking on the seabed, their bellies are studded with rounded denticles that provide an excellent supporting surface even on hard, uneven substrates, where they run no risk of remaining entangled.

A thickening of the epidermis and denticles in some parts of the body is found in the females of those sharks (such as *Prionace glauca*, *Carcharhinus sp.*) in which mating is preceded and accompanied by rough interactions and bites by the males. Defense against parasites, which are fairly numerous on the bodies of sharks, is another suggested function, though entirely secondary, and there is little evidence in support of this theory.

An important function associated with the sensory world of sharks is to protect some nerve receptors, like the sensitive crypts, which are always surrounded by two wide scales, one anterior and one posterior. The top part in particular appears to be modified so as to convey water toward the crypts, thereby making them more sensitive to stimuli. Further research has demonstrated that the relationship between scales and sense organs involves many other types of receptor. Scales which direct the flow of water toward the nares or other sensory systems (such as the ampullae of Lorenzini and the lateral-line organ) have been identified, together with scales which form a kind of barrier around the eyes designed to deviate water from these delicate organs to reduce the pressure on them.

In lanternsharks (such as *Etmopterus lucifer, E. spinax, Isistius brasiliensis, Centroscyllium ritteri* and *Dalatias licha*), some scales have an orientation and shape that aids diffusion of the light emitted by photophore glands, which have important defensive, intraspecific recognition, and sexual recognition functions in these species.

The function of the scales which is most widely studied because of its possible practical implications and, at the same time, is the most surprising, is reduction of swimming resistance. Strange as it may seem, structures which transform the shark's skin into a rasp also aid its propulsion, just as a dimpled golf ball travels faster and farther than a smooth one. If the placoid scales are analyzed mathematically, it will be found that their dimensions and sculptures are large enough to reduce microturbulence in the laminar water layer that surrounds the shark while

it swims, and at the same time small enough to prevent a significant increase in the wetted surface. These combined effects specifically increase the streamlining of sharks. Some particularly fast species, like *Isurus oxyrinchus* and *Carcharhinus falciformis*, actually seem able to vary the orientation of their scales while swimming by a process based on reduction of the size of their basal plate, making them more mobile and liable to change angle spontaneously under the thrust of the water.

Finally, the wide range of scales includes those associated with the pectoral fins. The denticles become almost smooth along the outer edge of the pectoral fins to adapt to the thinning of the boundary layer at this point and are modified again on the upper part to aid the upward thrust of the fins.

C - The placoid scales appear very early in life. In oviparous sharks, the embryos develop special placoid scales which help them break the shell when they hatch. In many adult sharks the scales on the pectoral fins later become almost smooth to help them glide through the water.

D - The placoid scales often become stronger around the eyes to protect these delicate sense organs.

D

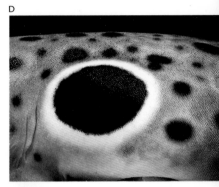

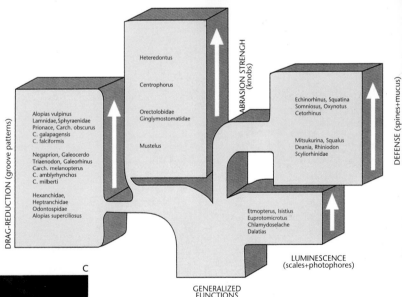

DRAG-REDUCTION (groove patterns)

Alopias vulpinus
Lamnidae, Sphyraenidae
Prionace, Carch. obscurus
C. galapagensis
C. falciformis

Negaprion, Galeocerdo
Triaenodon, Galeorhinus
Carch. melanopterus
C. amblyrhynchos
C. milberti

Hexanchidae,
Heptranchidae
Odontospidae
Alopias superciliosus

Heteredontus

Centrophorus

Orectolobidae
Ginglymostomatidae

Mustelus

ABRASION STRENGH (knobs)

Echinorhinus, Squatina
Somniosus, Oxynotus
Cetorhinus

Mitsukurina, Squalus
Deania, Rhiniodon
Scyliorhinidae

DEFENSE (spines+mucus)

Etmopterus, Isistius
Euprotomicrotus
Chlamydoselache
Dalatias

LUMINESCENCE
(scales+photophores)

C

GENERALIZED
FUNCTIONS

This diagram shows the development and adaptation of the placoid scales in the major shark families and genera. From their original, fairly simple function as a covering, *the placoid scales have adapted to perform more precise functions, depending on the lifestyle of the species: transformation into photophores (deepwater sharks),* *friction reduction (pelagic sharks), abrasion resistance (benthic sharks), and defensive functions and protection against parasites (spines and mucus).*

TEETH

Of all the parts of the shark, the teeth are the best known and have always constituted the highlight of more or less scientific descriptions designed to stimulate the imagination of readers of adventure and animal books.

This example is taken from a book published in 1881: "If the shark is an adult, it has six rows of these lethal weapons at the top and bottom–an arsenal well suited to tearing its victims apart. These teeth perform the various movements transmitted to them, according to the animal's desire, by the muscles situated around their base.

skin. The oral and pharyngeal cavities are studded with stomodaeal denticles, which present transitional characteristics between scales and true teeth. Another common denominator between the two formations is the fact that the teeth, like the scales, are not embedded in the jaw cartilage, merely strongly anchored to the skin by connective tissue fibers.

The teeth are composed of two main parts: a crown and a root. The root should not be confused with the tooth structure of the same name in mammals, as it is not connected to the jawbone. In modern sharks, with a few

exceptions, the tooth has a double root, considered by most experts to be the vestiges of the basal plate of the ancient cladodontid and hybodontid sharks.

The anatomical structure of the teeth, which necessarily resembles that of the scales, presents an internal cavity filled with pulp and covered with dentine, which is protected in turn by a thin layer of enamel (vitrodentine) on the crown. This substance is very hard and strong, as a result of the almost total absence of organic material, and is responsible for the success of sharks' teeth as ornaments.

The teeth form continuously throughout the shark's life. As they form, due to the combined effect of the cells of the dermis and epidermis, in a space inside the jaw cartilage, the teeth undergo simultaneous forward movement due to the continual growth of the gingival tissue to which they are firmly attached.

Thus the tooth moves forward

A

B

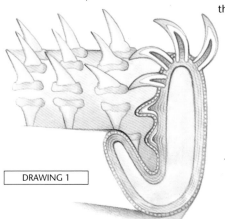

DRAWING 1

DRAWING 2

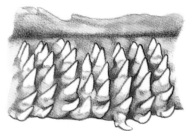

A - This mako shark jaw shows the tiered arrangement of the teeth. The functional teeth are the outermost, erect ones, while the inclined teeth arranged like roof tiles will only come into operation when the preceding ones fall out.

C

B - The typical triangular teeth of the top jaw of the great white shark appear to be widely spaced, but the gaps are occupied by the teeth of the lower jaw, which makes the creature's bite extremely effective.

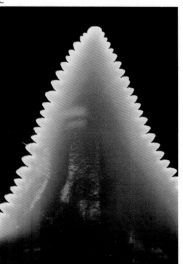

The shark lowers or raises the various rows of teeth; it can also raise part of a row and lower the other part. This far-sighted killer can therefore gauge the number and strength of the weapons it needs to rend its prey; against a weak, defenseless enemy it uses one row of teeth, but against a formidable adversary it uses the whole arsenal."

Unusual as it may seem, the connection between the outer surface of sharks and their teeth is perfectly logical. The oral cavity has teeth along the maxillary arches instead of the placoid scales on the

Drawing 1 - *Sharks' teeth are simply very large modified placoid scales. They are not embedded in the jaw cartilage, merely anchored to the dermis with connective tissue fibers. The outer covering consists of enamel that protects the layer of dentine which encloses pulp rich in blood vessels. Sharks' teeth are arranged in rows; the inclined rear rows, covered by a fold of the* buccal mucosa, are still being formed. As the front teeth are lost, the back teeth gradually move forward and straighten to become perfectly functional.

Drawing 2 - *Each jaw of the basking shark (Cetorhinus maximus) contains 4-9 irregular rows consisting of 200 or more tiny conical teeth .11-.23 in (3-6 mm) long, whose function is not yet understood.*

D

E

F

however *(Squalus* and *Isistius genera)* seem to replace an entire arch at once.

By contrast with other characteristics, the teeth present a wide range of shapes which are easily explained by the different dietary habits of each species, although it should be remembered that in most cases the prey, either whole or in pieces, is swallowed without any prior chewing. The teeth are specialized tools which may resemble sharp blades, with or without serrated edges suitable to tear large pieces of flesh from the prey; they may be long and sharp with lateral

cusps, in order to catch moving, darting prey like small fish and squid, or resemble grindstones designed to crush the shells of crustaceans and mollusks.

Apart from the differences between one species and another, there are also differences within individuals, as the teeth tend to change shape during growth, indicating that young and adult

DRAWINGS 3

c

b
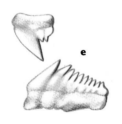

a
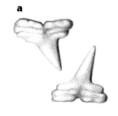

d
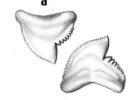

as it grows, gradually straightening as a result of simple mechanical tension until it becomes perfectly functional. This can easily be seen by examining a fresh or untreated shark jawbone, in which the functional teeth are preceded on the inside by a posterior set, which are increasingly inclined and partly hidden by the tissues of the oral mucosa. As a result of the continual growth of the original tissues and those surrounding them, the teeth are destined to fall out after a while, either spontaneously or as a result of traumatic breakage. It is often possible to establish relatively easily which species was responsible for an attack on cetaceans, seals, and even human beings, by examining the teeth that have remained embedded in the victim's flesh.

Tooth replacement is a natural phenomenon which takes place at different times and in different ways, depending on species. In general, it is estimated that the teeth are replaced individually every 8-15 days, and more often in young sharks. Some species,

f
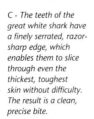

e

g
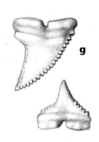

h

i

C - *The teeth of the great white shark have a finely serrated, razor-sharp edge, which enables them to slice through even the thickest, toughest skin without difficulty. The result is a clean, precise bite.*

D, E - *This photo sequence shows the arrangement of the teeth in the jaws of the tiger shark, from the outermost teeth to the innermost rows of gradually developing teeth.*

F - *The typical, unmistakable cockscomb-shaped tooth of the tiger shark, with its curved edge and highly accentuated cusp.*

Drawings 3 - *Sharks' teeth have different shapes and are one of the most important aids to understanding the biology and habits of these fish.*
(a) hammerhead shark,
(b) nurse shark,
(c) sand-tiger shark,
(d) tiger shark,
(e) bluntnose sixgill shark,
(f) gray shark,
(g) blue shark,
(h) great white shark,
(i) mako shark.

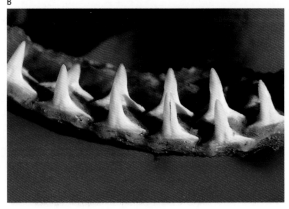

C

A, B, C - The photos show the powerful teeth of a mako (A) shark and of a sand-tiger shark (B and C).

DRAWING 1

sharks gradually adapt to their different diets.

In other cases the teeth of the upper jaw differ from those of the lower jaw, in order to produce the most efficient bite. In general, the bottom teeth are sharper and narrower, and often slightly curved to ensure a better grip, while the stronger top teeth have the task of slicing the prey. In some species, such as the sharks of the *Heterodontus* genus (which means "having different teeth"), the variation follows a different order, with a succession of shapes from the front to the back teeth. In view of their special characteristics, it is easy to see why the number and shape of the teeth is considered a useful way of recognizing species, and in some cases even gender. In the sharks of the *Deania* genus, the teeth of the males are more erect than those of the females,

Drawing 1 -
This reconstruction of the jaws of the Port Jackson shark (Heterodontus portusjacksoni) shows the variety and arrangement of its teeth; there are a few sharp teeth typical of predators in the front part, while the other teeth are plate-like and designed to grind and crush the shellfish (mollusks, echinoderms and crustaceans) that constitute the majority of this species' diet.

D - Through the half-closed mouth of this Port Jackson shark (Heterodontus portusjacksoni) *the front of its complex dentition can be seen; the teeth gradually become larger toward the back.*

D

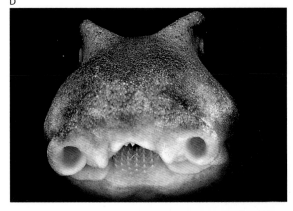

and the same applies to some catsharks of the *Halaelurus* genus. A marked dimorphism is observed in *Apristurus riveri*, the males of which have teeth twice as long as those of the females, with a single cusp instead of 3-5.

E

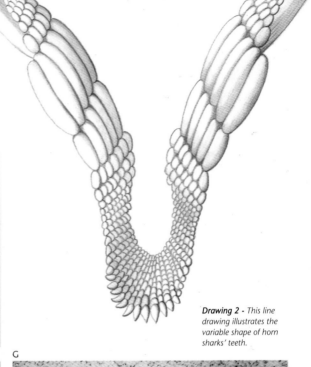

Drawing 2 - This line drawing illustrates the variable shape of horn sharks' teeth.

F

G

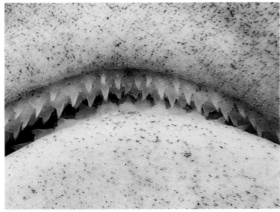

H

E - This swellshark (Cephaloscyllium ventriosum) has a large mouth with small sharp teeth which it uses to catch sleeping fish and crustaceans.

F - The functional teeth of this catshark can be arranged in a number of rows. This can be considered an adaptation to this small shark's need to hold onto its prey at all costs after catching it.

G - The Californian leopard shark (Triakis semifasciata) has close-set teeth with a strong central cusp surrounded by small lateral tips which it uses to capture a wide variety of prey. Young leopard sharks catch crustaceans, whereas the adults prefer fish.

H - The teeth of a hammerhead shark are regularly distributed along its rounded jaws.

THE MOUTH AND BITE
OF THE SHARK

The specialization that sharks' teeth have acquired would risk remaining almost unused if it was not accompanied by a simultaneous specialization of the jaws. Nearly all modern sharks present hyostylic jaw-suspension, in which the upper jaw is not attached to the cranium, allowing articulation in the posterior region with the hyomandibular cartilage. This has produced greater mobility of the jaws and the development of a protractile bite.

As a result of the inferior position of the shark's mouth, it was believed in the past that the fish had to perform strange contortions to feed, and descriptions like this could be read: "As the mouth of the shark is situated in the lower part of the snout, it has to turn over in order to grasp objects not situated beneath it." In fact, this position of the jaws is the result of their shortening, which took place at the same time as a lengthening and expansion of the snout. The snout can thus perform both a buoyancy and a sensory function by virtue of the movement of some receptors (eyes, olfactory cells, ampullae of Lorenzini) located in a forward position.

The belief that sharks had to turn over to seize their prey was partly due to the difficulty of direct observation and study of these species in the past, and partly to the characteristics which cause them to move their heads actively while swimming, not only from side to side but also up and down, in order to sound the surrounding environment in as much detail as possible. However, as is often the case, there is at least a grain of truth even in old wives' tales; in some cases, the white shark has actually been seen to approach a prey on the surface swimming belly uppermost, or lying on one side. The particular conformation of the cranium, considered as a whole, is such that when a shark attacks it seems to bend its head backward, while the lower jaw is pushed forward and comes into contact with the prey first.

As already mentioned, the bottom teeth mostly have a suitable shape to grip the prey, and the operating mechanism of the jaw is particularly suitable to exploit all their potential. For example, in the case of the gray nurse shark (*Odontaspis taurus*) and the porbeagle, the opening of the mouth causes a contraction of the front tissues of the lower jaw which makes the first rows of teeth protrude to the exterior, turning them into a kind of hooked trap which leaves the prey no way of escape. Next, the top jaw is lowered, bringing into operation the teeth designed to lacerate the prey.

This behavior, common to all predatory sharks, especially the pelagics, has been studied in detail in the white shark, in which it falls into five stages. The beginning of the attack coincides with a backward

A, B, C - As shown by this sequence of three photos, the bite of the great white shark takes place in accordance with a set series of movements: first the snout is lifted, then the bottom jaw is lowered and the teeth protrude, increasing the efficacy of the bite. In the last stage, the jaws clamp and the teeth meet, severing part of the victim's flesh.

A

movement of the head, produced by a flexion at the occiput. Immediately afterward, a depression in the lower jaw and a 30°-40° lift of the snout is observed. These actions transform the inferior mouth into a quasi-terminal mouth. The next stage involves forward and outward movements of the upper jaw, the teeth of which then protrude markedly from the oral cavity. This maneuver indicates that the mouth is about to be closed by simultaneous upward movement of the lower jaw. At the last stage, which corresponds to the end of the bite, the snout and head are lowered and the upper jaw returns to its original position ventral to the cranium.

In the case of repeated bites, this position is only taken up after the last bite. The entire sequence lasts for a much shorter time than it takes to describe it. In the time it's taken you to read these words, a white shark could have bitten over 30 times, in view of the fact that the time taken by each bite is under a second on average. When observing a shark attack and the way the shark violently worries the larger prey, it might be thought that the teeth, however sharp they may be, are not very strong, but the contrary is actually true.

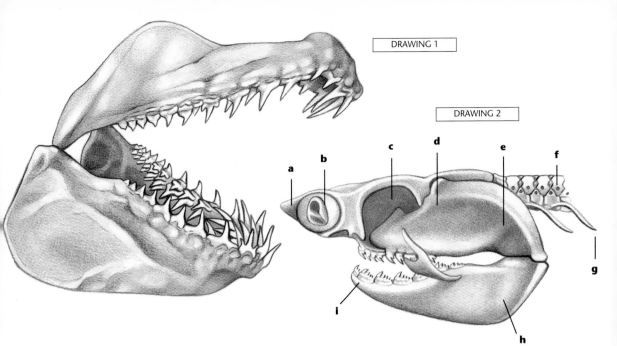

DRAWING 1

DRAWING 2

a b c d e f

g

i

h

Drawing 1 - The shape of the sand tiger shark's jaws and the muscles associated with them cause the lower jaw tissue to contract when the shark bites, with the result that the teeth protrude outward.

Drawing 2 - This drawing shows the cranium of Heptanchus maculatus and its various component parts. The nasal cartilage (a), the olfactory sac (b), the orbital processes (c), the palatoquadrate (d), the quadrate (e), and the first segments of the spinal column (f) with the gill rakers (g) can be seen in the upper part (neurocranium). The lower part (splanchnocranium) contains the upper jaw or Meckel's cartilage (h) and the labial cartilage (i).

B

C

The movements performed by the shark to detach morsels of its prey are equivalent to the action of a saw or knife which gradually slices through the part to be cut.

J.M. Snodgrass and P.W. Gilbert conducted some famous experiments to measure the force of a shark's bite. Using an instrument they invented themselves called a "shark-bite meter," which consisted of a plastic-covered steel and aluminium tube, they calculated the force of a requiem shark's bite at approximately 3 tons per square centimeter. On the basis of these findings one can only imagine, in the absence of more precise measurements and suitable instruments, what would be the force of a 16.4 ft (5 m) long great white shark which can effortlessly crush the femur of a horse or rip 44-66 lb (20-30 kg) morsels of flesh from seals or dolphins. Another fact which testifies to the power of the bite is the strength of the teeth which, measured on the Mohs hardness scale, is identical to that of steel.

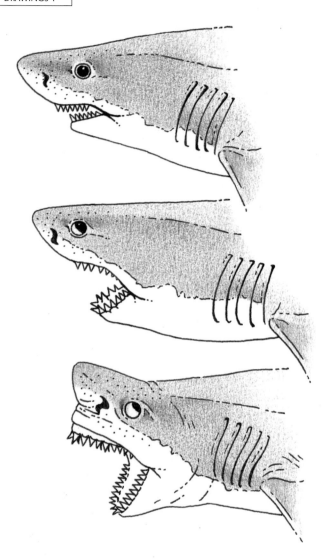

A

Drawings 1 - These three drawings show the jaw protrusion mechanism in sequence during the bite of the great white shark. This mechanism increases the size of the shark's mouth so that it can grasp the victim very effectively. The entire sequence lasts less than a second, and in the case of repeated bites, the snout remains raised in order to shorten the interval between bites.

A and B - These two closeups of a sand-tiger shark (Carcharias taurus) clearly show the awesome rows of teeth that tend to protrude from its mouth. In fact the teeth are fairly slender and serve mainly to catch fish, which are then swallowed whole.

B

SENSE ORGANS

DRAWING 2

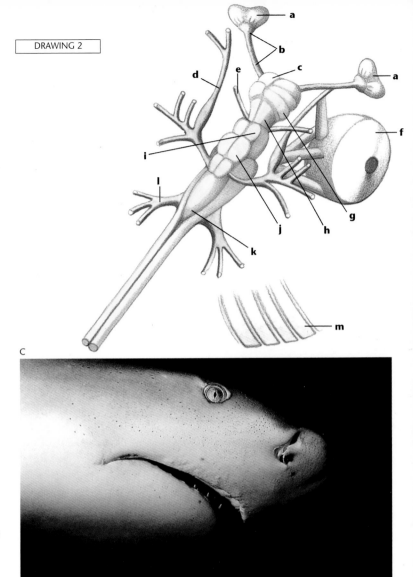

The attack and capture of a victim are only the last stage in what is often a long process of detection, which uses the shark's numerous senses. Some people jokingly describe sharks as "swimming noses," as accurate experiments have demonstrated the importance of the sense of smell to these creatures, also denoted by the fact that the olfactory lobes constitute much of the front section of the encephalon. There is no doubt about the shark's ability to smell substances dissolved in the water, and there is no lack of scientific and empirical proof, as demonstrated by the ground-bait techniques using blood employed by recreational fishermen and divers to attract sharks.

The olfactory organs, called the nares, are situated in an anterior position at the sides of the snout, usually near the mouth and sometimes communicating with it via a naso-oral groove. The round, oval, or elongated nares appear to be divided in two by a fleshy membrane that guarantees a continual inflow and outflow of water while the fish is swimming. In fact, however, the nares are single blind sacs whose inner surface is formed by numerous convoluted folds, covered with an olfactory epithelium consisting of elongated cells. Each of them has a receptor cilium which projects into the naris

C

D

Drawing 2 -
This drawing shows the encephalon and some of the main cranial nerves of a dogfish shark, namely, the olfactory sac (a), olfactory bulb and stalk (b), olfactory lobe (c), ophthalmic nerve (d), optic nerve (e), eyeball (f), cerebral hemisphere (g), diencephalon (h), optic lobe (i) cerebellum (j), medulla oblongata (k), vagus nerve (l), and branchial sacs (m).

C - This close-up of a lemon shark (Negaprion brevirostris) shows the slits corresponding to the ampullae of Lorenzini, the most unusual of the shark's many sense organs.

D - The long snout of the blue shark can be considered a single huge sensor. It contains the olfactory organs, the eyes, the endings of the inner ear, and the ampullae of Lorenzini (the electroreceptor organs).

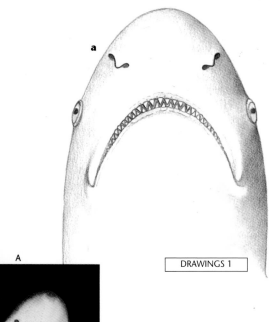

a

Drawings 1- *The nares (a), one of the shark's most important sense organs, are situated in a ventral position, between the tip of the snout and the mouth. Each naris consists of a blind slit divided into two parts by a fold of skin (the nasal valve), (b, c). While the shark is swimming, water is forced to pass through the nares along a mandatory route (d). In this way any odoriferous substances dissolved in the water stimulate the numerous olfactory cells arranged in the form of lamellae which line the nares (e), signalling the presence of prey or other sharks.*

A

DRAWINGS 1

b

c

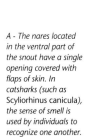

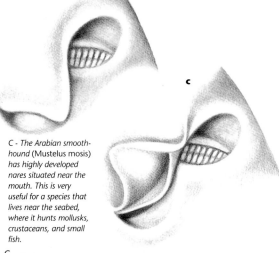

A - The nares located in the ventral part of the snout have a single opening covered with flaps of skin. In catsharks (such as Scyliorhinus canicula), the sense of smell is used by individuals to recognize one another.

B - The nares of Carcharias taurus are divided externally into two parts–an entrance and an exit–by a fold of skin. In this way water penetrates the naris as the shark swims and stimulates the olfactory epithelium which lines it.

C - The Arabian smooth-hound (Mustelus mosis) has highly developed nares situated near the mouth. This is very useful for a species that lives near the seabed, where it hunts mollusks, crustaceans, and small fish.

B

C

in direct contact with the water, while on the opposite side it continues into a nerve fiber connected to the olfactory nerve. The existence of the naso-oral grooves allows the nares to operate even when the shark is stationary on the seabed, as a result of the continual flow of water generated by the gills. This allows benthic sharks to "sniff" the surrounding environment, aided by the fact that their nares are more

complex, with a wealth of convolutions which greatly increase the receptive area. The olfactory cells are highly sensitive. Lemon sharks can detect an odoriferous substance even if it is diluted 10 million times, and many other species possess similar, if not greater abilities.

The substances that arouse the strongest reactions in sharks are naturally those present in the bodies of other animals, such as amino-

acids, hormones, amines, and plasma protein. Such compounds, once detected, generate variations in brain activity; these have immediate repercussions on the muscles of the gills, which rapidly close, and on the creature's movement, which suddenly accelerates.

These reactions are probably designed to distance the shark from or direct it rapidly toward the source from which the stimulus is received,

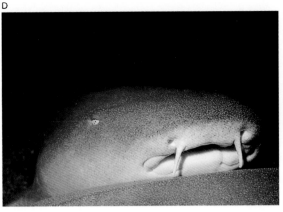

D

E

F

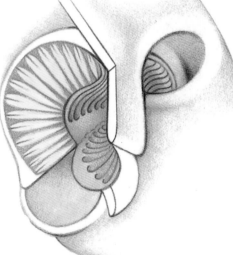

d

e

D - Nurse sharks (Ginglymostoma cirratum) *have a well-developed sense of smell which can detect odoriferous substances even at very weak concentrations (a few parts per million). This high sensitivity is very useful for species that hunt by night.*

E - The whitetip reef shark (Triaenodon obesus) *can maintain a continuous flow of water around the nares even when it lies motionless on the seabed.*

F - The rusty carpetshark (Parascyllium ferrugineum) *has cutaneous appendages near the nares which have a tactile and sensory function and increase the sensitivity threshold of the olfactory epithelium.*

minimizing the turbulence of the water it swims through so as not to disperse the odor trail. The odor is not necessarily associated with a prey, but also enables a shark to identify the gender of another shark and its level of maturity and readiness for mating.

Detection of the odor trail, at first tentative, becomes increasingly certain and fast, until the shark homes in on the source of the stimulus and manifests attack behavior. This behavior can even be generated in the absence of a true prey, merely by using very high concentrations of stimulants. The sensitivity of sharks to olfactory stimuli has led to numerous attempts to synthesize artificial substances which, when dissolved in the water, would serve as shark repellents. In practice, these substances already exist in nature and are quite efficient, as demonstrated by the Moses sole (*Pardachirus marmoratus*) which, if attacked, secretes a substance that temporarily paralyzes the mouth muscles, preventing the shark from biting, and the holothurian *Actinopyga agassizi*, whose Cuvierian ducts can release a substance potentially able to kill a small shark unless it swims off rapidly as soon as it smells it.

While the sense of smell is one of the most important of sharks' senses, their vision is equally acute. The eye of the shark is basically similar to that of other vertebrates, comprising cornea, iris, lens, retina, etc. Its size ranges from 1% of total body length in zebra sharks, typically found in clear tropical light. The lens is suspended in the eyeball by a system of muscles that maintain it in a position apparently suited to long-distance vision underwater. Although these muscles seem able to move it, it is not certain whether the shark can focus on nearby objects.

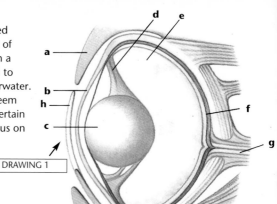

DRAWING 1

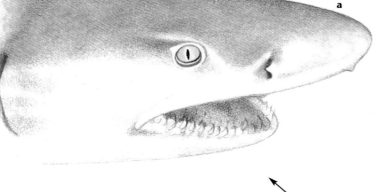

a

Drawing 1 -
The shark's eye consists of the same parts as those of all the vertebrates, namely, eyelids (a), cornea (b) lens (c), suspensory ligaments (d), vitreous humor (e), retina (f), and optic nerve (g). Some species also have a third eyelid, called the "nictitating membrane" (h).

The lens resembles a rigid sphere and accommodation can only take place if it is moved backward and forward on the horizontal plane.

A - Blue sharks, like many other sharks that live in pelagic waters, use their eyesight to a large extent to hunt their prey.

waters to 10% in the deepwater sharks and the big-eye thresher (*Alopias superciliosus*).
The shape of the pupil varies; it can be circular or oval with diagonal or vertical orientation and, unlike that of most bony fish, its size can be changed by the effect of the iris. The pupils of most sharks react quite slowly to light, but in those which live closest to the surface, where variations in brightness are more accentuated as the day goes by, the reaction is very fast.
A shark from the *Carcharinus* genus takes less than a minute to adapt its eyes to the dominant ambient

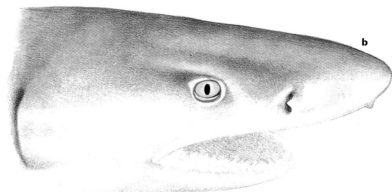

DRAWINGS 2

b

A

B

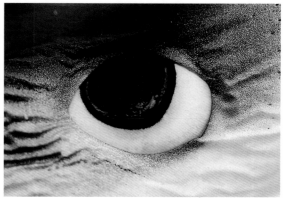

C

D

c

B - Requiem sharks mainly have round eyes and are equipped with a nictitating membrane, a kind of third eyelid that serves to protect these delicate organs when they attack their prey.

C - The eyes of hammerhead sharks are situated at the extremities of their broad heads. This position, together with the wide oscillations performed by the head, gives them a wide visual field.

D - The eye of this young hammerhead presents the circular shape typical of the family. The hammerhead's eyes also have a nictitating membrane.

E, F - Sharks' pupils have varying shapes. Pelagic sharks usually have rounder eyes than those which live near the seabed, and this feature can help evaluate the lifestyle of the various species.

Drawings 2 - Sharks that live in clear, shallow tropical waters are able to adapt their pupil diameter to the prevailing light conditions. As the intensity of the light decreases, the pupil diameter gradually increases, as can be seen in this sequence of drawings (a-d).

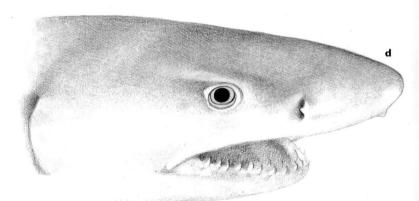

d

E

F

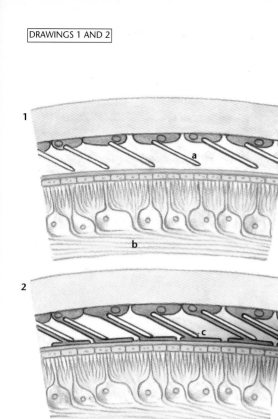

1

a

b

2

c

C

D

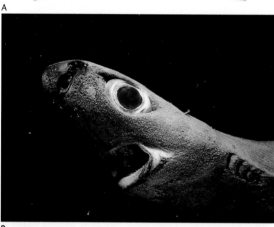

A

B

A possible exception seems to be the white shark, which has been observed to lift its head out of the water to look at objects on the surface. This suggests that it has a regulation system which adapts the eye to the different refraction of the light in the water and in the air.

The retina contains both cones and rods, which has given rise to the theory, based on a number of experiments, that sharks are able to distinguish colors and not just different shades of gray, as well as recognizing shapes, which they remember for a long time if suitably trained. An important specialized feature of the shark's eye is the "tapetum lucidum" situated behind the retina, which sharpens the vision in poor light conditions. The rays of light that cross the pupil are usually focused by the lens on the retina, where they excite the photoreceptors that transmit nerve stimuli to the optic lobes of the brain. In sharks, this route is to some extent altered by the tapetum lucidum, considered by some to be the most efficient in the animal kingdom. It consists of thousands of

*Drawing 1 - The eyes of many sharks (*Squalus *sp.,* Negaprion *sp.) have special reflecting plates (a) behind the retina which form a layer called the "tapetum lucidum." The task of this reflecting layer is to intensify the light radiation that strikes the retina (b) in poor light conditions. This explains why the eyes of many sharks appear luminous at night, like cats' eyes, if illuminated by a diver's torch.*

Drawing 2 - When the light increases, the reflecting plates are covered by a layer of black melanin (c) which makes them opaque.

*A - The velvet belly (*Etmopterus spinax*) is a typical deepwater shark, as demonstrated by its dark coloring and large eyes.*

B - Iago omanensis *is known as the bigeye houndshark because of its large eyes, an adaptation to life in deep waters.*

polygonal plates covered with crystals of guanine, a special substance that acts like the silvering on a mirror, and therefore has a high reflecting power. The light which has passed through the retina is thus reflected and the luminosity of the eye increases, producing an effect similar to that which can be seen in the eyes of a feline or cat in the dark. Seeing the luminous eyes of a shark by night, though unpleasant, demonstrates with certainty that you have entered its visual range, although it did not need to get so close before detecting your presence.

The plates of the tapetum have a variable orientation, depending on the area in which they are located; this meets the need to reflect light with the greatest efficiency, at the most suitable angle to avoid dispersion. In the species that live close to the surface, the plates are associated with sacs of dark pigment (melanin) which can be made to slide on the guanine, thus reducing the reflection capacity when the light is very strong. Sensitive electro-retinograms used to measure the sensitivity of the retina demonstrate the existence of two peaks corresponding to green and blue radiations–the wavelengths that most easily penetrate under the surface of the sea and reach the greatest depths. In many descriptions of shark attacks or underwater adventures, their icy stare is recalled. In fact, this is not due to the coldness or supposed ferocity of the fish, but to the fact that the eye can be closed temporarily with the nictitating membrane, a kind of third eyelid which covers the eye when it needs to be protected, such as during biting. The great white shark may appear to be in a sort of blind fury (although it isn't blind at all) because it protects its eyes during the final stage of the attack by rolling them inward.

E

F

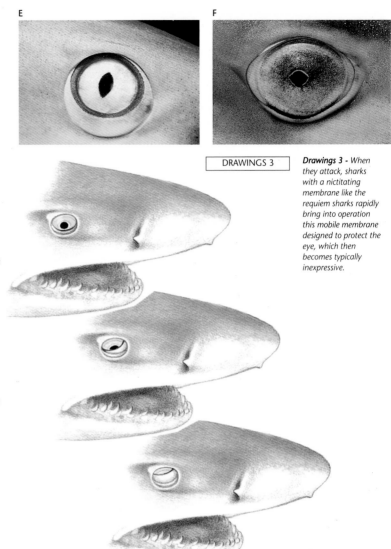

DRAWINGS 3

Drawings 3 - When they attack, sharks with a nictitating membrane like the requiem sharks rapidly bring into operation this mobile membrane designed to protect the eye, which then becomes typically inexpressive.

G

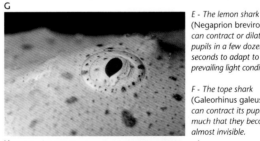

E - The lemon shark (Negaprion brevirostris) can contract or dilate its pupils in a few dozen seconds to adapt to the prevailing light conditions.

F - The tope shark (Galeorhinus galeus) can contract its pupils so much that they become almost invisible.

G - The Pacific angelshark has well-developed eyes, protected by small spines.

H - The hornsharks have oval eyes in a protruding position.

I - The catsharks of the genus Asymbolus have slight subocular protuberances.

C - In sharks, the size of the pupil can vary according to the prevailing light conditions. This regulation capacity is most accentuated in the sharks that live in surface waters in tropical areas.

D - The pupil of this rusty carpetshark (Parascyllium ferrugineum) is almost completely contracted.

H

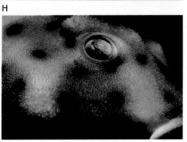

I

As well as sighting their prey and perceiving their odors, sharks can also identify victims or other sharks with different sensory systems, some of which are possessed by no other creature. One of their most efficient sensory complexes is the "lateral-line organ," a composite organ which runs along the body on both sides, from the eye to the base of the tail. It consists of ciliated cells sensitive to low-frequency pressure waves imperceptible to the human ear. Its function is mainly mechanical; it enables the shark to identify moving objects and locate them with great precision. Every moving body in water produces a series of vibrations which are transmitted through the surrounding medium, spreading out like the concentric ripples formed on a pond when a stone is thrown into it. The frequency of these vibrations depends not only on the size of the shark, but also on its state of health. This phenomenon explains the almost magical ability of sharks to appear within a few seconds when a swimmer is injured or a fish is caught. The vibrations produced by a fish in difficulty, detected by the lateral line, stimulate the cilia of its component cells, thus triggering the nerve fibers connected to them (over 6,000 in catshark). The impulses emitted by the nerve fibers are collected and interpreted by the nerve endings in the encephalon, which reacts by processing the distance and intensity data and directing the shark toward the source of the stimulus. The search

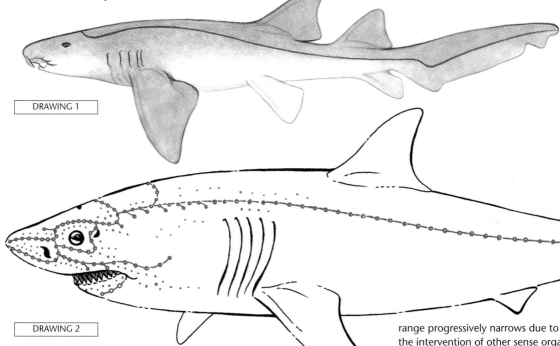

DRAWING 1

DRAWING 2

Drawings 1, 2 - *The lateral line organ, which extends from the head to the tail fin, is one of the shark's most important sense organs, acting as a kind of sonar. It enables sharks to detect the presence of other fish as a result of the vibrations they produce while swimming which are transmitted through the water, rather like the concentric ripples formed when a stone is thrown into a still pond.*

Drawing 3 - *The lateral line organ consists of a set of pores (a) opening to the exterior, which communicate with the mucus-filled inner canal of the organ (b). This canal is lined with sensory cells bristling with cilia (c) that protrude into the mucous layer. When the vibrations produced by a body moving in the water strike the lateral line organ, they are transmitted to the inner canal and stimulate the cilia of the sensory cells which activate the nerves (d) associated with them, causing the appropriate reaction by the shark.*

range progressively narrows due to the intervention of other sense organs which come into operation in an almost unchanging sequence (sound stimuli-smell stimuli-light stimuli), depending on their sensitivity threshold. The hearing organ of sharks, namely, the inner ear, is also highly developed; as well as perception of sounds, it governs balance and orientation. The auditory apparatus, which is invisible from the exterior apart from a few tiny endolymphatic pores on the top of the head, is closely connected with the lateral line organ. It is enclosed in the braincase and consists of a pair of organs situated just behind and above the eyes, formed mainly by three semicircular canals which control balance and orientation. The three canals are situated at right angles to one another, and are filled

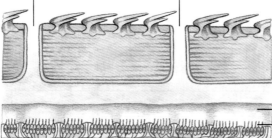

DRAWING 3 →

with a thick fluid. Each of them has an enlarged section called the ampulla, in which the sensory cells are concentrated; these cells are lined with cilia which plunge into a mass of mucus. Every movement of the shark, even a sudden acceleration, causes the fluid in the semicircular canals to shift and compress the mucus of the ampulla and the cilia, stimulating the nerve fibers to which they are connected and transmitting suitable impulses which the shark's brain converts into information about speed and position. A sac-like organ divided into three parts (the utricle, lagena, and saccule) is connected to the semicircular canals. The saccule is equipped with sets of ciliated cells sensitive to vibrations under 1,000 cycles per

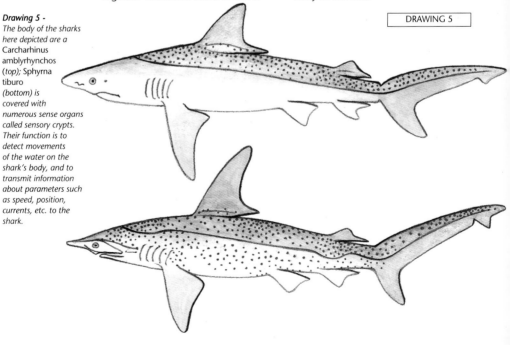

second (with a peak in the 25-100 cycles or Hertz band) which can easily be transmitted for a distance of hundreds of yards, and are in contact with dense particles comparable to the otoliths of fish.

As there is no structure resembling an eardrum, almost the entire body of the shark acts as the first receptor of vibrations, which are transmitted to the ear through the body tissues. In view of their common embryonic origin and similar innervation and morphology, the lateral line organ and inner ear are usually considered as two connected apparatuses and known as the "acoustico-lateralis system". When a sound is propagated in the sea, it produces pressure waves together with other kinds of waves

which vary, according to distance. This enables underwater sounds to be separated into two components: far and near. In the first case the effects of pressure prevail, mainly stimulating the inner ear, while the latter type of wave is more efficiently detected by the lateral line organ. The system also includes sensory crypts, mainly located near each of the endolymphatic pores on the top of the snout, parallel to the mouth, and along the pectoral fins. These crypts act individually and are believed to supply the shark with important information about its position, as they are particularly sensitive to the intensity and direction of the laminar water currents that flow along its body as it swims.

DRAWING 4

DRAWING 5

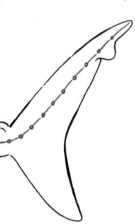

Drawing 4 -
Sharks' ears are rudimentary compared with those of the higher vertebrates. Vibrations are detected by the labyrinth through the tissues of the cranium, which contains the auditory organ considered by some experts to be an inner section of the lateral line organ, thus forming an "acoustico-lateralis" system.
The ear of the shark can be divided into two parts: the upper part consists of three semi-circular canals (a, b and c) and the utricle (d), which controls balance, while the lower part contains the saccule (e), which receives sounds transmitted along the endolymphatic duct (f).

Drawing 5 -
The body of the sharks here depicted are a Carcharhinus amblyrhynchos (top); Sphyrna tiburo (bottom) is covered with numerous sense organs called sensory crypts. Their function is to detect movements of the water on the shark's body, and to transmit information about parameters such as speed, position, currents, etc. to the shark.

65

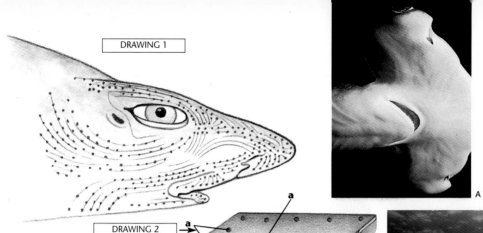

DRAWING 1

A - The shark's head is covered with tiny pores which communicate with nerve receptors highly sensitive to the electrical fields emitted by living creatures.

B - The "ampullae of Lorenzini" enable the blue shark to hunt by night or find prey hidden in the seabed.

A

B

DRAWING 2

a

b

c

d

Drawing 1 -
The shark's head is covered with pores, which constitute very special sense organs called the "ampullae of Lorenzini." These are electroreceptor organs able to detect the electrical fields produced by every living creature,

especially when the muscles contract. Sharks consequently have an efficient apparatus able to detect the presence of prey even at night or when hidden, and the predators are infallibly directed toward their food when it is very close to the mouth but out of visual range.

DRAWING 3

a   b   c   d

Drawing 2 -
This drawing shows the structure of the ampullae of Lorenzini in cross section. Each of them communicates with the exterior through a pore (a) connected by a canal (b) to the ampulla (c) lined with sensory cells. The sensory cells transmit the electrical signals received to the nervous system (d), which stimulates the appropriate motor responses by the shark.

Drawing 3 - Sharks are perfect predators, in which all the senses contribute to the success of the hunt. As shown in this drawing, the prey is first identified by the organs of the acoustico-lateralis system (a); the sense of smell (b) then directs the shark until the short-range senses such as sight (c), and the electrical sensors of the ampullae of Lorenzini (d) come into operation when it is a few yards away.

Some highly specialized organs which derive in some way from the lateral line organ are the ampullae of Lorenzini, named after the Italian doctor who first described them in his book *Osservazioni intorno alle torpedini fatte da Stefano Lorenzini Fiorentino* (Observations on Torpedo Fish by Stefano Lorenzini of Florence), published in 1678. The name "ampullae of Lorenzini" was only given to these organs by the German anatomist F. Boll in 1868, in homage to the Italian expert. They are small vesicles situated a few inches under the skin and connected to the exterior by a canal full of a gelatinous substance (which Lorenzini called a "humor").

The hundreds of pores visible on the head and snout of sharks constitute their opening to the exterior. In particular, these ampullae are electroreceptors which transmit the stimuli produced by very weak electrical fields through five nerve fibers leading to the facial nerve of the encephalon; the fields can measure as little as 0.02-0.13 microvolts per inch. To give an idea of their sensitivity, a battery which would seem totally flat to us would be considered a powerful source of energy by a shark.

The function of these organs is to identify prey and is based on the fact that living creatures emit an electrical field (including man, as demonstrated by the numerous diagnostic tests based on this phenomenon, such as the ECG, EEC, etc.). With the aid of the ampullae of Lorenzini, a shark is thus a living metal detector, able to identity the magnetic disturbances caused by the presence of a prey which,

Drawing 4 - Sharks can rapidly detect live prey, even when hidden in the sand, as a result of their ability to perceive electrical fields. However, this sense fails to operate if the prey is placed in an electrically insulated container, and the shark can be tricked if an artificial electrical field is created with two electrodes which simulate the existence of a fish.

Drawing 5 - Recent research seems to confirm the theory that the migrations of hammerhead sharks follow set routes, and that the ampullae of Lorenzini, which detect variations in the earth's magnetic field like a compass, enable the sharks to keep on course.

DRAWING 4

however much it tries to hide or camouflage itself, cannot conceal or inhibit the electricity produced by its body. This is how many sharks locate their prey, even if it is hidden under the sand. This has long been proved in tests which demonstrate that a shark can be tricked into following a moving artificial electrical field, or prevented from finding its prey by placing it in an insulated container. Finally, the electrical sense may also serve for orientation purposes.

An animal (which is a conductor) swimming in the earth's magnetic field emits an electrical field of varying intensity, depending on its direction of movement. Similarly, the great sea currents can have well-defined electrical fields. During an experiment designed to evaluate their orientation ability, a number of sharks were placed in a large tank and guided by researchers toward different points by altering the magnetic field. This ability, which means that sharks possess an internal geomagnetic compass, may explain the orientation ability of supposedly migratory sharks such as hammerheads and whale sharks, which gather in specific areas to mate at regular intervals.

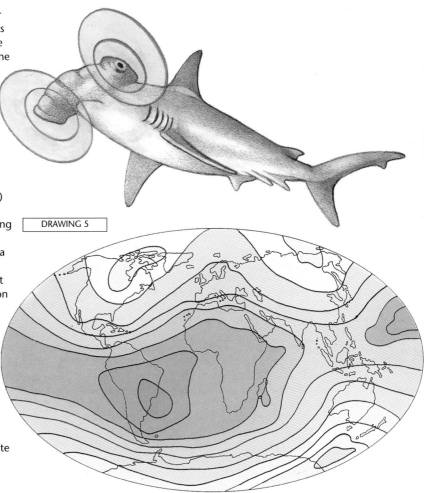

DRAWING 5

INTRODUCTION TO INTERNAL ANATOMY

The mouth of the shark constitutes the starting point of both the respiratory apparatus and the digestive apparatus, and is therefore an excellent place to begin a description of the creature's internal anatomy. The respiratory apparatus is basically limited to the gills. There are five gills, each consisting of a cartilaginous arch which supports a set of gill filaments. Each gill filament bears numerous perpendicular lamellae, which are densely vascularized as demonstrated by their red color. This complex structure is designed to increase the exchange surface between water and tissues as far as possible in order to enhance the efficiency of oxygen absorption, aided by the inner circulation which takes place in countercurrent. In a small *Squalus acanthias*, the area of the gill lamellae is estimated at 0.37 m² per kilogram

Drawing 1 - This drawing shows the positions of the shark's main internal organs. Olfactory bulb (a); Brain (b); Dorsal aorta (c); Spinal cord (d); Vertebrae (e); Stomach (f); Cloaca (g); Spiral intestinal valve (h); Pancreas (i); Liver (j); Esophagus (k); Heart (l); Gill (m).

DRAWING 1

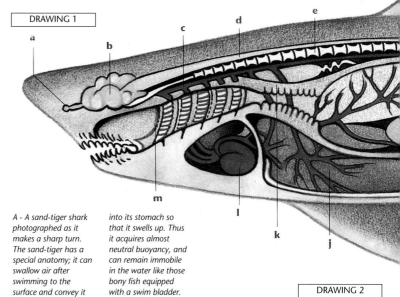

A - A sand-tiger shark photographed as it makes a sharp turn. The sand-tiger has a special anatomy; it can swallow air after swimming to the surface and convey it into its stomach so that it swells up. Thus it acquires almost neutral buoyancy, and can remain immobile in the water like those bony fish equipped with a swim bladder.

DRAWING 2

A

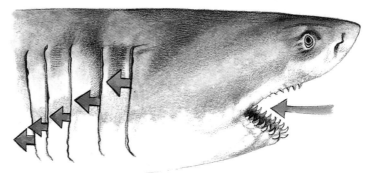

of fish. Water flows through the gills in two ways. Some species suck in water by expanding the pharynx and opening the mouth. During this stage, the gill lamellae adhere to the animal's body and can be considered closed. The mouth then closes, the pharynx contracts, and the water thus compressed is forced to pass rapidly through the gills and the gill slits. Sharks have five gills on average, although there are characteristic exceptions in the Chlamydoselachidae and Hexanchidae families, which include six-gill and even seven-gill sharks. It is a curious fact that the same mechanism as used for water flow is also used by the nurse shark to capture its prey, which is practically

inhaled. This "pumping" system is particularly common in sedentary sharks, whereas the pelagic species use a kind of respiration which exploits the shark's forward movement to pass water through the gills. This means that many sharks are obliged to swim continuously in order to pass enough water through their gills to meet their oxygen needs, which explains why many species are condemned to certain death by asphyxia if they are trapped in nets. Species like the sandtiger shark (*Eugomphodus taurus*) and the spurdog can change over from one type of breathing to the other, according to situation and behavior, in order to meet the body's metabolic needs with the minimum

energy expenditure.

Respiratory efficiency also depends on the amount of hemoglobin in the blood; the quantity of this substance, which bonds with and conveys oxygen from one point of the circulatory system to another and to all the organs, ranges from .11-.10 oz per 3.4 oz (3-5 g/100 ml) of blood in the case of the lazier sharks and those that live in the coldest and deepest waters to .21 oz per 3.4 oz (6 gm/100 ml) in the requiem sharks and hammerhead sharks, and reaches values comparable to those of mammals in the mackerel sharks and white shark, .49 oz per 3.4 oz (14 gm/100 ml) because of their particular physiology.

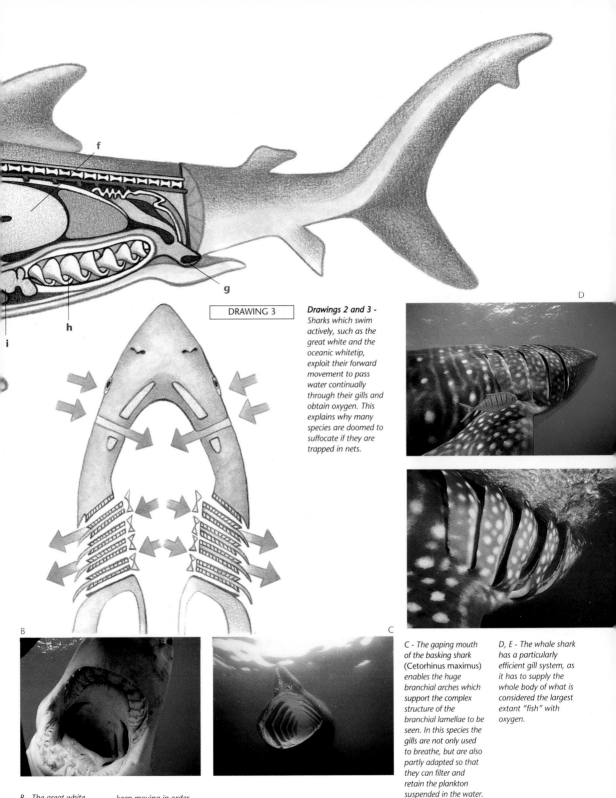

f

g

h

i

DRAWING 3

Drawings 2 and 3 -
Sharks which swim
actively, such as the
great white and the
oceanic whitetip,
exploit their forward
movement to pass
water continually
through their gills and
obtain oxygen. This
explains why many
species are doomed to
suffocate if they are
trapped in nets.

D

B

C

C - The gaping mouth
of the basking shark
(Cetorhinus maximus)
enables the huge
branchial arches which
support the complex
structure of the
branchial lamellae to be
seen. In this species the
gills are not only used
to breathe, but are also
partly adapted so that
they can filter and
retain the plankton
suspended in the water.

D, E - The whale shark
has a particularly
efficient gill system, as
it has to supply the
whole body of what is
considered the largest
extant "fish" with
oxygen.

B - The great white
shark is very efficient
and highly evolved in
various ways. However,
like the best swimmers
in the group it has to
keep moving in order
to pass enough water
through its gills to
guarantee an oxygen
intake sufficient for its
metabolism.

Drawings 1 - The nekto-benthic species and those which spend long periods motionless on the seabed, like the nurse sharks, can breathe by controlling the opening and closing of the mouth and gills. These drawings show their respiratory movements from the outside (a) and in cross section. At the first stage (a) the shark sucks in water by widening the pharynx and mouth. The resulting vacuum causes the branchial lamellae to adhere to the body, so that they can be considered closed. Then (b) the mouth closes, the pharynx contracts and the water, thus compressed, is forced to pass rapidly through the gills.

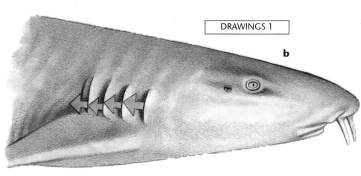

DRAWINGS 1

b

a

A - Sharks that spend long periods resting on the seabed (this photo shows Triaenodon obesus) breathe with a pump mechanism which enables them to force water through their gills by opening and closing the mouth rhythmically.

A

DRAWINGS 2

Drawings 2 - These drawings show the breathing movements in cross section and from outside which have been described on the previous page (Phase a, b).

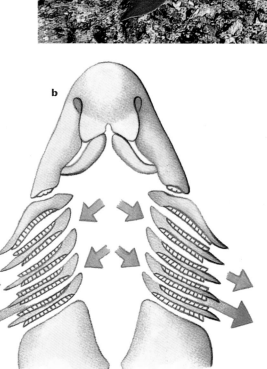

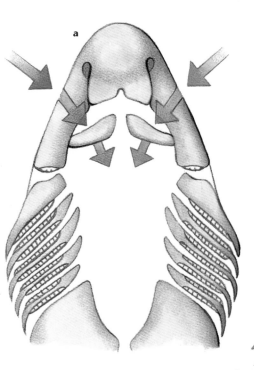

a

b

Food is also taken in by the mouth and is conveyed via the pharynx and oesophagus to the large, J-shaped stomach. Almost-whole fish, dolphins, and turtles have been found in the stomachs of some white and tiger sharks. The stomach is separated by the pyloric valve from the intestine, which is equipped with a special structure: the spiral valve. This is a spiral fold on the inner wall, designed to increase the absorption surface without lengthening the intestine. The number of coils ranges between a few and several dozen; the spiral valve can resemble a set of regular rings or a sort of scroll positioned lengthways to the intestine. The particular internal structure prevents the indigestible parts of the prey from travelling through the intestine, so they are regurgitated rather than being eliminated in the form of feces like

Drawing 3 - The gills, which in sharks have 5-7 gill slits opening to the exterior, form a barrier that separates the buccal cavity from the gill cavity, so that water is forced to flow through it. The barrier is constituted by thin filaments which are densely vascularized in order to absorb the oxygen dissolved in the water efficiently, and meet the body's metabolic needs with the minimum expenditure of energy.

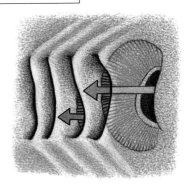

a

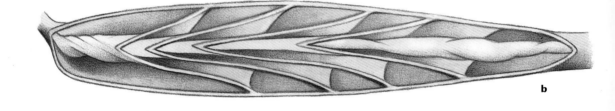

b

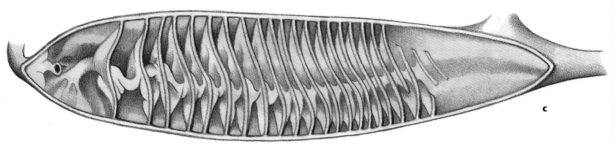

c

normal food residues. The largest gland of the digestive apparatus is the liver, one of the main economic resources provided by sharks; they are hunted partly for this gland, which is rich in oils and other valuable substances such as squalene.

Apart from its ordinary functions, this organ is of great importance to the shark's hydrostatic balance, as its size

and the high concentration of oily substances are exploited to reduce the creature's specific gravity and improve its buoyancy. The liver is also a useful energy reserve, allowing the shark to survive for long periods without feeding, as demonstrated by a whitetip shark deprived of food for over a month, which still survived although its liver mass was halved.

Drawings 4 - The shark's short intestine would not allow the absorption of nutrients if its area were not enormously increased by the spiral valve. This valve consists of a spiral fold in the absorbing mucosa which forms a series of coils (ranging from 4 in Prionace glauca to 45 in Alopias vulpinus) that are fairly regularly spaced (c), arranged in a bell shape (b), or set very close together to form a kind of scroll lying along the axis of the intestine (a).

FOUR SCENES FROM UNDERWATER LIFE

A - A nurse shark of the Indo-Pacific swims lazily through a shoal of totally unconcerned fish. Nurse sharks rarely hunt during the day, preferring to remain in their holes or swim around their territory.

B - A tawny nurse shark (Nebrius ferrugineus) inspects the coral-covered seabed that constitutes its habitat. Here it finds plenty of grottoes and crevices with sandy floors where it can remain immobile for long periods, while the variety of coral formations allows the development of a wealth of fauna able to meet its dietary needs.

The underwater twilight is growing darker. The nurse shark, which was lazy until not long ago, is now swimming in bursts. All its senses are on the alert as it seeks out possible prey in the dark. A large squirrelfish has also left its burrow and is swimming around in the water in search of food. As they come and go, the routes of the two fish suddenly cross. The nurse shark's behavior changes instantly. Its body stiffens, its tail lashes more quickly and it accelerates rapidly; the squirrelfish has become its target.

An indescribable pandemonium then begins, which sounds the alarm throughout the world of the reef. First comes the victim, which tries all possible ways of escape: accelerating, curving, reversing, and fleeing through the coral. Close behind is the nurse shark, which seems unstoppable. Its bulk makes it insensitive to obstacles, and coral colonies are smashed in the frenzy of the chase,

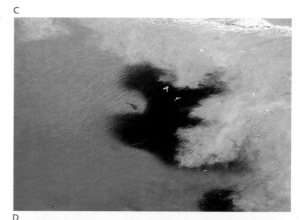

C

D

A

B

which reaches the inevitable conclusion. With a last burst of speed the nurse shark's jaws close on the squirrelfish, which is literally sucked into the shark's great maw by the violent undertow created as water is forced out through its gills. Slowly the sand settles, and nothing but broken coral branches remain to testify to what has happened. The darkness conceals the rest.

Albatrosses have gathered on one of the loneliest islands of the Pacific to mate, as they do every year. This is their island, and no one seems to threaten it. The eggs hatch rapidly and the chicks grow quickly, fed regularly by their parents. Their feathers gradually grow, and with them the instinct to try their wings. The first flights take them further and further away; first on dry land, then in the water. Suddenly, a small whirlpool forms in a place where a young albatross was swimming a few moments ago. Then a few ruffled feathers emerge, floating on the surface. Underneath them, the lazy shadow of a tiger shark swims slowly away from the scene of the crime.

C - In the inshore waters where large shoals of fish gather, sharks use special group hunting techniques. They surround the fish as if acting in liaison, making rapid incursions into the midst of shoal and taking advantage of the growing confusion to catch their prey without difficulty.

D - The tiger shark (Galeocerdo cuvier) is one of the most dangerous and aggressive species. Their voracity is proverbial, and hardly any creature or object can be considered immune from their attacks. All sorts of things have been found in their stomachs, including chickens, dogs, sheep, refuse, plastic, tin cans, bottles, and even pieces of iron.

Tiger sharks are considered the most adaptable sharks, and some have always made their appearance in the waters of the island at this period. It is not known what brings them there–perhaps a habit learned in the past–but they never fail to turn up punctually and take their toll of albatrosses every year.

The Farallon Islands, off the coast of California: another day begins for the sea lions. The waters are teeming with fish and provide the ideal place for sea lions to live with their own kind; this habitat is perhaps too welcoming, so that they forget to keep a constant watch on the surrounding waters.

Suddenly a whitish shape erupts from the blue sea, and only a rapid burst of speed, dictated by the survival instinct, distances the sea lion from the jaws of the great white shark–but not far enough. Although its sharp triangular teeth miss their victim, they leave a deep wound in the flesh of the sea lion; however, it still manages to reach the shore. It is an adult male, and there is

a good chance that it will recover and survive. Today, the great predator of the Farallon Islands will have to find another victim.

A flattish stretch of the seabed where sand and Zostera alternate, creating the ideal habitat for the great stingrays, which have room to stretch out their great bodies and find plenty of victims here. One of these fish is swimming over the seabed waving its fins, when suddenly, something makes it increase the rate of its movements. A large hammerhead shark erupts onto the scene and homes in on the stringray, striking it on a fin.

The attack is repeated once, twice, three times, and the stingray reacts more slowly every time. Yet it does not appear to be injured, and perhaps that is not even the hammerhead's intention. It merely lashes out at the ray repeatedly to daze it. Only then do its jaws come into action and it eats the ray, leaving the harder parts for some other shark, which will certainly turn up soon.

G

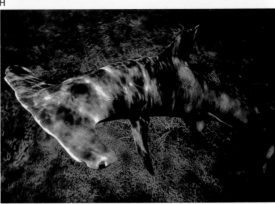

H

E

F

A

B

C

Sharks are considered to be the carnivores *par excellence*, situated at the top of the food chain. However, this is only partly true, although one shark, *Carcharhinus longimanus* (the oceanic whitetip), is believed to be the most common large predator in the world. In some limited areas, such as the Mediterranean, the white shark is certainly at the top of the marine food pyramids, as the adults feed on small cetaceans and tuna.

But in other seas, where they may find themselves competing with killer whales, it would be hard to deny the latter's supremacy. It would perhaps be more correct to describe sharks as important links in food chains rather than at the top, although this greatly reduces the exaggerated reputation for danger and ferocity still unfairly attributed to these fish.

According to some experts, many species should actually be considered "animals with saprophagous tendencies which do not have the patience to wait for their victims to die a natural death." This may partly explain observations of sharks' behavior with dolphins and sea lions, in which the prey was ignored or attacked without result because of its greater agility, and even the many cases in which potentially dangerous sharks have totally

ignored divers for no apparent reason in circumstances identical to those in which their most aggressive behavior has been manifested. The large predatory species are usually more or less solitary. This is mainly due to the need to avoid dangerous direct clashes between adults, and the need for better exploitation of resources, which can be highly specialized in some species.

This specialization can have different connotations from species to species, as demonstrated by the case of the great white shark, whose stomach contents have been found to include a wide variety of large and small fish, other sharks, seals, dolphins, and other cetaceans, sea lions, penguins, etc. This list might suggest that *Carcharodon carcharias* eats absolutely anything, but as we will see, it actually specializes in capturing whatever is most readily available.

The feeding behavior of individual species does not only depend on the availability of their prey; the available resources can best be exploited if individuals vary their feeding behavior as they grow. For example, young mako sharks (*Isurus sp.*) feed on small fish and cephalopods, while the adults catch swordfish, marlins, dolphins and porpoises.

D

A - The oceanic whitetip shark (Carcharhinus longimanus), *easily recognizable by its highly developed pectoral fins, is considered one of the most common marine predators. This species swims slowly but incessantly in surface waters, following the routes of shoaling fish (bonito, carangids, mackerel, and barracuda) and pelagic fish (dolphin fish and marlin) which it catches after rapid accelerations, often taking advantage of moments when its victims are intent on feeding.*

B - The copper shark (Carcharhinus brachyurus), *a common species in warm temperate seas, feeds on sardines, grey mullet, carangids, cod and benthic fish including rays, electric rays and soles. Recent research demonstrates that in some areas they make regular journeys, following the migratory routes of their prey.*

C - Carcharhinus brachyurus, *which grows to a maximum size of just under 10 ft (3 m) long, is considered dangerous to man and has been responsible for unprovoked attacks on swimmers and divers in Australia, New Zealand and South Africa.*

D - The mako (Isurus oxyrinchus) *is considered one of the fastest sharks; according to some experts its speed can exceed 43 mph (70 kph) over short distances. The huge power of its muscles is fully apparent when the shark leaps several yards out of the water.*

E - The sight of a great white shark approaching its prey always gives the impression of destructive power and strength. Once an attack begins, it is always carried through with determination, even if the prey proves to be inanimate bait.

F - This photo shows the functional set of teeth owned by the great white shark. Apart from the special movements its jaws can perform to increase their biting efficacy, the teeth dovetail perfectly to sever the victim's flesh with relative ease.

The white shark (inevitably used as an example because studies of this group of animals cover just over 10% of the known species) presents a clear differentiation in feeding habits. Individuals measuring up to 6.5 ft (2 m) long mainly feed on fish; those up to 10 ft (3 m) long catch large crustaceans and cartilaginous fish (small sharks and rays), while the larger sharks prefer cetaceans and seals. These observations, made in Australia, confirm the findings made in other areas among other populations. In the Mediterranean, the adults prey mainly on tuna fish, sharks, swordfish, and dolphins.

Along the coasts of South Africa, sharks present a similar change in favor of large warm-blooded prey on reaching sexual maturity, and the same occurs along the Californian and Atlantic coasts of America. These choices are partly due to the greater offensive capacity of the adults: they appear to choose prey that stays close to the surface so that they can make a surprise attack after a prior evaluation of their chances of

G

H

I

G - Shoals of carangids are just one of the prey on which the great white shark regularly feeds.

H - Colonies of sea lions are one of the favorite hunting grounds of the great white shark. The association between these or other similar mammals and the great white shark is regularly repeated in the worldwide distribution of sharks. Especially when the young are born, waters frequented by sea lions become a favorite spot with great white sharks, which have been found to use specific hunting strategies to capture this prey.

I - Although they belong to the same group (the Elasmobranchs), catsharks and many other sharks are by no means safe in waters patrolled by the great white shark, which feeds on the most abundant and readily available prey.

E

F

success, probably on the basis of their experience. Surface attacks appear to take place mainly in the daytime; at night, the white shark moves to deeper waters.

As regards the details of the shark's hunting technique, small prey (i.e., small in proportion to the size of the shark) are swallowed whole, while the larger ones are first killed and then devoured. This seems to be confirmed by the systems used by sharks to hunt the pinniped populations of the Californian coasts. Both sea lions and elephant seals live here, two species with different habits and sizes; the former are smaller, social creatures, while the latter are larger and solitary. Both are attacked by the white shark, but oddly enough, elephant seals are killed in greater numbers. Although the white shark's favorite victims are the young animals, it can take advantage of their inexperience and disregard for danger, adult specimens are also hunted in different and surprising ways, depending on species.

The favorite technique seems to be a surprise attack from below. If this first part is successful, it is followed by a phase of varying length that might be described as "remote surveillance," during which the shark waits for its victim to die. Observation of dead and injured specimens demonstrates that the areas of the body most often attacked, especially in the case of sea lions, are the pectoral region or the rear latero-dorsal region, while in the case of elephant seal the largest number of wounds is located in the front part of the body. This difference is due to the swimming technique of the two pinnipeds and the different use they make of their fins.

A

A - The great white shark often attacks its victims from below, to take them totally by surprise. As in the case of all sharks, all its senses are coordinated to complete the attack, which may begin far away, even before the great white shark can be seen.

B

C

Despite their smaller size, sea lions have a better chance of surviving an attack because they mainly use their front fins. A bite in the rear part of the body may therefore not be enough to stop them, as is the case with elephant seals.

In addition, the white shark is blind for a fraction of a second when its eyes roll inward for defensive purposes, and it has to rely on the ampullae of Lorenzini to locate its prey. This moment can make a significant difference to the survival of a sea lion, which can dart forward with a final burst of speed so that it is only wounded in the rear part of the body, whereas the slower elephant seal is injured in far more vital parts. Sea lions are also more social creatures, while elephant seals are solitary and may not benefit from the advantages of group. As regards the overlap of distribution areas between sharks and prey, observations conducted in Australia seem to confirm that seal colonies constitute a considerable attraction for white sharks, which patrol the areas frequented by these mammals; perhaps they perceive their odor due to substances produced by the animals on dry land, which are washed into the sea by the waves forming an odoriferous trail that can easily be followed.

5

8

B - Attracting a great white shark to a boat to take pictures like this one requires a great deal of patience and the use of bait rich in blood, like pieces of tuna fish which release a continuous flow of odoriferous particles into the water; these stimulate the shark's sensitive sense of smell and induce it to follow the trail to its source.

C - A great white shark shoots up to the surface, following the bait designed to attract it. This shark often raises its head above the surface, as if to observe what is happening in the vicinity.

The great white shark (1) is situated at the top of the trophic nets in all the seas in which it lives. Its feeding habits, especially in the case of the adults, are very variable, depending on the prey most readily available. For example, its prey mainly consists of pinnipeds along the Californian coast, fish in the Atlantic, and tuna and small cetaceans in the Mediterranean. The drawing therefore does not refer to a single food chain, but summarizes everything the great white shark mainly eats.

2) Sea lions;
3) Bottlenose dolphins and small cetaceans in general;
4) Penguins;
5) Elephant seals;
6) Cod and other Gadiformes;
7) Porpoises;
8) Piked dogfish and other sharks;
9) Salmon;
10) Mackerel;
11) Eagle rays;
12) Tuna and bonito;
13) Skates and rays.

A

B

C

D

Whereas the white shark usually seems to choose the prey which is most abundant locally and best meets its needs, the feeding habits of the omnivorous tiger shark (*Galeocerdo cuvier*), considered the most adaptable of all the sharks, are quite different.

As can be seen from studies of its biology, the tiger shark feeds on fish, sharks, rays, turtles, birds, seals, dolphins, sea snakes, cephalopods, lobsters, crabs, horseshoe crabs, gastropod mollusks, and jellyfish, not counting the numerous objects associated with human beings. Objects of definite human origin have been found in the stomachs of tiger sharks caught near ports and towns: tuna heads cut off by fishermen, tin cans, plastic bottles, rubbish of all kinds, domestic animals, and sometimes human beings. This capacity is largely due to its size (the tiger shark can potentially

A - A tiger shark is swimming on a sandbank. This species is considered one of the most dangerous and aggressive, but if food resources are plentiful, humans are rarely among its prey.

B - The typical teeth of the tiger shark (Galeocerdo cuvier), shaped like a rounded blade with a serrated edge, can be glimpsed in its large mouth.

C, D, E - Tiger sharks are voracious predators which never pass up the chance of feeding on bait left on the seabed to attract them. The shark's attack techniques vary from species to species and according to the size of the prey. Small prey is swallowed whole, while large prey is torn into large pieces after being killed or prevented from escaping.

E

grow to as much as 20 ft/6 m long) and the structure of its teeth which, though not as large as those of the white shark, are equally terrible.

Their subtriangular shape and serrations complement the action of the jaws which, after grasping the prey, move rapidly from side to side, imparting a to-and-fro movement to the teeth, thus acting as a saw, and can cut through even apparently indestructible parts like the thick shell of the turtle.

F

G

H

F - Lobsters might seem to be an unusual prey for a shark like the tiger shark, but they have often been found in the stomachs of sharks caught near the reef.

G - Octopus and squid are easy prey for many sharks, and tiger sharks are no exception, although on average these mollusks only represent 3%-5% of their catch.

*H - A whitetip reef shark (*Triaenodon obesus*) can represent an excellent meal for a big tiger shark. Although the remains of other sharks are not uncommonly found in the stomach of the tiger shark, experts believe that most are only attacked when caught in nets.*

I - Even the robust shell of the turtle gives little protection against the jaws of the tiger shark, whose teeth can easily cut through the shells of these marine reptiles.

J - Skates and rays (this photo shows a Dasyatis americana*) constitute another potential victim of the tiger shark, which has the strangest feeding habits of all the sharks.*

I

J

This drawing shows the main prey of the tiger shark (1), as demonstrated by a series of studies conducted in Australian waters for over 20 years. (2/3) birds (seagulls, terns and albatross); (4) carangids; (5) squid;

(6) bottlenose dolphins and small cetaceans; (7) dugongs; (8) grunts; (9) snappers; (10) turtles; (11) dogfish sharks; (12) sea snakes; (13) octopus; (14) lobsters; (15) skates and rays.

A - Young tiger sharks, recognizable by their much more evident striped pattern, catch more fish, birds, and squid than the adults. As in many other species of shark, the tiger shark not only adapts to the prey most abundant locally, but selects it on the basis of its energy value and the expenditure of energy required to catch it.

A

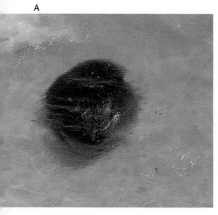

A

B

However, experts agree that in the world of sharks, the rule is specialization rather than adaptability. This is particularly true of families such as the Carcharhinidae (requiem sharks), which in many areas are represented by several species. A study conducted on the shark populations of the Gulf of Carpentaria along the northern coast of Australia showed that the three species of requiem shark present have such different feeding habits

D

C

that they can coexist with no competition at all. Of the three species studied, *Carcharhinus dussumieri* is a predator of benthic species, with a marked preference for crustaceans; *C. tilstoni* prefers to catch its prey (bentho-nektonic fish) in mid-water; while *C. sorrah* tends to be pelagic and feeds on clupeids, mainly penetrating into the estuary areas where these small gregarious fish gather.

A - The sharks that usually live in groups have in some cases developed the ability to act in a coordinated manner, surrounding shoals of fish and forcing them to crowd into a small volume of water.

B - The gray reef sharks (Carcharhinus amblyrhinchos), together with the blacktip, are the sharks best known by divers, and those involved in shark feeding activities.

C - Bait dangling near the seabed soon becomes an irresistible attraction for sharks living in the vicinity.

D - One of the most striking manifestations of a shark attack is the "feeding frenzy," which is even more evident when a group of sharks is involved.

E - A mixed group of Caribbean reef sharks (Carcharhinus perezi) and blacktip sharks (Carcharhinus limbatus) are swimming round in circles while they wait for the diver to bring their usual ration of fish, thus initiating the shark-feeding show.

F - The small area in which these gray reef sharks are swimming is due to the presence of bait and the consequent feeding frenzy, which causes them to make increasingly rapid, sometimes uncontrolled movements.

E

F

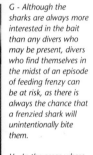

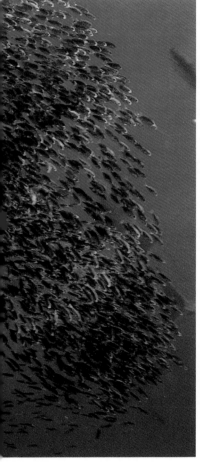

G

G - Although the sharks are always more interested in the bait than any divers who may be present, divers who find themselves in the midst of an episode of feeding frenzy can be at risk, as there is always the chance that a frenzied shark will unintentionally bite them.

H - In the areas where shark feeding is most often practiced, sharks eventually acquire conditioned behavior, associating the presence of divers with feeding.

H

A

D

A - The wealth of life on the coral reef allows the development of numerous food chains, each of which can be exploited by a particular species of shark to reduce competition.

B - A rapid movement brings the hunt by this requiem shark to a successful conclusion, while the ubiquitous remoras are all ready to take advantage of its leftovers.

B

C - Although stingrays have large poisonous spines, they are virtually helpless against sharks, although sharks do not usually attack such large stingrays unless they are already weakened.

D - An episode of feeding frenzy involves a large number of fish in addition to sharks. The food fragments scattered around by the sharks attract numerous fish, which fight over the meal of the larger predators just as frenetically.

C

E - Carangids are
among the favorite
prey of small and
medium-sized sharks.
Although they are not
easy to catch because
of their speed and
agility, carangids can
meet a shark's dietary
requirements
for quite a long time.

F - Sole might enjoy
relative immunity from
shark attack if it were
not for the fact that
their camouflage skills
are useless against
predators equipped
with electric sensors.

G - An octopus outside
its lair is easy meat for
the smaller, more agile
reef sharks and those
which hunt by twilight
and at night.

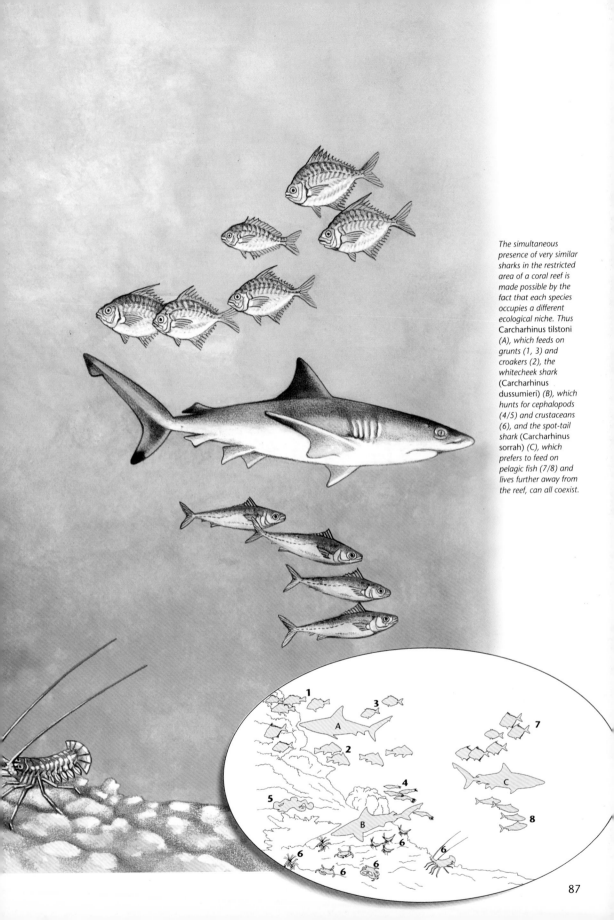

The simultaneous presence of very similar sharks in the restricted area of a coral reef is made possible by the fact that each species occupies a different ecological niche. Thus Carcharhinus tilstoni (A), which feeds on grunts (1, 3) and croakers (2), the whitecheek shark (Carcharhinus dussumieri) (B), which hunts for cephalopods (4/5) and crustaceans (6), and the spot-tail shark (Carcharhinus sorrah) (C), which prefers to feed on pelagic fish (7/8) and lives further away from the reef, can all coexist.

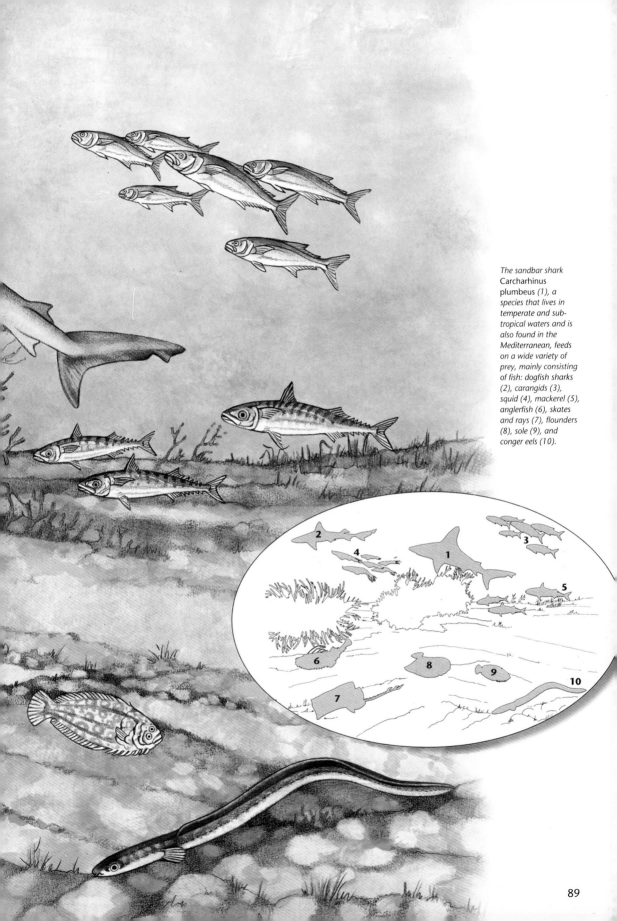

The sandbar shark Carcharhinus plumbeus (1), a species that lives in temperate and sub-tropical waters and is also found in the Mediterranean, feeds on a wide variety of prey, mainly consisting of fish: dogfish sharks (2), carangids (3), squid (4), mackerel (5), anglerfish (6), skates and rays (7), flounders (8), sole (9), and conger eels (10).

A - Port Jackson sharks are small sharks with a tall, conical head. They are rather lazy, and swim around near the seabed at night in search of their prey.

Heterodontidae (horn sharks) specialize in feeding abundantly on sea urchins and mollusks, whose shells they can easily crush with their grindstone-like teeth. The cookie-cutter shark (*Isistius brasiliensis*) clings to the bodies of large fish and cetaceans with a kind of sucker formed by its lips; it then uses its numerous teeth to sever a piece of flesh, leaving a highly characteristic imprint, traces of which have been found on the plastic sheaths of telephone cables laid at great depths, and even on submarines.

Thresher sharks employ an unusual and almost unique hunting system; they use their long, mobile tail to concentrate their prey (small fish) or stun them. As a result of this practice they often get caught in the hooks of long lines when they try to take advantage of the fish caught in them.

Port Jackson sharks (Heterodontus sp.) (1) have special teeth that enable them to eat organisms with robust protective structures, such as echinoderms (2), mollusks (3), and crustaceans (4), without difficulty.

B - Bullhead sharks, which are practically defenseless apart from the robust spines preceding their dorsal fins, are often attacked by larger sharks.

This photo shows an attack by an ornate wobbegong (Orectolobus ornatus) on a Port Jackson shark (Heterodontus portusjacksoni) in Australian waters.

C - Bullhead sharks are capable of crushing the strongest mollusk shell. The larger shells are split at the weakest point so that the mollusk can easily be extracted. In this photograph a Port Jackson shark is cannibalizing an egg of another shark.

Thresher sharks have developed a special hunting technique that exploits the exceptional size of their tail fin. They feed on shoals of small fish and squid; after sighting a shoal, the sharks swim round and round it, gradually tightening the circle so that the victims are crowded into an ever smaller space. When the shoal is very densely packed, the thresher shark lashes out violently with its tail, stunning and killing the fish so that it can seize them without difficulty.

A - Thresher sharks (Alopias sp.) are easily recognizable by their tail; the highly developed, elongated top lobe accounts for around 50% of the total length of the fish.

B - Shoals of fish constitute one of the most frequent targets for attacks by sharks, especially pelagic species like hammer-heads and mackerel sharks, each of which has developed its own techniques for exploiting this abundant but elusive resource with the minimum expenditure of energy.

C - Although barracudas are considered typical predatory fish, they are just one of the tiers in the food pyramids headed by sharks. A rapid incursion by a hungry shark into a shoal of barracuda always leaves a few victims behind.

C

A

D

B

E

D, E - As these photos show, mating and death are inextricably linked in the life cycle of sea creatures. Every winter, large numbers of opal squid (Loligo opalescens), sometimes millions of them, assemble off the Californian coast to mate. On moonless nights the squid mate, lay and fertilize their eggs heedless of every other stimulus, such as fear, hunger, and fatigue. The blue shark (Prionace glauca) takes advantage of this state to catch huge numbers of squid, until it cannot swallow any more. The feast goes on for several nights, and cruel as it may seem, is an example of the essential rules of Nature, designed to keep its resources in balance.

93

A

A - The basking shark (Cetorhinus maximus) is one of the largest known sharks; it can exceed 40-42 ft (12-13 m) long. Despite its awesome size it is totally harmless, as it feeds on plankton.

B - The basking shark feeds as it swims. It swims with its mouth open for nutritional rather than respiration reasons. When it encounters waters particularly rich in plankton, the basking shark opens its mouth wide, allowing the plankton to flow into its mouth, after which it is filtered by the gill rakers.

C - This photo shows part of the filtering apparatus of the basking shark. It is situated at the branchial arches and the gill slits (the dark parts inside the mouth) through which the entire mass of water conveyed to the mouth passes, transporting food and oxygen simultaneously.

B

C

The technique used by the basking shark, whale shark, and megamouth is very unusual, but is the only way to give these giants of the shark world a sufficient energy intake. They rely on the most abundant resource offered by the sea, namely plankton, for their sustenance. These species have very small teeth, and huge mouths which they open wide as they cruise along. The gills are highly modified, to become large filter units.
The gills of the basking shark have thousands of horny spines (gill rakers) with a characteristic shape which serves to trap small organisms carried in the water that flows through its mouth and gills.

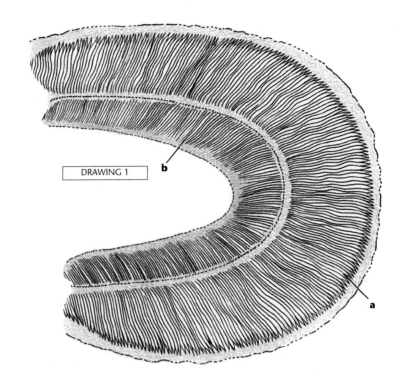

DRAWING 1

b

a

DRAWING 2

When swimming with its jaws wide open at cruising speed, a basking shark can filter 10 tons of water an hour in this way.

Oddly enough, the basking sharks caught in winter have no gill rakers, which raises the question of what these animals do in the coldest months of the year, and how they feed. According to some widely accepted theories, basking sharks may stop eating in winter, and leave the surface for the deeper layers of water. Here they may go into a kind of hibernation until the gill rakers re-form, by a mechanism which might be compared to seasonal molting.

Drawing 1 -
This drawing shows the structure of a basking shark's branchial arch (a). It consists of a rigid arch which on one side supports the flexible and densely vascularized branchial lamellae (b), which have a respiratory function, and on the other side supports the more rigid horny gill rakers which act like a comb or sieve, and are designed to intercept and retain small planktonic organisms, especially crustaceans, which are then swallowed. (modified from Massimo Demma).

Drawing 2 - Shows the flow of water through the basking shark's gills. As it swims with its mouth gaping to a greater or lesser extent, masses of water are conveyed into its jaws and forced through the gills. The gill rakers act as a filter, retaining the plankton.
They also perform a protective function by eliminating particles that might damage the more delicate branchial lamellae (modified from Massimo Demma).

A

A - A whale shark
(Rhiniodon typus)
swims to the surface,
perhaps in pursuit of
a swarm of plankton,
which are often most
plentiful in the first few
yards of water.

B - The prey of the
whale shark includes
small pelagic fish like
anchovies and sardines
which are swallowed
together with great
mouthfuls of water;

the shark takes
advantage of their
gregarious habits,
which cause them to
close ranks when
attacked.

C - The large mouth
of the whale shark is
situated in a terminal
rather than a ventral
position as in most
sharks; this is an
adaptation to the
plankton-eating habits
of the species.

E

The whale shark is more active:
instead of keeping its mouth open
while it swims and taking advantage
of the current of water thus created,
it opens and closes its jaws before
and after swimming through a swarm
of plankton, especially krill, or a shoal
of small fish. In this species the filter
which serves to trap the food consists
of spongy tissue, a kind of close-
meshed net with 2-3 mm wide
mesh attached to the cartilage
walls of the gill arches.

On several occasions whale sharks
have been observed eating while
moving vertically up and down in
the water, sucking in their prey and
occasionally raising their heads above
the surface so that water can flow out
of their gills. The presence of whale
sharks near large swarms of krill (a
kind of universal food for the
inhabitants of the sea, from fish to
whales) may confirm the empirical
observations of many fishermen, who
once used these sharks as natural
indicators of good fishing waters.
The last example of a filter-feeding
shark, the megamouth, also has gill
rakers to trap food particles.

B

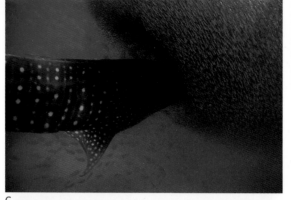

C

D

D - The fish which
often surround the
mouth of whale sharks
are unlikely to be
swallowed by the big
shark; they exploit the
large mass of the shark
to protect themselves,
and make the most of
its leftovers.

E - The interior of the
whale shark's mouth
immediately gives the
impression of a well-
designed trap for the
capture of plankton
(especially crustacean
and krill larvae) and
small fish.

F

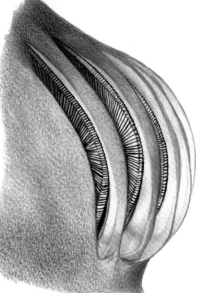

G

F - The bulk of the whale shark, with its unmistakeable pattern of white spots, appears even more impressive when compared with the size of the diver. Water carrying both oxygen and nourishment passes through the large gill slits, which can be seen in front of the pectoral fins.

H

G - When the gill slits dilate under the pressure of the outgoing water, it is possible to catch a glimpse of their complex structure, consisting of thousands of filter plates.

H - The latest, though certainly not the last shark to be discovered is the mysterious

megamouth (Megachasma pelagios). *This species, found by chance for the first time in Hawaiian waters in 1976, feeds mainly on euphausiids (very common shrimps), following them in their daily movements between deep and surface waters.*

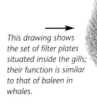

This drawing shows the set of filter plates situated inside the gills; their function is similar to that of baleen in whales.

97

Eating to survive: At the sight of a group of gray sharks darting in all directions in a feeding frenzy, or the terror that seems to overcome a shoal of tuna chased by a mako or a white shark, it is easy to see why the shark has always been considered a voracious, tireless predator.

In practice, it does *not* spend all its time eating, and this seems to be confirmed by the large number of sharks caught with empty stomachs. Lengthy observations in aquariums and in nature have led to the

B

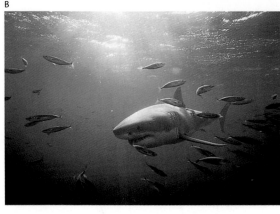

A

*B - The great white
shark owes much of its
efficiency as a predator
to its physiology, which
resembles that of the
land creatures that
can regulate their
temperature
independently.*

discovery that a shark eats on average every 4-7 days. This is due to the existence in all species of trophic rhythms, according to which intense hunting periods stimulated by increasing hunger alternate with digestion times which are quite long, because of the particular structure of the digestive apparatus and the shark's ability to store its prey intact in an unknown way for long periods, regardless of the effect of ambient temperature and the type and size of the victim

DRAWING 1

DRAWING 2

+4°c
+5°c
+6°c
+3°c +2°c +1°c

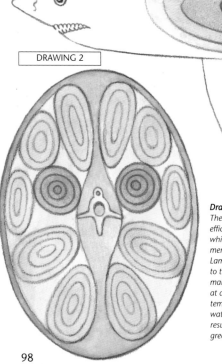

*Drawings 1, 2 -
The extraordinary
efficiency of the great
white shark and other
members of the
Lamnidae family is due
to their ability to
maintain their bodies
at a higher
temperature than the
water they live in. This
result is achieved by
greater development*

*of the red muscles
at the sides of the
spinal column, and
a special type of
blood circulation
(countercurrent
circulation) which
enables the blood in
the veins to warm up
before reaching the
heart, so that the
internal muscles are
progressively warmer.*

swallowed. Although there is no doubt that an adult shark can eat more than a younger one, this difference is due to the larger size of the adult's stomach rather than to real need. As in man, food consumption is highest during the early years of life, when it is essential to provide sufficient nourishment to the actively growing body, and then declines in adult age.

Despite the difficulties involved in this type of survey, which requires detailed examination of the stomach contents of as many specimens and species as possible and recording of data relating to length, weight, age, gender, season, etc., it can be said that food intake is much

C

lower than generally believed, amounting on average to 1-10 times the body weight a year.

For example, a sandbar shark just over 19 in (50 cm) long, weighing under 5 lb (2 kg), eats the equivalent of 5 times its own weight in a year, while in an adult the proportion falls to 3 times. A small hammerhead weighing 110 lb (50 kg) eats 550 lb (250 kg) a year, while an adult porbeagle of a similar weight eats 220 lb (100 kg) of fish and invertebrates in the same period, i.e., approximately 10 oz (300 gm) a day. A nurse shark eats just over the equivalent of its own weight, while a mako, one of the most voracious species of shark, devours an amount of food equivalent to 10-11 times its own weight in a year.

These considerable differences are influenced by numerous variables such as water temperature; cold water slows the metabolism of the fish, and thus their requirements. The period of life may also be significant, as the females of some species seem to feed more before and during mating. Finally, it has been observed that sharks are able to perform a kind of energy saving process, for example, by seeking the waters with the most favorable temperature and moving as far as possible by following the currents. White sharks and other members of the Lamnidae (mackerel shark) family have a very unusual energy metabolism, which gives them some exceptional abilities.

Species	Length (ft)	Weight (lbs)	Food Eaten (lbs/day)	Food Eaten (lbs/yr)
Mako *Isurus oxyrinchus*	5.75	138.9	4.41	1609.65
Lemon (immature)	4.93	176.4	2.43	837.90
Lemon *Negraprion brevirostris*	2.30	22.1	0.66	220.50
Lemon	9.00	330.8	7.72	2646.00
Scalloped hammerhead *Sphyrna lewini*	6.57	110.0	1.50	547.28
Blue *Prionace glauca*	6.14	107.2	0.61	222.04
Nurse *Ginglymostoma cirratum*	8.21	336.0	0.99	362.28
Sand-tiger *Carcharias taurus*	4.50	110.3	1.50	547.28
Sandbar (juv)	4.93	72.3	0.32	115.10
Sandbar (pups)	1.84	3.9	0.04	16.10
Sandbar (pups)	1.81	3.7	0.05	19.18
Sandbar (juv. & pups)	4.73	75.0	0.65	235.93

Fish, by definition, are cold-blooded animals, but there are some exceptions, represented by tuna fish, among the teleosts, and mackerel sharks, whose body temperature is 41°-50° F (5°-10° C) higher than that of the environment they live in; this has been demonstrated by heat sensors concealed in bait and fed to some sharks so that their internal body temperature could be measured. Higher body temperature is accompanied by a larger amount of red muscle (up to 12% of the axial muscles), mainly situated around the spinal column, though with some differences depending on species. These muscles are vascularized by a dense network of blood vessels which act as heat exchangers, allowing the blood that circulates in these parts of the body to maintain a higher temperature.

D

To give some idea of the efficiency of this network, in a small porbeagle around 3.3 ft (1 m) long, its area can be estimated at over 4 square yards. The large number of blood vessels is associated with the size of the heart, which is larger than in all the other sharks and provides a higher oxygen supply to the red muscles, which are therefore more efficient and capable of producing heat.

As a result of their special physiology, mackerel sharks can swim longer than other sharks and at a higher average cruising speed because they are partly free of the changes that temperature would impose on their life as fish and thus do not need to remain in the most favorable layers of water. As can be seen, hardly anything in shark biology, in the broadest sense of the term, is unexplained or can be considered superfluous. Every aspect serves to explain another.

Experience shows that any interference by man with the life of a species can have unexpected consequences, which often run

C

D

A

B

counter to our interests. The ideas we had about sharks until recently caused their true role in food chains to be underestimated, as is clearly shown by a number of episodes.

One of the most flourishing activities in some parts of Tasmania used to be lobster fishing. Shark fishing was introduced during the first half of the 20th century and, although it eventually declined upon becoming unprofitable, it continued for a long time. At about the same time, lobster catches declined sharply for no apparent reason. The experts called in to investigate the situation discovered that the surrounding seabeds were inhabited by an unusually large number of octopus, specific predators of lobsters. It was easy to see what had happened: the drastic reduction in sharks, which are predators of octopus, had upset a balance, and the most evident result was the decline in the lobster population.

An indirect effect is the reduction in record shark catches along the Natal coast, caused partly by the installation of shark netting and partly

E - The Caribbean reef shark and blacktip shark (Carcharhinus limbatus) populations rarely overlap so markedly, unless unnatural conditions are created like an episode of feeding frenzy caused by abundant shark feeding.

by the unlamented cessation of whaling along these coasts, which constituted an irresistible attraction for large sharks, often seen feeding on the remains of captured whales. The use of shark netting may have led to a change in shark populations; the numbers of smaller sharks, no longer kept under control by large ones, have increased, and they have proved potentially dangerous because their small size 3.6-3.9 ft (1.1-1.2 m) enables them to cross the barriers and reach bathing areas easily.

E

F

G

F - Blue sharks are fast swimmers, and this enables them to catch equally good swimmers like mackerel, which constitute one of their most frequent prey during the migration period.

G - Blue sharks feed on a large number of vertebrates and invertebrates. As in the case of many sharks with a wide feeding spectrum, the relative abundance of individual prey varies during the year.

MATING: DIFFERENT METHODS TO ACHIEVE A SINGLE PURPOSE

For many sharks, the mating period is almost the only time when they come into contact with members of their own species. At this period, the distribution and behavior barriers which usually lead to segregation of the genders (a distinctive feature of the lives of many species of shark) break down because the instinct to ensure the continuance of the species becomes impelling.

The mating period mainly seems to be associated with variations in ambient temperature that elicit a hormonal response designed for reproduction, which often coincides with the beginning of the migration period. However, although studies conducted on this subject have led to the discovery that reproductive cycles exist, the full details of how sharks reproduce are still not known. Some species mate all year round and others only at certain seasons; the females of some species can give birth year after year once they reach

A, B, C, D - Judged by human standards, the shark world appears extremely violent. Even the foreplay before mating is hardly gentle, as demonstrated by this sequence of photos, showing the courting behavior of a pair of nurse sharks. Before the actual copulation, when the male inserts one of its claspers into the female's cloaca for a few minutes, both sharks perform a violent courting ritual involving biting and chasing one another. The most active and the first to take the initiative is the male, whereas the female is mainly passive, at least in the initial stages, relying on her thick epidermis to withstand the male's rough advances.

sexual maturity, while in others, reproductive stages alternate with rest stages of varying lengths.

As often happens in animals with aggressive tendencies (and the reproduction of sharks is more similar to that of felines than that of the majority of fish) mating is not exactly a gentle process. Mating between the male and female presumably takes place after an initial approach; this cannot be described as "courtship," which has never been observed, but is certainly designed to send signals destined to reduce intraspecific aggression.

Mating is only possible if the two individuals take up the right position. In the smaller and more agile sharks, the male can actually wrap itself round the female, while in the larger species the male and female have to position themselves parallel to one another, side by side, with the ventral part facing.

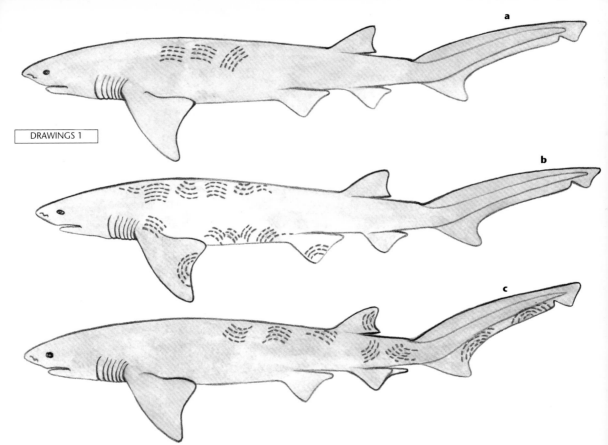

DRAWINGS 1

Taking up the right position is not easy, however, and the task of inducing the female to do so is up to the male. To this purpose the male bites the female and tries to exploit the characteristics of the seabed in all possible ways, at least according to the few direct observations of the mating behavior of sharks, which have always taken place near the seabed. In practice, both partners often come out of the encounter the worse for wear, with significant, clearly visible bites and scratches on the body, usually on the back and sides and near the fins. This is mainly because the greater aggressiveness of the male is matched by the larger size of the female, and because females reach the stage of reproduction in perfect shape. The females also have another defense weapon, namely, a much thicker skin–sometimes twice as thick as the male's.

Drawings 1 -
The adult broadnose sevengill shark (Notorynchus cepedianus) presents characteristic curved or parallel longitudinal wounds on the body. These are rare in immature females (a), and far more evident and numerous in adult females (b). The wounds are due to bites inflicted by the males at the time of mating, and the females often react with equal violence, leaving evident traces on the back and fins of their mates (c).

DRAWINGS 2

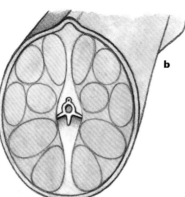

Drawings 2 -
The violent foreplay and bites which precede mating in many species of shark have led to the development of forms of passive defense by the females (a), which have a thicker epidermis than the males (b).

103

Gender identification, which is difficult in many animals, is quite easy in sharks. The males are recognizable by their claspers, two symmetrical appendages deriving from the development of the inner margin of the ventral fins, which rolls up; in adult sharks they are supported by pieces of hard cartilage. They usually face backward, but at the time of mating they are rotated forward and outward by muscles connected to the ventral

Drawings 1 -
The ventral fins of male sharks (1) present two typical extensions called claspers (a), which constitute their most evident secondary sexual characteristics. At the time of mating, one of the claspers is brought forward (2) to help water enter the siphon (b) through a specific orifice (c); it is then introduced into the female's vagina, where it opens like an umbrella to anchor it in position (3). The siphon then begins to contract (4), expelling water and sperm.

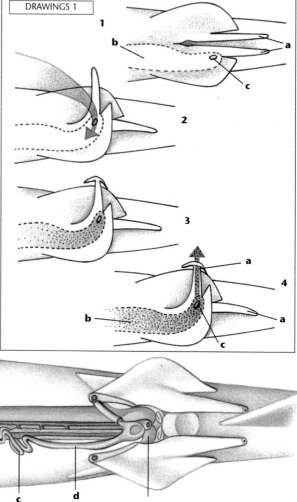

DRAWINGS 1

DRAWING 2

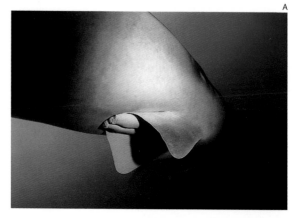

Drawing 2 - This drawing illustrates the internal anatomy of the reproductive system of a male shark, consisting of the following organs: testicle (a), epididymis (b), vas deferens (c), seminal vesicle (d), and sperm sac (e).

fins. This uncovers the opening of each siphon, a kind of subcutaneous pouch of the claspers which communicates with the exterior and can fill with water as a result of the forward swimming movement of the shark. The pouch is therefore filled passively, not actively.

What happens actively is that the claspers are introduced into the female's cloaca until their ends are in close contact with the innermost part of the female's genital apparatus. The already solid contact then becomes even more stable,

A - This photo shows the ventral fins of a male whale shark with evident claspers. These organs, which enable the sex of the shark to be distinguished easily, derive from the development of the inner edge of the fins, which is supported by hardened cartilage in the adults.

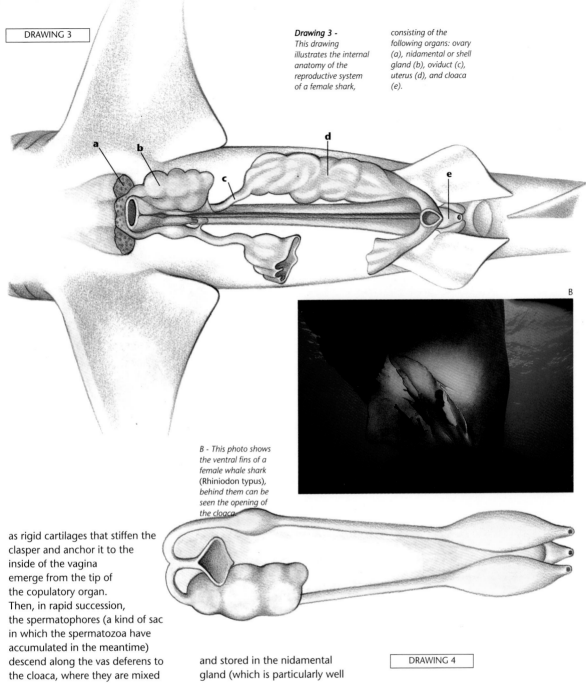

Drawing 3 - This drawing illustrates the internal anatomy of the reproductive system of a female shark, consisting of the following organs: ovary (a), nidamental or shell gland (b), oviduct (c), uterus (d), and cloaca (e).

B - This photo shows the ventral fins of a female whale shark (Rhiniodon typus), behind them can be seen the opening of the cloaca.

DRAWING 4

as rigid cartilages that stiffen the clasper and anchor it to the inside of the vagina emerge from the tip of the copulatory organ. Then, in rapid succession, the spermatophores (a kind of sac in which the spermatozoa have accumulated in the meantime) descend along the vas deferens to the cloaca, where they are mixed with water from the siphon which is forced through the claspers. Thus a large number of spermatozoa, released on contact with the water from the sheath enclosing them, are projected into the lower female genital tracts; from there they can travel to the uterus and the nidamental gland, where they will encounter the ova.

Gamete fusion and fertilization do not always take place after mating. Spermatozoa may be accumulated and stored in the nidamental gland (which is particularly well developed in oviparous species) for a very long period; it can even be as much as two years, as in the case of the small-spotted catshark *Scyliorhinus canicula.*

A similar phenomenon also takes place in the much larger and more specialized porbeagles, in which fertilization can be delayed for several months, in *Rhizoprionodon taylori,* and probably in other requiem sharks too.

Drawing 4 - The female reproductive apparatus, drawn as it might appear if isolated. Note the single opening in the infundibulum and the two uteri, which do not always function in the same way in sharks.

Drawings 1 and 2 - These drawings illustrate a whale shark (Rhiniodon typus) egg and embryo on the basis of material found by chance in the Gulf of Mexico in 1953.

However, the latest research suggests that the find was the result of a miscarriage, and that the whale shark is actually an ovoviviparous species.

DRAWING 2

DRAWING 1

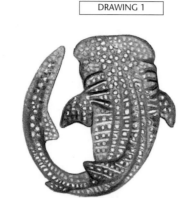

A

B

C

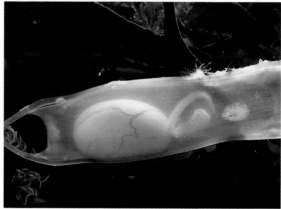

D

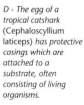

A - The catsharks' eggs are a rare spectacle to the divers in the Mediterranean, particularly on seabeds rich in red gorgonians. The fans of these cnidarians are among the catshark females' favorite support to deposit their eggs.

B - A characteristic egg of a bullhead shark (fam. Heterodontidae), attached to a colony of ascidians by strong filaments, which are only destroyed after it hatches.

C - The embryo and the large yolk sac that contains its food supply can be seen in catshark eggs after a few weeks.

D - The egg of a tropical catshark (Cephaloscyllium laticeps) has protective casings which are attached to a substrate, often consisting of living organisms.

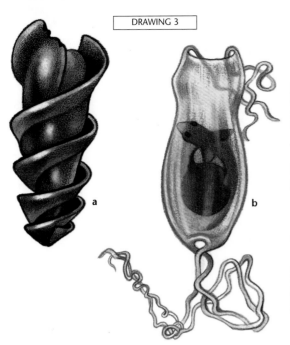

DRAWING 3

G

Drawing 3 - Oviparous sharks often lay eggs with a characteristic shell, which in many cases allows at least the genus, if not the species, to be identified rapidly. This drawing shows the curious helical eggs of the genus Heterodontus *(a), which hatch in 9-12 months, and the eggs of the catsharks (b), with their flattened, roughly quadrangular, cirrus-covered shell, which hatch 6-8 months after being laid.*

The ova, whose size ranges between 0.039 in (1 mm) in *Scoliodon* and 3.9 in (100 mm) in nurse sharks (Ginglymostomatidae) and the frill shark *Chlamydoselachus anguineus*, are produced either in both ovaries, as in the case of *Squalus acanthias*, or only in the right-hand ovary, which is the functional ovary in most species.

From here, the ova are released into the abdominal cavity and directed by ciliated cells toward one or both oviducts, along which they descend until they reach the nidamental gland where fertilization finally takes place, and gestation begins or the eggs are laid. Immediately afterward, a protective covering is secreted by the female's nidamental gland (which for this reason is also called the shell gland);

E - The small-spotted catshark (Scyliorhinus canicula) swims frantically away from the underwater photographer. The shark pups, though defenseless, are already able to live independently and imitate the behavior of the adults.

F - Mediterranean catsharks often attach their eggs to gorgonians in order to exploit the currents that continually wash over the fans of these invertebrates.

G - After a few months the catshark pup manages to break the protective casing surrounding it, and embarks on its first movements in free waters.

in oviparous species it resembles a very strong horny theca, while in viviparous species it may be reduced to a thin membrane, which is sometimes very large, as in the case of the whitecheek shark *Carcharhinus dussumieri*. In this species, the fertilized eggs, which have a diameter of 0.78 in (20 mm), are wrapped in a membrane that may be over 15.76 in (40 cm) long and is kept folded in the front part of the uterus. This "pseudoshell" then gradually unfolds as the size of the embryo increases. After fertilization, the stages leading to the formation and development of the embryo usually take place normally, but some species, such as the Australian sharpnose shark, can inhibit its growth for up to 7 months so that the birth coincides with the most favorable environmental conditions for the pups.

The reproductive biology of sharks

E

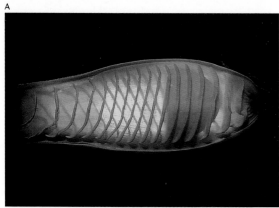

is much more sophisticated and varied than might be expected of such a small and relatively unspecialized group of vertebrates. The most striking feature of the whole subclass is the choice of a reproductive strategy quite opposite to the "R" strategy typical of fish such as tuna and cod, which rely on millions of small eggs scattered over the sea for the survival of the species. The sharks' strategy, conventionally indicated by the letter "K," involves the birth of a relatively small number of young (only

A - The horny sheath which constitutes the outer covering of the eggs of the South Australian swellshark Cephaloscyllium laticeps has a characteristic geometrical pattern.

B, C, D, E, F - These photos show five stages in the development of the egg of a swellshark (Cephaloscyllium ventriosum). Photo B shows the stage of development reached by the embryo after 3 months, and the large yolk sac. After 7 months (C) the embryo appears almost fully developed, while the

nutritional function of the yolk sac is about to end. The swellshark pup's back is decorated with a double row of denticles, used to cut the shell open when it hatches. At the end of the development period (D), the shark pup slowly makes its way out (E-F); when free of the shell it can start swimming independently.

G - The egg of a crested bullhead shark (Heterodontus galeatus), with its typical spiral shell, is attached to the organisms encrusting the seabed with adhesive filaments.

H - The color of the bullhead shark's eggs varies from species to species, but they all have an unmistakable spiral shape. In some cases when the eggs are laid, the mother forces the egg into a crevice in the seabed before the shell hardens, and it remains there until it hatches.

I - When its development is complete, the bullhead shark pup leaves its shell and embarks on life as a free creature.

one or two in some species) which are already able to lead independent lives as a result of the large amount of energy devoted to them by their mothers.

There are two basic types of reproduction: oviparous and viviparous. Oviparous species such as catsharks, horn sharks, zebra sharks, and carpet sharks lay large eggs (e.g., 4.7 in [12 cm] high and 2.4 in [6 cm] in diameter in *Heterodontus francisci*) of shapes varying from family to family. They usually have a strong shell or theca made of horny material which is permeable to water and oxygen, inside which the embryo grows until fully developed. When this stage is reached the perfectly formed miniature shark, already capable of catching its first prey, cuts its way out of the shell with special serrated scales on the snout or fins, which drop off not long afterward. Viviparous reproduction is far more complex. In some species the embryos depend for their development solely on the yolk reserves associated with the ovum. A typical case is that of the spiny dogfish (probably the most widely studied shark because of its large numbers and commercial interest) in which several fertilized eggs are enveloped in a common egg membrane when they reach the uterus, where a kind of spindle or candle is formed which opens after 6 months to release the embryos. They continue to develop independently from one another at the expense of the yolk sac, which provides their nourishment until just before their birth, some 22 months after fertilization, the longest gestation period known among sharks.

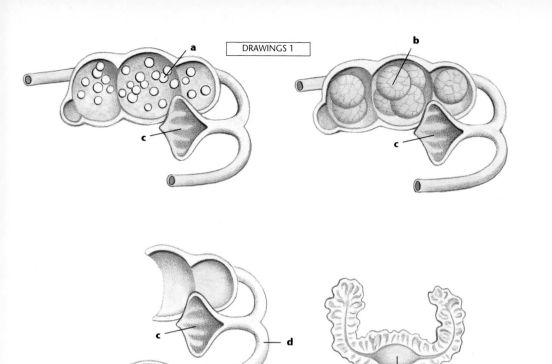

DRAWINGS 1

Drawings 1 - These diagrams illustrate the stages of development preceding the birth of a requiem shark. The ova (a, b) gradually mature in the ovaries, are released at the time of ovulation, and migrate through the infundibulum (c) in the oviduct (d) until they reach the nidamental gland (e), where fertilization takes place and the ovum is surrounded by a thin shell (f). At this point the ovum reaches the uterus (g) and the shell expands, surrounding the embryo which is protected by a fluid covering (h). Subsequently, the embryo develops and increases in size by feeding on the contents of the yolk sac (i). The empty sac is eventually implanted in the wall of the uterus where a placenta (j) develops, partly formed by the covering shell (k), which will provide the fetus with the nutrients it needs until the birth.

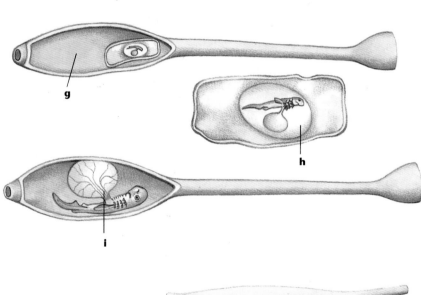

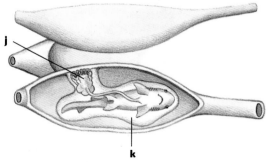

110

The case in which the eggs are very small and have small yolk sacs is quite different. In this case there is a very close relationship between mother and embryos, and situations typical of the more evolved mammals are observed in some species.

The uterus specializes, grows, and produces long filaments deriving from the soft mucous membrane that penetrate the gill slits of the young, instilling a nutritious milky substance into them.
As a result of this system, the tiger shark can give birth to up to 82

large pups of 20-29 in (51-76 cm). In requiem sharks and hammerheads the embryo initially develops independently, then the yolk sac and the egg membrane adhere to the uterus and turn into a placenta. As a result, nutrients and oxygen pass directly from mother to embryo

DRAWING 2

Drawing 2 -
In viviparous sharks, the embryos establish close contact with the mother through the umbilical cord and the placenta. In this way the young are fed inside the mother's body with a system that in many ways resembles the one that has evolved in mammals.

DRAWING 3

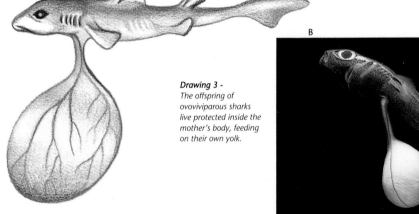

Drawing 3 -
The offspring of ovoviviparous sharks live protected inside the mother's body, feeding on their own yolk.

B

A

A - An embryo of the velvet belly, an ovoviviparous species of shark found in the Atlantic and the Mediterranean, where it can live at a depth of up to 6,564 ft (2,000 m).

B - A shark embryo with its yolk sac.

through the umbilical cord, which contains blood vessels and specialized transport cells.
In the species with placentas, the uterus is divided into compartments (gestation chambers) by the transformation of the individual egg membranes.
These chambers can be positioned crossways or lengthways, but the embryos always have their heads facing forward.
    A wholly anomalous case, typical of the shark world, is oophagy, a

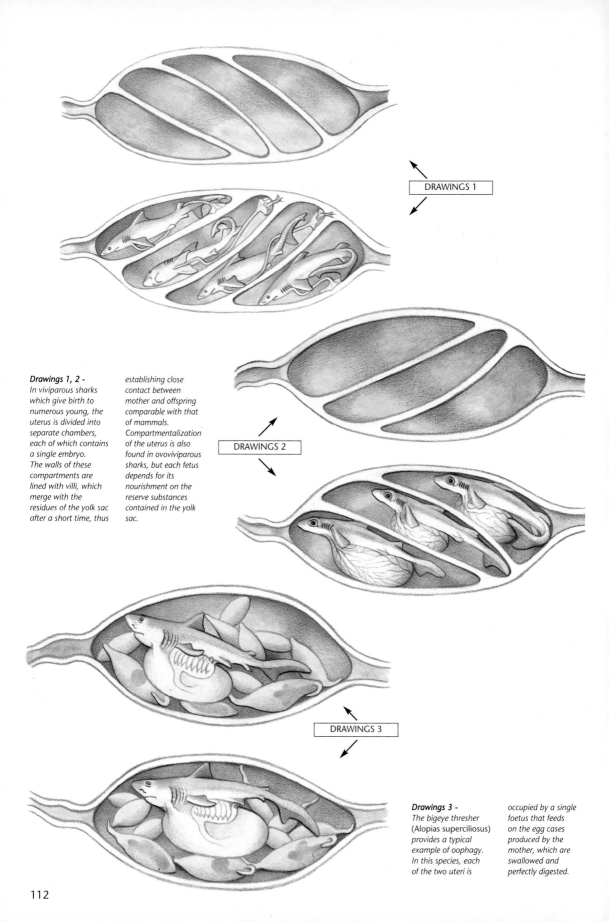

DRAWINGS 1

DRAWINGS 2

DRAWINGS 3

Drawings 1, 2 -
In viviparous sharks which give birth to numerous young, the uterus is divided into separate chambers, each of which contains a single embryo. The walls of these compartments are lined with villi, which merge with the residues of the yolk sac after a short time, thus establishing close contact between mother and offspring comparable with that of mammals. Compartmentalization of the uterus is also found in ovoviviparous sharks, but each fetus depends for its nourishment on the reserve substances contained in the yolk sac.

Drawings 3 -
The bigeye thresher (Alopias superciliosus) provides a typical example of oophagy. In this species, each of the two uteri is occupied by a single foetus that feeds on the egg cases produced by the mother, which are swallowed and perfectly digested.

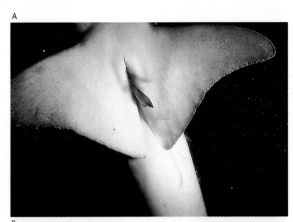

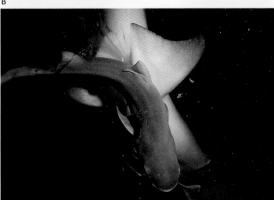

A - This rare photo shows a lemon shark, a typical viviparous species, about to give birth.

B - A small lemon shark makes its first movements outside the mother's uterus. The newborn shark remains motionless on the seabed next to its mother for a few minutes, then swims off abruptly, severing the umbilical cord.

C - When a shark pup is born it emerges from the uterus snout first, and immediately starts to breathe. The slight reddish halo that surrounds mother and pup is due to the expulsion of the placenta, which will be eaten by remoras and other fish.

D - This pregnant female has given birth to a litter of 10 pups in rapid succession. Two of them can still be seen near the mother. Shortly after the birth the shark pups are perfectly capable of surviving alone, although many are rapidly eaten by other sharks.

C

D

kind of intra-uterine cannibalism. In thresher and mako sharks, for example, the ovaries can produce a large number of eggs, but only the embryos which hatch first can continue to develop, by feeding on the other eggs as they are produced.

This kind of nutrition and reproduction also seems to be typical of the white shark; this is a fairly recent discovery, resulting from the lucky find of a pregnant female in New Zealand and rapid intervention by specialists in the field, which fills one of the many gaps in our knowledge about the life of the species.

The reproduction and embryo development process of the sand-tiger shark *Eugomphodus taurus* (Odontaspididae) is even more specialized, and from the human standpoint even more horrific; the embryos fight one another right from this early stage, feeding on one another (embryophagy or adelphophagy) until only two (the strongest) are left, one in each uterus.

ECOLOGY AND BEHAVIOR

The full details of shark ecology are still largely unknown. As will be seen in the chapter devoted to orders and families and in the fact sheets, at least one species of shark inhabits every sea and ocean, without exception, and some sharks are even found in freshwater environments. Each habitat is exploited in a special way by each species, as is being discovered in increasingly detailed studies of sharks. Basking sharks appear along the British coasts in late spring, and disappear in autumn after exploiting the summer plankton harvest. Sand-tiger sharks migrate seasonally, following their prey, and white sharks also present a variable distribution pattern, heading further and further north as the temperature increases. The seasonal migrations of whale sharks (*Rhiniodon typus*), which appear at Ningaloo Reef off the Australian coast with astonishing regularity, have recently been discovered. The reason for this seasonal rendezvous is very unusual, namely, the appearance of huge amounts of planktonic shrimps and small fish attracted by the mass reproduction of the corals forming the nearby reef at the same period. Lengthy migrations are also performed by mako sharks,

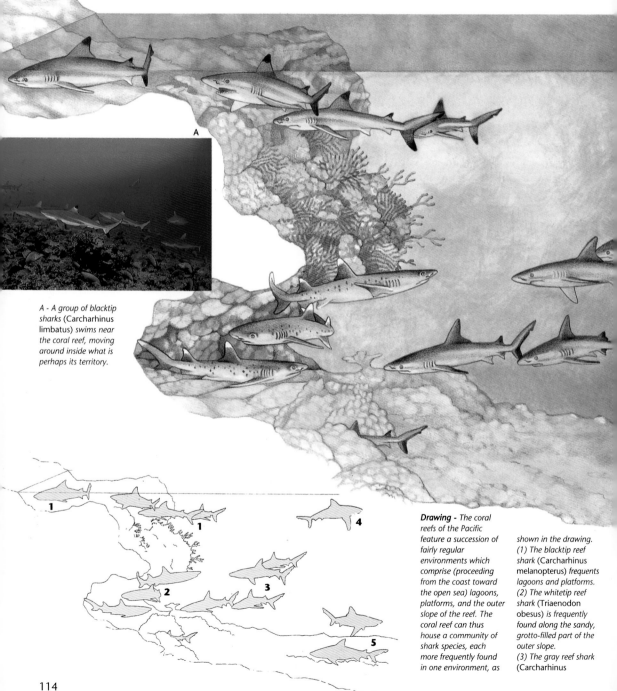

A - A group of blacktip sharks (Carcharhinus limbatus) *swims near the coral reef, moving around inside what is perhaps its territory.*

Drawing - *The coral reefs of the Pacific feature a succession of fairly regular environments which comprise (proceeding from the coast toward the open sea) lagoons, platforms, and the outer slope of the reef. The coral reef can thus house a community of shark species, each more frequently found in one environment, as shown in the drawing. (1) The blacktip reef shark (Carcharhinus melanopterus) frequents lagoons and platforms. (2) The whitetip reef shark (Triaenodon obesus) is frequently found along the sandy, grotto-filled part of the outer slope. (3) The gray reef shark (Carcharhinus*

which follow water masses that remain at a temperature of 57°-71° F (17°-22° C). Tagging of some specimens has demonstrated that the populations of the West Atlantic perform journeys of 1,242 mi (2,000 km) and more in clockwise circular routes as they follow the water masses of the Gulf Stream and the eddies that detach from them and return toward the coast–a very effective way of saving swimming energy.

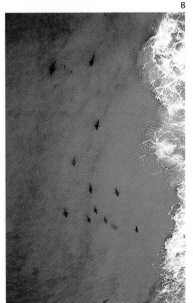

B

C

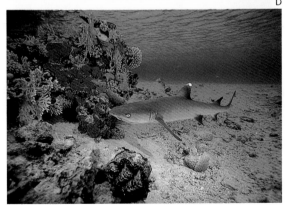

D

amblyrhynchos) *prefers the deeper waters of the platform and the outer slope. (4) The silvertip shark (Carcharhinus albi-marginatus) is mainly found along the outer* *reef at a depth of over 27.35 in (25 m). (5) The tiger shark (Galeocerdo cuvier) lives in the deep waters of the reef, from which it can swim right to the surface.*

B - *An entire group of requiem sharks has ventured into shallow water at the outermost limit of the surf zone of this Australian beach. Because of situations like this, many Australian beaches are protected by barriers of shark netting.*

C - *These Galapagos sharks (Carcharhinus galapagensis) seem to be trying to approach the photographer to discover his intentions and demonstrate who these waters really belong to.*

D - *A whitetip reef shark swims among the coral in search of a grotto with a sandy floor where it can rest.*

The discovery that many sharks have specific heat requirements has explained some of the mechanisms that lead individual species to exploit only certain environments and certain resources. For example, blacktip reef sharks minimize contact with the larger mako sharks by swimming in waters with an average temperature ranging between 71.6° and 80.6° F (22°-27° C). Similar segregation takes place along coral reefs, where the various species of reef shark (the blacktip, whitetip, and gray reef shark) each occupy a precise territory or have different feeding habits and noctidiurnal rhythms, some species being most active by day, and others by night. These rhythms are often typical not only of the species but also of individuals, as seems to be demonstrated by studies in which the movements of tagged specimens have been found to present a considerable degree of regularity. This kind of behavior is most frequent in reef sharks, where the type of seabed is perhaps conducive to the establishment of territories and specific types of behavior.

For example, whitetip reef sharks chase away silky sharks from possible prey, whereas both species accept the approach of their own kind without difficulty. White sharks seem to establish a precise hierarchy in their small subpopulations, as a result of which individuals feed in decreasing order importance, from the dominant to the least important member of the group.

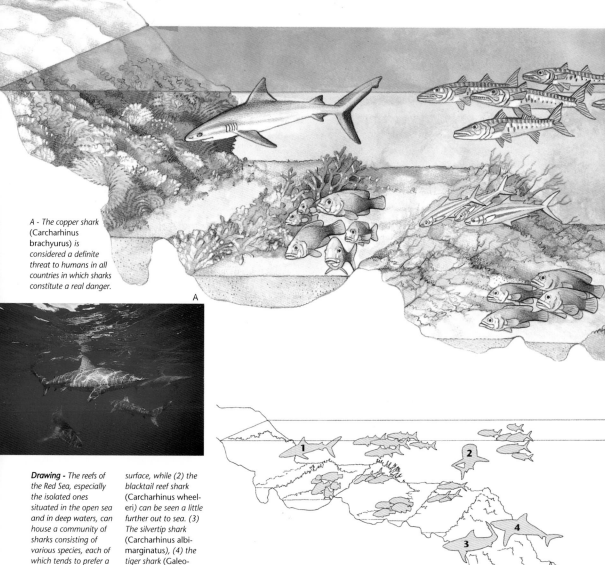

A - The copper shark (Carcharhinus brachyurus) *is considered a definite threat to humans in all countries in which sharks constitute a real danger.*

A

Drawing - *The reefs of the Red Sea, especially the isolated ones situated in the open sea and in deep waters, can house a community of sharks consisting of various species, each of which tends to prefer a particular part of the reef. Thus (1) the blacktip reef shark* (Carcharhinus melanopterus) *swims in the waters nearest the surface, while (2) the blacktail reef shark* (Carcharhinus wheeleri) *can be seen a little further out to sea. (3) The silvertip shark* (Carcharhinus albimarginatus), *(4) the tiger shark* (Galeocerdo cuvier), *and (5) the hammerhead shark* (Sphyrna lewini) *are found at a depths of over 65-98 ft (20-30 m).*

116

B

C

*B - Silvertip sharks
(Carcharhinus
albimarginatus)
dominate the coral reef
at depths exceeding
65-82 ft (20-25 m),
excluding smaller
sharks from their
territory.*

D

*C - In view of its habits,
the tiger shark can be
considered the
dominant shark of the
coral reef, even though
it is not the most
frequent in numerical
terms.*

*D - Hammerheads are
considered the most
recent sharks in terms
of evolution; they
appeared around
25 million years ago.*

117

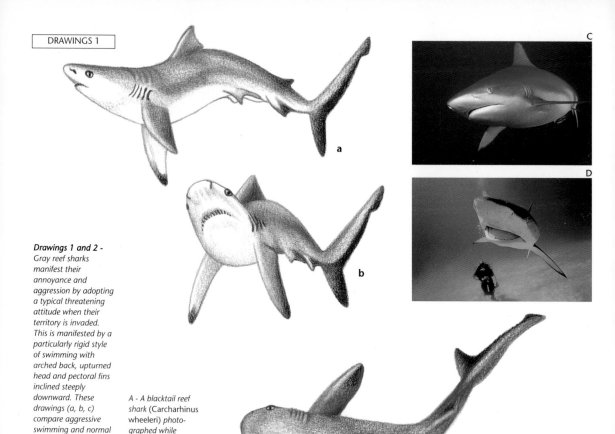

Drawings 1 and 2 -
Gray reef sharks manifest their annoyance and aggression by adopting a typical threatening attitude when their territory is invaded. This is manifested by a particularly rigid style of swimming with arched back, upturned head and pectoral fins inclined steeply downward. These drawings (a, b, c) compare aggressive swimming and normal swimming (d, e, f), viewed from different angles.

A - A blacktail reef shark (Carcharhinus wheeleri) *photographed while swimming normally, quite unconcerned by the divers' presence.*

B, C, D -
The downwardly inclined fins and nervously arched back of this gray shark indicate its growing aggression.
By adopting this behavior, the shark endeavors to drive off the intruder by threatening it.
Only if its signals are misunderstood or underestimated does the shark intensify its threatening action, swimming faster and approaching closer to the intruder until it eventually makes a direct attack, which appears to be limited to a few bites.

A particular kind of defense behavior is manifested by the gray reef shark (*Carcharhinus amblyrhynchos*). This species is famous for being the only one so far known to present stereotyped threatening behavior, called an "exaggerated swimming exhibition," which always precedes an attack. This exhibition is performed whenever the shark feels threatened or its movements are restricted. It involves shaking the head and tail to simulate burst swimming, vertical movements of the pectoral fins or arching of the back, after which the shark swims in a horizontal spiral or a series of rapid figures-of-eight.

Other sharks, including the white shark, present similar forms of threatening behavior, but they

d

e

E - A group of hammerhead sharks silhouetted against the surface. Hammerheads are among the most gregarious sharks known and can form groups of a hundred or more sharks. The reason for this aggregation is not known with certainty, but many experts believe that it is associated with migration and reproductive patterns.

f

F

all seem to be limited to only some of the phases described above. However, these initial findings demonstrate that territorial sharks, and presumably also those that live in groups, such as the hammerhead, have developed intraspecific and possibly interspecific communication systems whose code so far remains unbroken.

Increasing interest in the shark world, together with the fact that more and more species are being declared protected (including those representing a definite threat to humans, such as the great white shark), suggests that the search for this communication code is destined to give the desired results in the short term, and to do justice to these extraordinary creatures.

F - A shoal of scalloped hammerheads (Sphyrna lewini) swimming in Mexican waters along the Pacific coast. Sights like this are becoming increasingly rare because these sharks are now fished in large numbers.

G - Because of their gregarious nature, hammerhead sharks have developed a number of behavior codes which are used within the group to reduce aggression.

G

THE DIFFERENT KINDS OF SHARK

Finding one's way through over 350 species of known sharks (and many more probably still remain to be discovered) is by no means easy, especially when you find out how many differences there are between one form and another, and how complex their lives are. It is a practically impossible task to reconcile in a single chapter the gigantic, harmless whale shark with the tiny, spined pygmy shark *Squaliolus laticaudus,* or the great white shark and the tiger shark with the good-natured basking shark.

Fortunately, order is imposed by systematics, the branch of biology officially introduced by Linnaeus in 1758, which gives a forename and surname to all species, and then groups them into larger and larger categories on the basis of common morphological characteristics. In the case of sharks, these characteristics include the spines, teeth, fins, and cranium, as well as more sophisticated and less evident characteristics such as those deriving from biochemical, immunological, and genetic studies. Officially, sharks are divided into eight orders. The order is a systematic category which biology dictionaries define as "each of the divisions of a class, generally distinguished by the ending '-formes'. The order is some-times divided into suborders, which are subdivided into families. Conversely, a number of orders can be grouped in a superorder or subclass."

On the basis of comparative studies, the subclass of the Elasmo-branchii could also be divided into four superorders, three of which only include sharks (*Squalomorphi, Galeo-morphi,* and *Squatinomorphi*), while the last (*Batoidea*) comprises those particular selachians, skates, electric rays, manta rays, etc., which have evolved to a dorso-ventrally flattened shape like discs. The debate between experts is wide open, and some families or even species may well be reassigned to different categories; this has happened frequently in the past, as we see by comparing systematic lists drawn up only a few years apart.

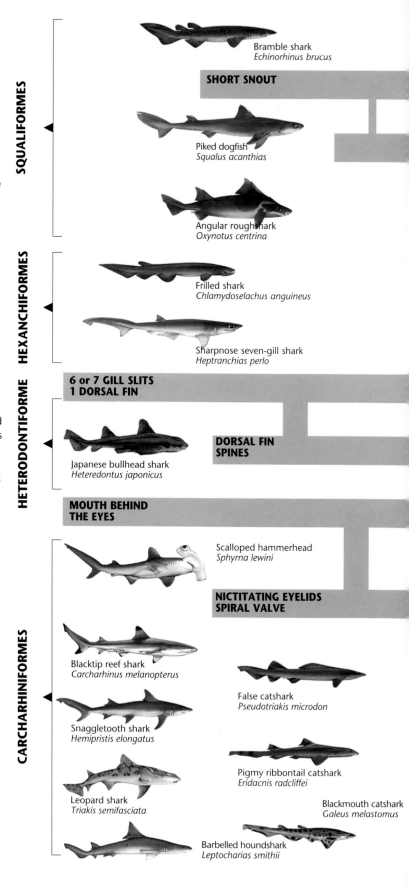

SQUALIFORMES

Bramble shark
Echinorhinus brucus

SHORT SNOUT

Piked dogfish
Squalus acanthias

Angular roughshark
Oxynotus centrina

HEXANCHIFORMES

Frilled shark
Chlamydoselachus anguineus

Sharpnose seven-gill shark
Heptranchias perlo

HETERODONTIFORME

6 or 7 GILL SLITS
1 DORSAL FIN

Japanese bullhead shark
Heteredontus japonicus

DORSAL FIN
SPINES

MOUTH BEHIND
THE EYES

CARCHARHINIFORMES

Scalloped hammerhead
Sphyrna lewini

NICTITATING EYELIDS
SPIRAL VALVE

Blacktip reef shark
Carcharhinus melanopterus

Snaggletooth shark
Hemipristis elongatus

Leopard shark
Triakis semifasciata

False catshark
Pseudotriakis microdon

Pigmy ribbontail catshark
Eridacnis radcliffei

Blackmouth catshark
Galeus melastomus

Barbelled houndshark
Leptocharias smithii

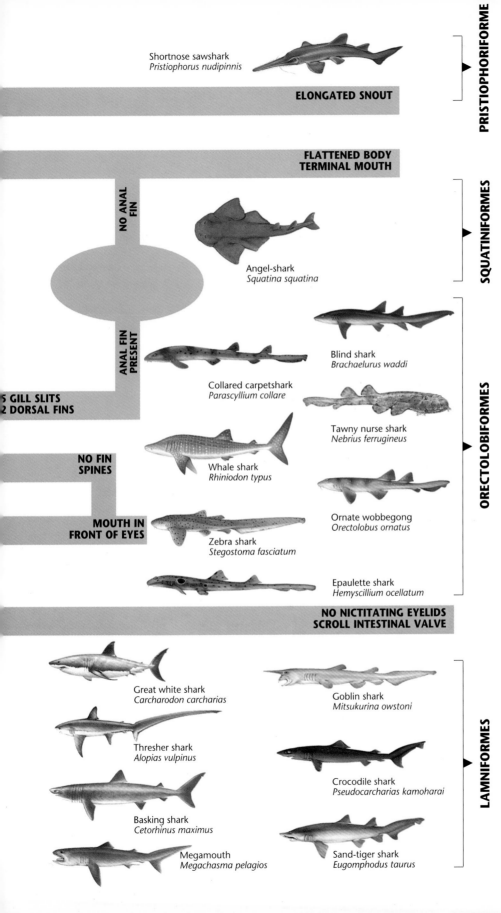

Shortnose sawshark
Pristiophorus nudipinnis

ELONGATED SNOUT

**FLATTENED BODY
TERMINAL MOUTH**

**NO ANAL
FIN**

SQUATINIFORMES

Angel-shark
Squatina squatina

**ANAL FIN
PRESENT**

Blind shark
Brachaelurus waddi

Collared carpetshark
Parascyllium collare

**5 GILL SLITS
2 DORSAL FINS**

Tawny nurse shark
Nebrius ferrugineus

ORECTOLOBIFORMES

Whale shark
Rhiniodon typus

**NO FIN
SPINES**

Ornate wobbegong
Orectolobus ornatus

**MOUTH IN
FRONT OF EYES**

Zebra shark
Stegostoma fasciatum

Epaulette shark
Hemyscillium ocellatum

**NO NICTITATING EYELIDS
SCROLL INTESTINAL VALVE**

Great white shark
Carcharodon carcharias

Goblin shark
Mitsukurina owstoni

Thresher shark
Alopias vulpinus

Crocodile shark
Pseudocarcharias kamoharai

LAMNIFORMES

Basking shark
Cetorhinus maximus

Megamouth
Megachasma pelagios

Sand-tiger shark
Eugomphodus taurus

The variety of their shapes constitutes the first characteristic useful in distinguishing if not individual species, at least the representatives of the various orders and families of sharks. The diagram opposite is based on the main diagnostic characteristics (e.g., the number of gill slits, the presence or absence of the anal fin, the presence or absence of spines associated with the dorsal fins), which enable one order to be distinguished from another and the main families attributed to each one. As is standard practice in all "keys" to the recognition of living organisms, the application mechanism is based on the presence or absence of a given anatomical feature. For example, the Hexanchiformes are recognizable by the fact that they have one dorsal fin and 6-7 gill slits.

HEXANCHIFORMES
(FRILLED AND COW SHARKS)

It is fairly common practice for a descriptive analysis of organisms to start with the most primitive (although this term has only a relative value) and move on gradually to those with more complex or highly evolved characteristics. According to this system, we should begin with the Hexanchiformes, widely considered to be the most direct descendants of the sharks of the Mesozoic. The members of this order can be distinguished more easily than other sharks by the fact that they have a single spineless dorsal fin, an anal fin, and above all six or seven gill slits as opposed to five. This group, considered the least specialized because of its skeletal structure (especially that of the cranium and spinal column) and its digestive and excretory systems, comprises two families (Chlamydoselachidae and Hexanchidae) and five species. The former is a single-species family whose only member is *Chlamydoselachus anguineus*, a strange shark with a slender body and a fierce appearance because of its snake-like head, apparently separated from the body by a kind of lacy frill, which is why it is known as the "frilled shark." The frill is actually constituted by the six gill slits, whose frilly edges act as a kind of operculum, protecting the delicate respiratory

three-pointed hooks.

The four sharks in the Hexanchidae (cow shark) family are equally divided between those with seven gills (*Heptranchias perlo* and *Notorynchus cepedianus*), a unique characteristic that makes this species unmistakable, and those with six gills (*Hexanchus griseus* and *H. vitulus*). The six-gill sharks, which can reach 15 ft (5 m) long, prefer to live in deep waters, over 650 ft (200 m) down, and feed on fish, sharks, skate, squid, and crustaceans. The seven-gill sharks have slightly different habits; they can also be found in inshore waters as little as 3.2 ft (1 m) deep, and present a clearly seasonal

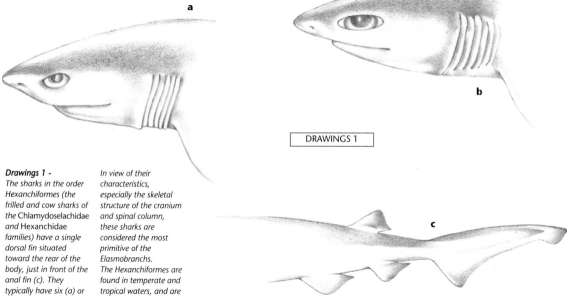

DRAWINGS 1

Drawings 1 - The sharks in the order Hexanchiformes (the frilled and cow sharks of the Chlamydoselachidae and Hexanchidae families) have a single dorsal fin situated toward the rear of the body, just in front of the anal fin (c). They typically have six (a) or seven (b) gill slits.

In view of their characteristics, especially the skeletal structure of the cranium and spinal column, these sharks are considered the most primitive of the Elasmobranchs. The Hexanchiformes are found in temperate and tropical waters, and are locally fished for meat.

A - The broadnose sevengill shark (Notorhynchus cepedianus) is common in the temperate waters of the globe, from the east Pacific coasts to the Chinese and southern Australia coasts. A population is also present in the west Atlantic, between Brazil and Argentina.

organs beneath. The frill shark is able to live at depths of over 3,282 ft (1,000 m), and its unusual shape seems to be suited to its lifestyle (at least as far as its biology is known). Its snaky body is incapable of swimming for long distances, but allows it to move easily on uneven surfaces. The arrangement of the fins, concentrated at the rear of the body, suggests an aptitude for burst swimming, a technique that enables it to catch its prey (presumably fish and cephalopods) like lighting; its large mouth has 13-14 rows of mainly functional teeth resembling

behavior pattern, moving into bays and sheltered areas in spring and summer. This takes place in conjunction with the appearance of other, smaller species of shark which, perhaps not by chance, have been found in the stomachs of these great sharks; they can even catch seals, salmon, and dolphins because of the rapid acceleration of which their bodies are capable. Unusually, cow sharks caught in different areas possess different coloring, which seems in some way to adapt to the predominant characteristics of their habitat.

HETERODONTIFORMES (BULLHEAD SHARKS)

This order comprises a single family (Heterodontidae, the horn sharks) and eight species, found in warm temperate and tropical waters in the west Indian Ocean and the east Pacific. These sharks, considered to be among the most primitive and related to extinct species of the Devonian, are easily distinguished by the fact that both dorsal fins have a strong anterior spine and the anal fin is also present.

Typical features are the very large head, with a strong bony crest above the eyes, and the mouth, located in an anterior position and joined to the large nares by marked naso-oral grooves. Because of the odd shape of the snout, when seen from the front these sharks recall a bull or a pig, after which various species in the order are named.

Bullhead sharks are typical bottom-dwelling creatures; they have special dentition with small, sharp front teeth and large flattened rear molars that enable them to feed mainly on shellfish (sea urchins, bivalves, gastropods, and crustaceans), which they

C - The distribution of Heterodontus francisci (the horn shark) is limited to the Californian Pacific coast.

Its coloring is brownish, with small dark spots all over the body. It mainly lives in surface waters, and has nocturnal habits.

C

Drawings 2 -
The Heterodontiformes (bullhead sharks) are found in the warm temperate and tropical waters of the Indo-Pacific. They are easily distinguished by the fact that both dorsal fins have a robust spine (c). They have an anal fin. The head has a robust bony crest above the eyes (a); the mouth is situated in an anterior position and connected to the nares by naso-oral grooves (b).

a

b

DRAWINGS 2

c

B

sometimes dig out from the base of rocks using the armor on their heads. As a result of their feeding habits, they cause a great deal of trouble to mollusk farmers by stealing their harvests, as suggested by the nickname of "oystercrusher" given to the Port Jackson shark (*Heterodontus portusjacksoni*); this shark lives in Australian waters where it performs lengthy migrations, returning to the same mating site every year.

B - The Port Jackson shark (Heterodontus portusjacksoni), a typical species of the south Pacific, is found along the south-eastern coasts of Australia and off New Zealand. These sharks perform long migrations in the mating season, when the females swim as far as 500 mi (800 km) to reach the breeding grounds. Even the young seem to have specific

territorial requirements; after hatching, they gather in sheltered areas inside bays and estuaries.
The Port Jackson shark, which is protected by its robust dorsal spines and camouflage coloring and by its nocturnal habits, has few natural enemies, mainly other sharks. Its favorite prey consists of organisms with hard shells such as sea urchins and starfish, crabs, and mollusks.

ORECTOLOBIFORMES
(CARPET SHARKS)

This order comprises seven families (which according to some experts should be reduced to five) and 33 species, found mainly in inshore tropical waters. All these sharks have a subterminal mouth situated in front of the eyes, and a marked naso-oral groove which joins the mouth to the nares and the spiracles. Another typical characteristic is that they possess nasal barbels (crucial in distinguishing between species

A - Stegostoma fasciatum owes its popular and apparently undeserved name of zebra shark to the special coloring of the juveniles, which are dark and decorated with marked yellow stripes. This species is found from the Red Sea to the Great Barrier Reef of Australia, and has benthonic habits, as can be deduced from the long tail fin and flattened underbelly.

1

2

Drawings 1, 2, 3 - Wobbegongs (Orectolobidae) are sharks typically adapted to bottom- dwelling life. Their characteristic feature is the cirri surrounding the mouth like the fringes of a carpet.

B, C - The order Orectolobiformes (carpet sharks) comprises 5-7 families characterized by a sub-terminal mouth, an evident naso-oral groove, and nasal barbels of varying lengths, ranging from the short ones of the Brachaeluridae to the long ones of the nurse sharks and wobbegongs.

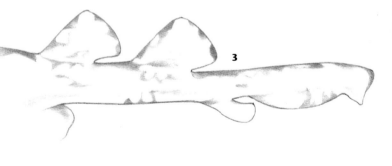

3

belonging to this order and other sharks) of varying sizes, from the short ones of the Australian blind sharks (Brachaeluridae) to the evident appendages of the nurse sharks (Ginglymostomatidae) and the numerous uneven whiskers of the wobbegongs (Orectolobidae), whose mouths appear to be surrounded by a thick moustache.

Although these characteristics are common to all the carpet sharks, it is hard to find another order containing such a variety of sharks, especially in terms of size; this group contains sharks only a few dozen inches long like the Parascyllidae (collared carpet sharks) as well as the huge whale shark, the largest fish known, which can grow to as much as 50 ft (18 m) long. Apart from a few exceptions, they are bottom-dwelling fish, as demonstrated by their flattened bodies, elongated tails and coloring, among the brightest in the world of sharks, which usually have very dull colors. Particularly colorful are the wobbegongs (Orectolobus sp.), frequently found in Australian waters, and the zebra shark (Stegostoma fasciatum) of the Indo-Pacific, although the body of the latter is only decorated by alternating light and dark stripes when young.

124

D - A tawny nurse shark of the Indo-Pacific (Nebrius ferrugineus), photographed as it swims through the coral reef just a little way above the seabed.

E, F - These Atlantic nurse sharks rest on the sandy sea bottom in the waters of the Bahamas. This behavior is due to the nocturnal habits of nurse sharks, which are particularly active and voracious at night.

Within this group the history of the nurse shark is interesting. Originally there were considered to be three separate species, but the number has now been reduced to two: *Ginglymostoma cirratum* and *Nebrius ferrugineus*. The former in particular has an unusual distribution pattern; although the individual sharks belong to the same species, three different populations can be distinguished on the basis of some somatic characteristics and different coloring. These populations, present along the African Atlantic coasts, the American Atlantic coasts and in the Pacific, from California to Peru, are probably the result of the continental

G

H

G - Nebrius ferrugineus is able to perform rapid, abrupt accelerations if disturbed too much by divers, who may be injured in a collision with this shark, which can grow to 9.8 ft (3 m) long, or be attacked. Its bites, though not deep, are painful, because the small teeth are very sharp, and the shark is not easily persuaded to let go.

H - The ventrally flattened shape and subterminal mouth are adaptations to a sedentary life. In particular, the mouth has been transformed into a powerful suction pump with which the nurse shark captures many of its prey, even if they are hiding under the sand or among corals or rocks.

D

E

F

drift which caused the formation of the Atlantic, and the subsequent emergence of land which joined the northern and southern parts of the American continent and separated the Caribbean Sea from the Pacific area. This phenomenon may seem to be a mere curiosity, but as we shall see when discussing the Carcharinidae, it is by no means an exception among sharks.

The example of nurse sharks can be used to demonstrate how shark systematics are continually developing. The reduction from three species to two, proposed by some experts, requires the creation of a new genus, *Pseudoginglymostoma*, to which the third species of nurse shark, *Ginglymostoma brevicaudatum*, is reassigned; this nurse shark is said to differ from the others because it has smaller eyes, shorter barbels, and three-cusp teeth, and reaches sexual maturity at a much smaller size (3.2 ft [1 m] as opposed to over 6.5 ft [2 m]). To go still further, it has been suggested that the Ginglymostomatidae and Stegostomatidae families should be eliminated, and their genera reassigned to the same family as the whale sharks (Rhiniodontidae).

LAMNIFORMES (MACKEREL SHARKS)

The sixteen species of mackerel shark, whose length ranges between one and 32 ft (10 m), are grouped in seven families. Although this is considered to be the order of the great white and mako sharks, those species cannot be said to be truly representative of the group as a whole. Mackerel sharks have five gill slits and no naso-oral grooves, barbels, or nictitating membrane; they have two spineless dorsal fins, and the first dorsal fin is situated between the ventral or pectoral fins or above the pectoral fins. This order includes the sand-tiger sharks (Odontaspididae), which threateningly bare their long pointed teeth when they open their protractile jaws, surmounted by a long snout, the thresher sharks (Alopiidae), whose long tails, resembling an elegant train, are actually a terrible weapon that lashes the water, stunning the small fish on which they usually feed, and the Lamnidae (mako, great white, and porbeagle sharks), the most typical representatives of this order. The Lamnidae are by far the most specialized sharks, and include the great white (*Carcharodon carcharias*), the last link in many food chains. Its body, moulded by the water, looks as though it might have been designed by a team of engineers who left out nothing that would help make it perfect, including a central heating system that optimizes the energy consumption of the powerful body, driven forward with implacable determination by the great sickle-shaped tail fin. This fin is a distinguishing feature of the family; it is also found in the mako sharks and porbeagles. The very fast mako sharks with their tapered bodies, and especially the shortfin mako (*Isurus oxyrinchus*), are a popular target of

B

C

DRAWINGS 1

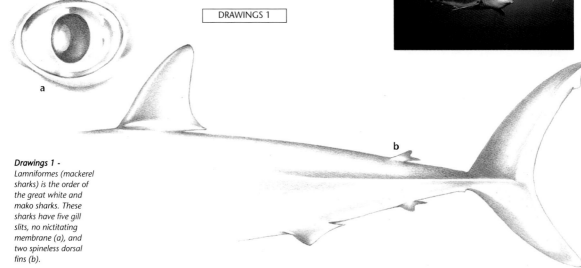

a

b

Drawings 1 -
Lamniformes (mackerel sharks) is the order of the great white and mako sharks. These sharks have five gill slits, no nictitating membrane (a), and two spineless dorsal fins (b).

A

A - A specimen of Carcharias taurus shows the typical pointed, curved teeth which have won it the popular name of sand-tiger shark. Despite this name and its fearful teeth, the sand-tiger shark is not considered particularly dangerous to human beings, which it tends to avoid. The unusual biological features of this species include the aggressive behavior of the young, which feed on their siblings when still in the uterus.

game fishermen following in the footsteps of Hemingway, who pursue it as far as the waters of the Gulf Stream. The porbeagles (*Lamna sp.*), which live in temperate and cold waters, have large gill slits, and are capable of such rapid acceleration that they can catch the almost equally fast mackerel, which they resemble because of the shape of their tails.However, it would be wrong to think that all mackerel sharks are alike. For example, the little crocodile sharks (Pseudocarchariidae) have a tapering body, huge eyes, a long conical pointed snout, and a mouth bristling with prominent, sharp, pointed teeth. Mainly distributed in pelagic waters from the east Atlantic to the entire Pacific, crocodile sharks seem to be quite rare, but this may be due to their habits, and the fact that they are of little interest except to zoologists.

The goblin shark (Mitsukurinidae) is something of an anomaly, and its little-known history recalls that of the more famous coelacanth. Considered the ugliest of the extant sharks, the goblin shark has a long, flat, pointed snout in which its tiny eyes almost disappear. Its body is soft and flaccid. Its long protractile jaws, similar to the jaws of hooked pliers, have large, sharp teeth. On the whole, this shark would not look out of place in a horror film.

merely a normal report of an unknown species. However, some palaeontologists discovered a number of similarities, especially in the shape of the head and teeth, between the description of the goblin shark and that of a fossil shark dating back to 100 million years ago, which was discovered in 1887. This meant that the fossil shark (called *Scapanorhynchus*) was, if not the same species, definitely a member of the same genus as the extant shark. In theory, according to the Zoological Nomenclature Rules, this name should have taken precedence, but as a compromise it was decided to keep both names; *Scapanorhynchus* would be used to indicate the extinct species, and *Mitsukurina* the extant species.

DRAWING 2

It was entirely unknown until 1897, when a specimen was caught in the depths of the dark Kuro Shiwo current off Yokohama. Professor Kakichi Mitsukuri, to whom it was delivered, took it from Japan to the United States, where Prof. David Starr Jordan recognized its uniqueness and named it *Mitsukurina owstoni*, adding this new species to the catalogue of known sharks. A few years later another specimen was captured by Dom Carlos I, King of Portugal, during one of his oceanography cruises, a hobby he shared with the more famous Prince Albert I of Monaco, founder of the Oceanographic Museum.

Apart from its weird appearance, the discovery so far seemed to be

Although the species is found in most oceans, from the Atlantic to the Indo-Pacific, it is so rare that very little is known of its life. It reaches the respectable length of 11.8 ft (3.6 m), and some specimens can even exceed 13 ft (4 m). Its diet seems to consist of fish, prawns, and squid which it catches with its highly protractile mouth. The function of the strange shape of the snout is unknown; some experts believe that it may serve to perceive the electrical fields emitted by its prey. This would be logical, as it seems to be able to live at a depth of over 3,282 ft (1,000 m), and in such an environment the light is so dim that senses other than sight would be needed to identify its prey.

The basking shark and the megamouth are much larger, but wholly inoffensive, although they belong to an order of large predators. The megamouth (*Megachasma pelagios*, Megachasmidae family), was discovered in 1976, but was only given its official name six years later. This time-lag suggests that further additions to the shark lists may be made in the next few years; in fact, rumor has it that unknown sharks have been captured in Australia and Argentina.

The megamouth is a large oceanic shark with a soft, cylindrical body, a round, blunt snout, and an enormous mouth with numerous small hooked teeth which may help it filter the euphausiids and other planktonic organisms it feeds on and traps with the numerous comb-like spiny formations situated along its gill slits. The six specimens (five males and a female) captured between Japan and California have raised many questions, but supplied few answers about their biology. Everything suggests that this species belongs to

C

D

A, C, D - The basking shark (Cetorhinus maximus) is one of the largest known sharks. Despite its bulk, it is practically harmless, feeding solely on plankton which it filters from the water by swimming forward with its mouth wide open. This species, which can live in cold as well as warm waters, seems to go into a kind of hibernation in the winter months, when it moves to deep water.

B - The chance capture of a specimen of an unknown species in 1983 demonstrated that the shark world still holds many surprises. The new species, five specimens of which have now been found, was named the megamouth (Megachasma pelagios) because of its huge mouth.

A

B

deep tropical waters, but the specimen captured and released off the Californian coast in October 1990 did little to confirm this theory; it remained fairly close to the surface as long as the sensors with which it was tagged continued to transmit.

The case of the basking shark (*Cetorhinus maximus*, Cetorhinidae family) is very different. This shark has been known for a very long time and is actively hunted for its liver oil, used by the cosmetics industry and to make sophisticated hydraulic systems for high-flying aircraft. The basking shark, which often takes the blame for attacks by great white sharks because of its size, is a typical example of how humankind is far more dangerous to sharks than they are to us. Fishing reports show that catches along the Irish coasts reached a peak of 1808 specimens in 1952, five years after fishing of the species began. In 1975 only 35 were caught; too few to make the business profitable, but perhaps enough to reduce the recovery ability of the species drastically. At the same period the basking shark was hunted in

Norway at the rate of 4,000 a year, using techniques banned in whaling as they are considered too cruel. Unfortunately, this indifference toward the shark world is proving hard to eliminate. It was not until 1995 that the first voices were raised in defense of this group by a specialist association theoretically concerned with fauna protection issues, namely, the experts of the Convention on International Trade in Threatened and Endangered Species (CITES). An official debate on shark fishing took place only in 1997, while the first ad hoc conference about sharks is not to be held until 1999, during the World Fishing Congress organized by the Food and Agriculture Organization (FAO) and the United Nations.

SQUALIFORMES (DOGFISH SHARKS)

The dogfish sharks, typical of the deep waters of tropical and temperate seas but also found in Arctic and Antarctic waters, are divided into three families, containing a total of over 90 species. They are distinguished by having five gill slits and two dorsal fins, usually preceded by a spine; the anal fin is absent. They have a short mouth and a long snout. They mainly live in deep waters, over 330 ft (100 m) down, and often between 985 and 3,000 ft (300-700 m), with maximum depths of almost 9,846 ft (3,000 m). Many of these abyssal species present typical adaptations to life in deep waters such as large eyes and luminous organs, as in the case of the *Etmopterus* genus.

Another group of deepwater sharks are the Echinorhinidae or bramble sharks, whose name refers to their denticles of various sizes, often with a sharp central spine.

There are two species in this family: *Echinorhinus brucus* and *E. cookei*. The former, until recently considered the only species, is just over 9.5 ft (3 m) long and is found in all temperate and tropical seas, while the latter, which can reach 13 ft (4 m long), has so far only been sighted in the Indian Ocean. Both species live near continental slopes, at depths of between 1,312 and 2,954 ft (400 and 900 m), and appear to stay near the seabed, only coming up to the surface at night. Their feeding habits seem to confirm this tendency, as their stomach contents have been found to include benthic bony fish, small sharks, octopus, crabs, and the egg cases of skate and catsharks.

The Squalidae are the true dogfish. They include both small and gigantic species such as the Greenland shark (*Somniosus microcephalus*), which can grow to 20-23 ft (6-7 m) long; it has a cylindrical body, ranging from strong to slender, or a slightly compressed shape. One of the best-known species is the spiny (or piked) dogfish (*Squalus acanthias*), which has a tapering body, a pointed snout and a wide mouth. The spines of the dorsal fins after which the fish is named are connected to poison glands; the shark uses them as defense weapons by turning them in the direction of the enemy with particular body movements. Its coloring is grayish with occasional white blotches on the back, while the belly is paler. This species performs typical seasonal migrations associated with temperature, avoiding waters with a temperature of under 44° F (7° C) or over 59° F (15° C). It is capable of covering very long distances, as demonstrated by one specimen, tagged off the American Pacific coast, which was captured eight years later near Japan.

The Oxynotidae (rough sharks) are small sharks with an odd appearance, which is perhaps why they were cited by famous authors of the ancient world such as Aristotle, Oppian, and Aelian, who wrote about fish for various reasons. The five species have squat bodies with a subtriangular cross section due to the tall dorsal fin, which almost entirely surrounds the strong, forward-facing spine situated about halfway along its base. In the second dorsal fin, the spine faces backward as usual. The mouth is transverse and possesses labial papillae with a spongy texture; these probably assist in the capture of benthic inverte-brates and small fish, which are then crushed by the triangular teeth. The upper teeth are narrower and sharper and arranged in increasingly num-erous rows, while the lower teeth are wider and pointed. The bodies of the Oxynotidae are covered with very rough placoid scales, which is why they are known as rough sharks. This family is very widespread, being found from the Atlantic to the Pacific, but its distribution is very uneven, so that it may be considered locally rare.

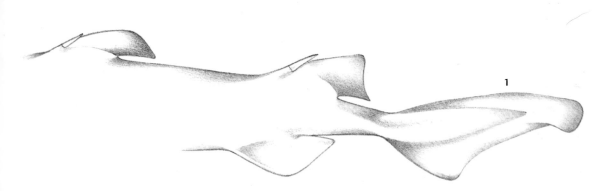

Drawing 1 - The Squaliformes (dogfish) are typical of the deep waters of tropical and temperate seas, but also live in Arctic and Antarctic waters. On the whole they are distinguished by having five gill slits and two dorsal fins, usually preceded by a spine. They have no anal fin. Their size is almost variable, from 13 ft (4 m) to 10-12 in (25-30 cm). Their body is rather cylindrical as they are less active species which are to be found near the seabed.

SQUATINIFORMES (ANGEL SHARKS)

This order contains only one family (the Squatinidae) and a number of species which, according to various authors, may be 11, 13, or 15. These sharks have a flattened body similar to the rays, no anal fin, and two dorsal fins. Their common name of angel sharks is due to the large pectoral fins, which extend forward above the ventral gills. The large, terminal mouth is flanked by barbels of varying lengths, and the palisade teeth are

A - Angelsharks are most active at twilight, when they swim close to the seabed with wide, snaky movements of the tail fin. They usually swim quite slowly, but still manage to capture their prey as a result of the lightning-fast protrusion of the mouth.

B

C

DRAWING 1

Drawing 1 -
The Squatiniformes (angelsharks) have a flattened body similar to that of the rays. They have two dorsal fins and no anal fin.
The name angelshark derives from the large pectoral fins, which extend forward above the ventrally situated gills. The mouth is terminal, and flanked by barbels of various lengths.

small and even, with a wide base and a triangular tip. By contrast with most other sharks, in this species the lower lobe of the tail is larger than the upper lobe. Although they sometimes grow to 7.9 ft (2.4 m) Squatinidae do not exceed 4.9 ft (1.5 m) long on average. As clearly shown by their shape, which has often caused them to be classed with the rays, they live on the seabed, between a few yards and 4,560 ft (1,390 m) deep, preferring muddy or sandy substrates in which they bury themselves, especially during the day. They mainly seem to hunt by lying in wait and then darting out of the sediment to catch their prey (fish, crustaceans, and cephalopods) with a mouth that can open very wide. They are found in temperate and tropical waters, except for the central Pacific and much of the Indian Ocean.

A

B - Angelsharks (this photo shows the Australian angelshark Squatina australis) have modified their hunting techniques to suit their shape; they lie in wait for their prey on the seabed, well camouflaged.

C - The snout of Squatina australis is characterized by sensitive fringed barbels.

PRISTIOPHORIFORMES (SAW SHARKS)

The sharks in this order also comprise a single family, with five species (the genera *Pristiophorus* and *Pliotrema*). These are practically inoffensive benthic sharks which, like the sawfish, have a characteristic head modified into a long flattened rostrum with lateral protuberances resembling the teeth of a saw; in saw sharks, these "teeth" are thin, pointed, and sharp. The shape of the upper part of the body recalls that of other sharks, but it presents as ventrally flattened, partly because of the absence of an anal fin as a result of its bottom-dwelling life. There are two dorsal fins, and the tail has a wide upper lobe. The long rostrum is characterized by a pair of long barbels situated in front of the nares. The small, transverse mouth has narrow pointed teeth used to catch small fish and crustaceans; the prey are identified among the sediment and seaweed of the seabed with the barbels, and probably uncovered and perhaps stunned by the movement of the rostrum. These sharks usually live at moderate depths, even a few dozen yards from the surface, but can be found at over 2950 ft (900 m). The various species are found in the west Pacific, the west Indian Ocean, and the Atlantic. Oddly enough one species, the South African *Pliotrema warreni*, has six gills, a characteristic which takes us back to where we started, with the six-gilled Hexanchiformes.

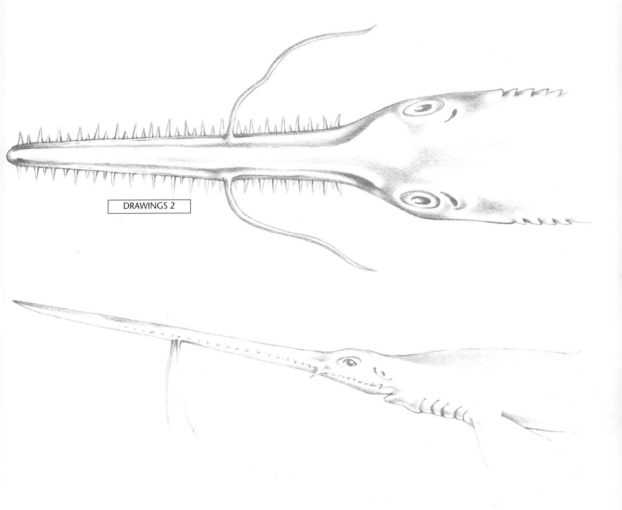

DRAWINGS 2

Drawings 2 -
The Pristiophoriformes (sawsharks) are benthic sharks easily recognizable by the modified head which is transformed into a long flattened rostrum with lateral protuberances resembling the teeth of a saw. The rostrum has a pair of long barbels situated in front of the nares. These structures are densely covered with sensory cells that have touch and taste functions.

CARCHARINIFORMES (GROUND SHARKS)

The order Carchariniformes includes the majority of the extant shark species. It comprises some 197 species grouped into eight families, including the one which contains the eponymous sharks, the Carcharinidae (requiem sharks), which could also be called the diver's sharks in view of the frequency with which they are sighted by divers. Ground sharks have a long, tapering body, two spineless dorsal fins, one anal fin, five gill slits, and an elongated snout with a well-developed mouth that reaches almost to behind the eyes. The eyes have a lower nictitating membrane which can be raised for protective purposes; this makes the eyes of these sharks wholly inexpressive, as if they were wearing a mask. This order, which is distributed in tropical and temperate inshore waters but also includes some more markedly benthic or oceanic species and even some capable of living in fresh water, comprises small primitive sharks like catsharks, those considered

"intermediate," like weasel sharks and blue sharks, the powerful, highly evolved requiem sharks (one of the names used to indicate the Carcharinidae, the group which probably comprises the largest number of species potentially dangerous to humans), and the hammerheads.

About half the known species are assigned to the Scyliorhinidae family. These sharks are commonly known as catsharks because of their elongated eyes, sometimes yellow or green, and their coloring, which features a wide variety of patterns: spots, stripes, streaks and curlicues. Their affinity with domestic cats is oddly manifested in the nursehound (*Scyliorhinus stellaris*), which makes a noise rather like a cat hissing if it is removed from the water. Catsharks are small, with sedentary habits, and measure up to 5.25 ft (1.6 m), although there are some dwarf species which do not reach 12 in (30 cm). In view of their numbers these sharks are more or less ubiquitous, and found in temperate, tropical and boreal waters, from a few yards down to a depth of nearly 6,564 ft (2,000 m).

A - The nursehound (Scyliorhinus stellaris) is one of the sharks most familiar to divers in the Mediterranean and off the European Atlantic coasts. Easily distinguished by its spotted pattern, the nursehound belongs to the family Scyliorhinidae, one of the many families in the order Carchariniformes (ground sharks).

B - The leopard shark (Triakis semifasciata) is regularly encountered by divers in the cold waters of California and the underwater kelp forests. These fairly active sharks often gather in large shoals, mingling with piked dogfish and smooth-hounds.

C - Catsharks are generally lazy, and unsuited to an active life of continual movement. They are frequently encountered near sandy, muddy, and detrital parts of the seabed where they remain motionless for long periods, especially when the light is brightest.

D - This photo shows the extraordinary agility of the catfish, which can roll up its body for defensive purposes. The same technique is used by the male during mating, when it curls its body round the female.

E - The striped catshark (Poroderma africanum) *is a typical inhabitant of the waters off the Cape of Good Hope, where it lives at a depth of up to 330 ft (100 m). The sharks in this species prefer rocky parts of the seabed containing numerous grottoes and crevices where they rest by day, coming out at night to hunt crustaceans.*

F - This small catshark (Scyliorhinus retifer), *has a typical pattern which seems to show chain links on its skin, thus its name, the chain catshark. This species, found along the Atlantic coasts of America from New England to Nicaragua, is a member of the group of small ground sharks; it grows to a maximum of 18.5 in (47 cm) long.*

G - The small-spotted catshark (Scyliorhinus canicula) *is found in the Mediterranean and the east Atlantic. It lives on muddy or detrital parts of the seabed and can reproduce all year round. It lays eggs contained in subrectangular shells covered with cirri, which cling onto the first thing they touch after being laid.*

F

E

G

Some species have a very wide bathymetric distribution range, up to as much as 2,950 ft (900 m), which may be explained by the existence of seasonal vertical migrations. Their widespread distribution is demonstrated by the fact that many species are identified by geographical names, such as the Atlantic ghost catshark (*Apristurus atlanticus*), the Japanese catshark (*A. japonicus*), the Madeira catshark (*A. maderensis*), the South China catshark (*A. sinensis*), and the Panama ghost catshark (*A. stenseni*), not to mention the Australian, Borneo, Arabian, New Zealand, and West African species.

Less numerous are the Triakidae (houndsharks), a family of sharks ranging in size from small at 12 in (30 cm) to medium-large at 6.5 ft (2 m), which are found in the temperate and warm area of all oceans. They prefer sandy, muddy and rocky inshore waters, although some go as deep as 6564 ft (2,000 m) and more. They feed on benthic crustaceans and fish. The two best-known species in this family are the leopard shark and the smoothhounds.

The former (*Triakis semifasciata*) is one of the most common species in the inshore waters of California, and one of the sharks most frequently found in aquariums because of its coloring, while the latter (*Mustelus sp.*) includes some of the species most commonly fished by humans for food.

The Proscylliidae (finback sharks) and the Hemigaleidae (weasel sharks) each comprise six species, but there are no other similarities between them. The Proscylliidae, divided into four genera, are very similar to true catsharks, from which they are distinguished by the position of the first dorsal fin, which is situated further toward the front of the body. They measure from just over 7 in (20 cm; 24 cm in the case of *Eridacnis radcliffei*) to 4 ft (1.2 m). Their elongated body terminates at the rear with an almost horizontal tail fin, which has only a vestigial ventral lobe. They all live between 165 and 3,000 ft (50-700 m) deep in the tropical and warm temperate seas of the Atlantic and Indo-Pacific. They are all ovoviviparous apart from the graceful catshark (*Proscyllium habereri*), which is oviparous.

Weasel sharks have a moderately elongated body with a rounded or slightly pointed snout. The tail fin has an upward-facing upper lobe and a well-developed terminal lobe. The ventral lobe is equally well developed. Most of these sharks are no more than 4.6 ft (1.4 m) long, apart from *Hemipristis elongatus*, found from east Africa to the coasts of Australia, which measures up to 7.8 ft (2.4 m) long. These sharks live in inshore waters, usually in the Indo-Pacific, apart from the Atlantic weasel shark (*Paragaleus pectoralis*), which is found at depths of up to a hundred yards. They are all viviparous and feed on fish, cephalopods, crustaceans, and echinoderms.

The false catsharks (Pseudo-triakidae) and barbelled houndsharks (Leptochariidae) are two families each containing a single species: *Pseudotriakis microdon* and *Leptocharias smithii*. The former is a large shark that can reach 10 ft (3 m) in length and is found at depths of 650 to 5000 ft (200-1,500 m) from the north Atlantic to the Indo-Pacific. Its most evident feature is the long, low, keeled dorsal

133

fin which starts above the pectoral fins and extends as far as the ventral fins. *Leptocharias* measures up to 2.69 ft (82 cm), and has a pair of barbels near the nares. It is typical of the West African coasts, where it lives on muddy seabeds between 33 and 246 ft (10-75 m) deep, especially close to river estuaries.

The true Carchariniformes, as the name suggests, are the Carcharinidae (requiem sharks), a family that comprises 48 species of sharks large and small, from 3.2 ft (1 m) to 16-19 ft (5-6 m); they have round eyes with a nictitating membrane, and usually have no spiracles or barbels. The dorsal fin is always further forward than the ventral fins, and the tail fin has a well-developed ventral lobe. These elegant swimmers have a tapering body which usually ends in a pointed, flattened snout. This is considered the most important of the shark families, and dominates the tropical fish communities in terms of number of species and individuals. They are present in all tropical and temperate seas, and also frequent a wide variety of inshore habitats, ranging from the

A

A - The Zambezi or bull shark (Carcharhinus leucas) is one of the most common members of the requiem shark family, as it can live in the fresh waters of great rivers like the Zambezi, the Congo, the Mississippi, and the

Amazon as well as the sea. This adaptability is associated with a well-deserved reputation as a maneater because of the numerous attacks for which it has been responsible in South Africa, Australia, and the United States.

estuaries of rivers, which some species swim up for long distances and long periods (*Carcharinus leucas*) or stay in permanently, like the Ganges shark (*Glyphis gangeticus*), to muddy bays and the clear waters of coral reefs. Among the sharks mentioned above, *C. leucas* is particularly interesting for its strange behavior. This species is also incorrectly called the "freshwater shark" because of the large number of sightings in this habitat, which is very unusual for what are almost exclusively marine animals. They have been found in the Zambezi river so often that they are also known as the "Zambezi shark," in the Congo, the Mississippi, the Amazon where they swim up to a distance of 1860 mi (3,000 km) from the river mouth, and

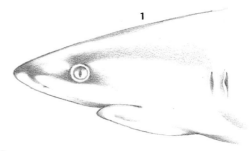

1

Drawings 1, 2, 3 -
The Carcharhiniformes (ground sharks) have a long, fusiform body, two spineless dorsal fins (2), one anal fin, five gill slits, and an elongated snout (1) with a well-developed mouth that almost reaches to behind the eyes.
The eyes have a lower nictitating membrane (3). This order, which is found in tropical and temperate inshore waters but also includes more markedly benthic or oceanic species and even some able to live in fresh water, includes the catsharks, the weasel and tope sharks, and the requiem sharks, which are the most representative group.

B - The silky shark (Carcharhinus falciformis) is a large shark, over 9.8 ft (3 m) long, typical of the circumtropical inshore and oceanic waters of the Atlantic and Indo-Pacific. It is a great nuisance to tuna fishermen, as it follows the shoals and eats large numbers of the tuna trapped in the nets.

even in Lake Nicaragua, where they sometimes stay for weeks before returning to the sea. Requiem sharks usually live within 330 ft (100 m) of the surface, though some species can go as far as 1,300-2,600 ft (400-800 m) deep, while others again are typically pelagic. They are voracious predators, feeding on a wide variety of organisms, especially fish, cephalopods, and crustaceans, and even their own kind.

With the sole exception of the tiger shark, which is ovoviviparous, all the other requiem sharks are viviparous. The largest genus of the family is *Carcharhinus*, which comprises 29 species. The best-known include *Carcharinus plumbeus*, which has a dorsal carina and is typically found in warm temperate and tropical waters above the continental shelf, the small *C. porosus*, scarcely 3.9 ft (1.2 m) long, and *C. falciformis*, which has very fine placoid scales that make its skin feel almost smooth; this is a pelagic, or rather semi-pelagic species, nearly always found in water masses

B

C

influenced by the coast, which feeds on deep-sea fish, squid and pelagic crustaceans. The emblematic oceanic shark *C. longimanus*, so called because of its well-developed pectoral fins, has similar habits. Like the previous species, this shark is considered a pest by tuna fishers as it intercepts their catches, causing considerable financial loss. The gray reef shark (*C. ambly-rhynchos*), the blacktip and blacktail reef sharks (*C. melanopterus* and *C. wheeleri*), and the whitetip reef shark (*T. obesus*) are frequently found along coral reefs. They are so common in the Indo-Pacific area that it is easier to list the areas where they are not found, namely, the Arabian Gulf, Easter Island, and Rapa. The gray reef shark generally prefers the deeper parts of the reef, while the blacktip and blacktail share the shallower areas, such as lagoons, with the whitetip. The whitetip is considered

F

3

2

F - Gray reef sharks (Carcharhinus amblyrhynchos) are quite social creatures living in groups, especially in the daytime. The widespread popularity of diving has *made these sharks very familiar and increased knowledge of their biology, leading to the discovery of some unusual forms of threatening behavior.*

C - The oceanic whitetip shark (Carcharhinus longimanus) is one of the most common sharks in the pelagic realm, together with the blue shark and the silky shark. This species is easily recognizable by its long, wide pectoral fins, which may be an adaptation designed to increase its buoyancy at low speed.

D, E - A blacktip reef shark (Carcharhinus melanopterus) displays the black-tipped fins after which it is named. This species lives on coral reefs in the tropical waters of the Indo-Pacific, where it can sometimes be encountered in water less than 3.3 ft (1 m) deep.

C
D
E

the typical reef shark, because it not only feeds on coral-dwelling fish but also lives permanently on the reef, where it is easily found by day in caves and other secluded spots; at night it ventures into areas normally inaccessible to other sharks to hunt its prey. Other members of the same genus are the silvertip shark (*C. albimarginatus*), the spinner shark (*C. brevipinna*), and the spot-tail shark (*C. sorrah*), all of which are fairly sedentary, and the dusky shark (*C. obscurus*), which is found in both the Atlantic and the Pacific. It frequents the nontropical areas of both these oceans and the seas dependent on them, such as the Mediterranean, performing long northward or southward migrations in the warmer periods. The blue shark (*Prionace glauca*) is a very common, well-known requiem shark. Some special aspects of its behavior have been discovered such as gender segregation, the existence of special mating areas like the one in the Adriatic, and long distance ability.

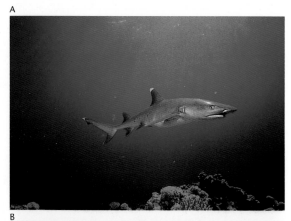

A

B

C

D

E

growth of individuals.

A characteristic feature of requiem sharks resulting from their number and widespread distribution is the large number of sister species, i.e., species of such similar appearance that it is hard to tell them apart. The prevalent hypothesis is that they originated from different populations of a single species following the separation for geological reasons of their territories, which are often the only truly discriminating feature in deciding which is which. Among the best-known pairs of sister species identified by experts are
C. leucas and C. amboinensis,
C. limbatus and C. amblyrhynchoides,
C. amblyrhynchos and C. wheeleri,
C. dussumieri and C. sealei,
Rhizoprionodon longurio and
R. lalandii, Nasolamia velox and
C. acronotus.

A - The whitetip reef shark (Triaenodon obesus) is mainly found in the Indo-Pacific. It prefers coral beds containing grottoes with sandy floors, where it remains motionless for long periods.

B - The silvertip shark (Carcharhinus albimarginatus) is commonly found on coral reefs, where the slope of the reef is steepest. It can grow up to 10 ft (3 m) long.

Much of this information is owed to the relative popularity of the species, which has a reasonable commercial value and is also popular with game fishermen. The link between scientific discoveries and game fishing has become particularly close in the past few decades as a result of the widespread use of "tag and release" techniques; after being caught the sharks are tagged with special signals and immediately released, enabling fishermen to indulge in their sport and researchers to study the sharks, monitoring their movements and the

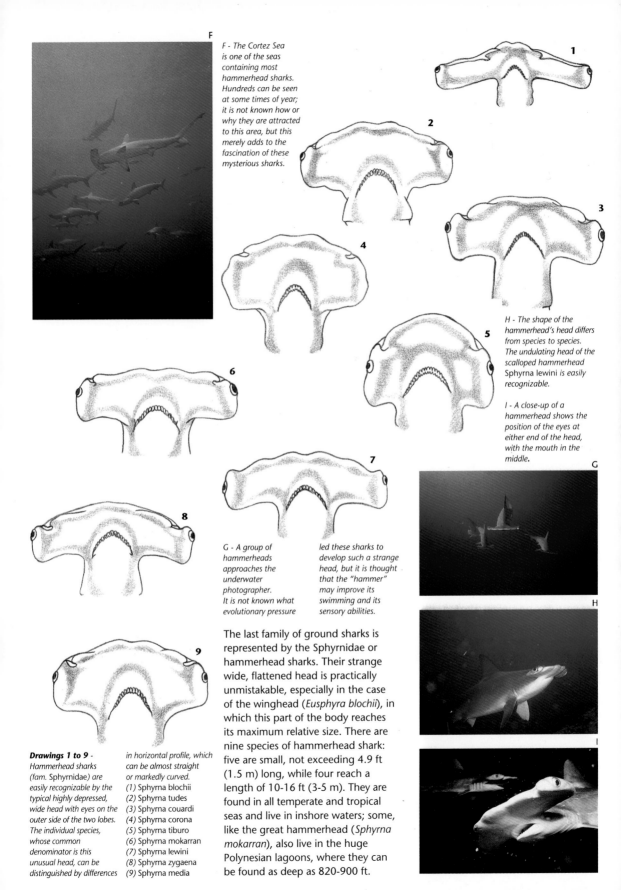

F - *The Cortez Sea is one of the seas containing most hammerhead sharks. Hundreds can be seen at some times of year; it is not known how or why they are attracted to this area, but this merely adds to the fascination of these mysterious sharks.*

1

2

3

4

5

H - *The shape of the hammerhead's head differs from species to species. The undulating head of the scalloped hammerhead Sphyrna lewini is easily recognizable.*

I - *A close-up of a hammerhead shows the position of the eyes at either end of the head, with the mouth in the middle.*

6

7

8

9

G - *A group of hammerheads approaches the underwater photographer. It is not known what evolutionary pressure led these sharks to develop such a strange head, but it is thought that the "hammer" may improve its swimming and its sensory abilities.*

G

H

I

Drawings 1 to 9 - *Hammerhead sharks (fam. Sphyrnidae) are easily recognizable by the typical highly depressed, wide head with eyes on the outer side of the two lobes. The individual species, whose common denominator is this unusual head, can be distinguished by differences in horizontal profile, which can be almost straight or markedly curved.*
(1) Sphyrna blochii
(2) Sphyrna tudes
(3) Sphyrna couardi
(4) Sphyrna corona
(5) Sphyrna tiburo
(6) Sphyrna mokarran
(7) Sphyrna lewini
(8) Sphyrna zygaena
(9) Sphyrna media

The last family of ground sharks is represented by the Sphyrnidae or hammerhead sharks. Their strange wide, flattened head is practically unmistakable, especially in the case of the winghead (*Eusphyra blochii*), in which this part of the body reaches its maximum relative size. There are nine species of hammerhead shark: five are small, not exceeding 4.9 ft (1.5 m) long, while four reach a length of 10-16 ft (3-5 m). They are found in all temperate and tropical seas and live in inshore waters; some, like the great hammerhead (*Sphyrna mokarran*), also live in the huge Polynesian lagoons, where they can be found as deep as 820-900 ft.

CHLAMYDOSELACHIDAE FAMILY
Frilled shark - *Chlamydoselachus anguineus*

A shark with a typically elongated, almost eel-shaped body and a short, truncated snout. The mouth is terminal, and the teeth have three elongated, diverging cusps. The characteristic six gills have jagged edges and extend to the throat. There is a single dorsal fin opposite the anal fin. A prominent carina runs along the belly. The caudal fin is elongated and pointed. The color is grayish. It lives near the seabed, between 390 and 4,200 ft (120 and 1,280 m) deep. It feeds on cephalopods and benthic fish. It is ovoviviparous and measures up to 6.4 ft (196 cm) long. It is found in the east Atlantic, the Indian Ocean (South Africa), and the Pacific (Japan, New Zealand, California, and Chile), with a cluster distribution.

THE SHARKS
AND THEIR FAMILIES

HEXANCHIDAE FAMILY
Sharpnose seven-gill shark - *Heptranchias perlo*

A shark with a pointed, tapering head and very large eyes. It has a single dorsal fin. The seven pairs of gills are the distinctive, unmistakable feature of this species. The mouth is very narrow and parabolic. The lower teeth have several cusps of graduated heights. The color is grayish. It lives near the seabed between 85 and 2,360 ft (27-720 m), but has also been reported at depths of over 3,280 ft (1,000 m). It feeds on fish and squid. It is ovoviviparous and measures up to 4.5 ft (137 cm) long. It is found in tropical and temperate seas, from the Atlantic to the Indo-Pacific.

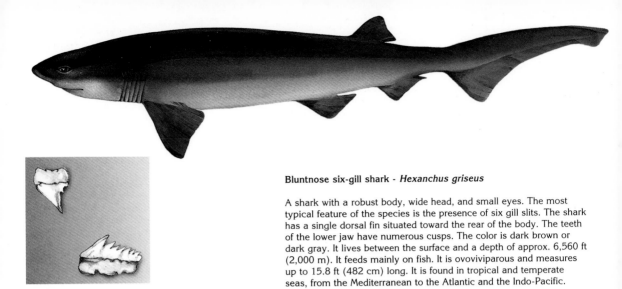

Bluntnose six-gill shark - *Hexanchus griseus*

A shark with a robust body, wide head, and small eyes. The most typical feature of the species is the presence of six gill slits. The shark has a single dorsal fin situated toward the rear of the body. The teeth of the lower jaw have numerous cusps. The color is dark brown or dark gray. It lives between the surface and a depth of approx. 6,560 ft (2,000 m). It feeds mainly on fish. It is ovoviviparous and measures up to 15.8 ft (482 cm) long. It is found in tropical and temperate seas, from the Mediterranean to the Atlantic and the Indo-Pacific.

Broadnose seven-gill shark - *Notorynchus cepedianus*

A shark with a large, rounded or thickset head and small eyes. The most typical feature of the species is the presence of seven gill slits. There is a single dorsal fin, situated toward the rear of the body. The mouth is large and arched. The teeth of the lower jaw are large and have small cusps. The coloring features small black spots. This shark is considered potentially dangerous, but is actively fished for its meat. It lives between the surface and around 160 ft (50 m) deep. It feeds mainly on fish. It is ovoviviparous and measures up to 9.5 ft (290 cm) long. It is found in temperate seas, from the south Atlantic to the central and eastern Indo-Pacific.

ECHINORHINIDAE FAMILY
Bramble shark - *Echinorhinus brucus*

A shark with a thickset, cylindrical body and a short snout. The head is depressed, with an arched mouth. There are two posterior dorsal fins, the first of which is situated opposite the ventral fins. The anal fin is absent. The last gill slit is larger than the others. The body surface is covered with bony shields, with a central spine. The coloring is dark gray, brown, or olive, sometimes with dark spots. It lives near the seabed, between 60 and 2,950 ft (18-900 m) deep. It mainly feeds on fish and smaller sharks. It is ovoviviparous and measures up to 10.2 ft (310 cm) long. It is found in temperate seas, especially in the east Atlantic.

139

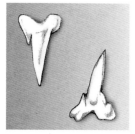

SQUALIDAE FAMILY
Hooktooth dogfish - *Aculeola nigra*

A small shark with a fusiform, slightly compressed body and a short, flattened snout. The mouth is large, with numerous narrow hooked teeth. The two dorsal fins are set close together, and each has small anterior spines that are only partly exposed. The anal fin is absent. The tail fin is asymmetrical, and the upper lobe is well developed. The coloring is black. It lives near the seabed, between 360 and 1,840 ft (110-560 m) deep. It probably feeds on small fish and benthic invertebrates. It is ovoviviparous and measures up to 1.97 ft (60 cm) long. It is found in the east Pacific, along the coasts of Chile and Peru.

Gulper shark - *Centrophorus granulosus*

A shark with a cylindrical body and a moderately long, depressed snout. The eyes are elliptical. There are two dorsal fins, set well apart, with a robust anterior spine. The posterior tip of the pectoral fins is elongated and pointed. The anal fin is absent. The coloring is purplish-brown. It lives near the seabed, between 330-660 ft (100-200 m) and 4,000 ft (1,200 m) deep. It feeds on deep-water fish. It is ovoviviparous and measures up to 4.9 ft (150 cm) long. It is found in temperate seas, from the Atlantic to the west Indian Ocean and Southern Japan.

Black dogfish - *Centroscyllium fabricii*

A small shark with a fusiform but robust, compressed body and a medium-long rounded snout. The mouth is arched, and has tricuspid teeth. There are two dorsal fins, with an anterior spine. The tail fin is well developed, with an elongated upper lobe and a marked notch. The coloring is blackish-brown, with a few photophores. It lives in deep inshore waters at a depth of 590 to 5,250 ft (180-1,600 m). It feeds on crustaceans, cephalopods and, unusually, jellyfish. It is ovoviviparous and measures up to 3.51 ft (107 cm) long. It is found in the north Atlantic, along both the European and the American coasts.

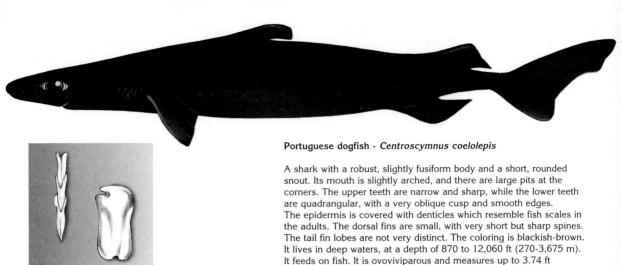

Portuguese dogfish - *Centroscymnus coelolepis*

A shark with a robust, slightly fusiform body and a short, rounded snout. Its mouth is slightly arched, and there are large pits at the corners. The upper teeth are narrow and sharp, while the lower teeth are quadrangular, with a very oblique cusp and smooth edges. The epidermis is covered with denticles which resemble fish scales in the adults. The dorsal fins are small, with very short but sharp spines. The tail fin lobes are not very distinct. The coloring is blackish-brown. It lives in deep waters, at a depth of 870 to 12,060 ft (270-3,675 m). It feeds on fish. It is ovoviviparous and measures up to 3.74 ft (114 cm) long. It is found in the Mediterranean and the Atlantic, especially along the European and African coasts.

Kitefin shark - *Dalatias licha*

A shark with a fairly cylindrical body, a short rounded snout and a depressed head. The eyes are large and greenish. The mouth is surrounded by lips with fringed papillae. The upper teeth are narrow and sharp, and the lower teeth are erect, triangular and serrated. There are two spineless dorsal fins. The anal fin is absent. The coloring is dark brown or blackish. It lives in deep water, often near the seabed, between 660 and 5,900 ft (200-1,800 m) down. It feeds mainly on fish, but also catches cephalopods and crustaceans. It is ovoviviparous and measures up to 5.97 ft (182 cm) long. It is found in warm temperate and tropical seas from the Atlantic to the Indo-Pacific, from Mozambique to Hawaii.

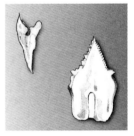

Birdbeak dogfish - *Deania calcea*

A shark with a fusiform body, a very elongated, flattened, spatula-shaped snout, and large eyes. The mouth is slightly arched, and the upper teeth are smaller than the lower teeth. The first dorsal fin is long but low. Both dorsal fins have an anterior spine, which is more developed and curved on the second dorsal fin. The anal fin is absent. The coloring is brownish-gray. It lives between 240 and 4,760 ft (73-1,450 m) deep. It feeds on deep-water fish and prawns. It is ovoviviparous and measures up to 3.64 ft (111 cm) long. It is found in the east Atlantic, S. Africa, and the Pacific, Japan, Australia, and Chile.

Velvet belly - *Etmopterus spinax*

A small shark with a subcylindrical body and a depressed, elongated mouth. The eyes are elliptical. The mouth is slightly arched. The upper teeth have a number of points. The two dorsal fins have an anterior spine. The first dorsal fin is smaller than the second. The anal fin is absent. The coloring is brownish above and black below. It lives near the seabed, mainly between 660 and 1,640 ft (200-500 m) deep, but has also been sighted at 6,560 ft (2,000 m). It feeds on small fish, squid and crustaceans. It is ovoviviparous and measures up to 1.97 ft (60 cm) long. It is found in the Mediterranean and the east Atlantic, from Scandinavia to South Africa.

Cookiecutter shark - *Isistius brasiliensis*

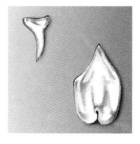

A small shark with a subcylindrical body and a short, rounded snout. The eyes are large. The mouth is rounded, and has thick lips that enable the animal to cling to the epidermis of its prey while its sharp teeth go to work. The dorsal fins are small and attached to the body at the rear, above the ventral fins. The anal fin is absent. The tail fin is almost symmetrical, with well-developed lobes. The coloring is brownish-gray, with a dark stripe in the branchial region. The central part of the abdomen is studded with greenish photophores. It lives in pelagic waters, at a depth of 280 to 11,490 ft (85 to 3,500 m). It feeds on large fish and cetaceans, clinging to their body with its mouth and tearing off pieces of flesh with a typical circular shape. It is ovoviviparous and measures up to 1.6 ft (50 cm) long. It is found in the Atlantic and the Indo-Pacific, from Mauritius to the Galapagos.

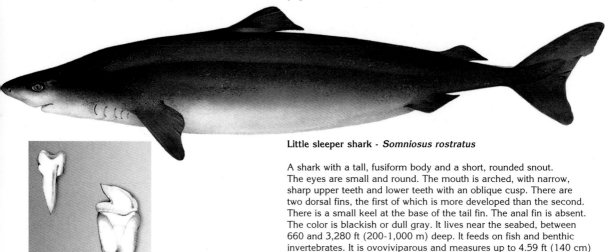

Little sleeper shark - *Somniosus rostratus*

A shark with a tall, fusiform body and a short, rounded snout. The eyes are small and round. The mouth is arched, with narrow, sharp upper teeth and lower teeth with an oblique cusp. There are two dorsal fins, the first of which is more developed than the second. There is a small keel at the base of the tail fin. The anal fin is absent. The color is blackish or dull gray. It lives near the seabed, between 660 and 3,280 ft (200-1,000 m) deep. It feeds on fish and benthic invertebrates. It is ovoviviparous and measures up to 4.59 ft (140 cm) long. It is found in the Mediterranean and the east Atlantic, and along the coasts of Japan.

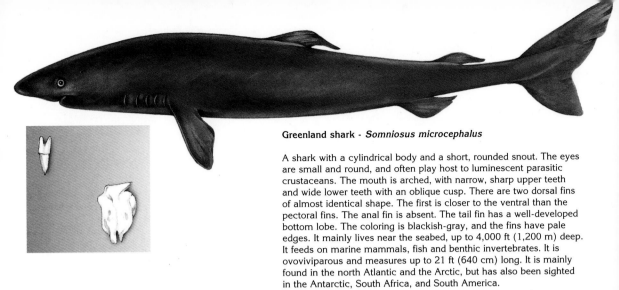

Greenland shark - *Somniosus microcephalus*

A shark with a cylindrical body and a short, rounded snout. The eyes are small and round, and often play host to luminescent parasitic crustaceans. The mouth is arched, with narrow, sharp upper teeth and wide lower teeth with an oblique cusp. There are two dorsal fins of almost identical shape. The first is closer to the ventral than the pectoral fins. The anal fin is absent. The tail fin has a well-developed bottom lobe. The coloring is blackish-gray, and the fins have pale edges. It mainly lives near the seabed, up to 4,000 ft (1,200 m) deep. It feeds on marine mammals, fish and benthic invertebrates. It is ovoviviparous and measures up to 21 ft (640 cm) long. It is mainly found in the north Atlantic and the Arctic, but has also been sighted in the Antarctic, South Africa, and South America.

Spined pygmy shark - *Squaliolus laticaudus*

A very small shark with a fusiform body and a long, conical, pointed snout. The mouth is small, with pointed upper teeth and razor-like lower teeth. In this species, only the first dorsal fin has an anterior spine, while the second is very long and low. The anal fin is absent. The tail fin is almost bilobate. The coloring is blackish, while the edges of the fins are paler. The ventral surface is studded with photophores, which are less frequent on the sides and back. It lives in deep inshore waters, at a depth of 660 to 1,640 ft (200-500 m). It feeds on deep-water fish and squid. It is probably ovoviviparous and measures up to 9.9 ft (25 cm) long, which makes it one of the smallest known sharks. It is found in the Atlantic (Madeira, the Bay of Biscay, Bermuda, Brazil, and Argentina) and the Indo-Pacific (Somalia, Japan, and the Philippines).

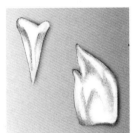

Piked (or spiny) dogfish - *Squalus acanthias*

A shark with a fusiform body and a long, pointed snout. The eyes are well developed. The mouth is wide, and the teeth of both jaws are fairly similar. There are two dorsal fins, each with a robust anterior spine, which is more developed on the second dorsal fin. The anal fin is absent. The tail fin has a lateral keel and a dorsal pits. The coloring is grayish, with white spots on the flanks. It prefers to live near the seabed, at a depth of up to 2,950 ft (900 m). It mainly feeds on fish. It is ovoviviparous and measures up to 5.25 ft (160 cm) long. It is probably the most common shark, present in all seas apart from tropical waters: it cannot survive at temperatures exceeding 59° F (15° C). It can swim for long distances, up to 4,030 mi (6,500 km).

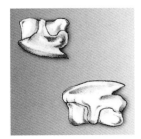

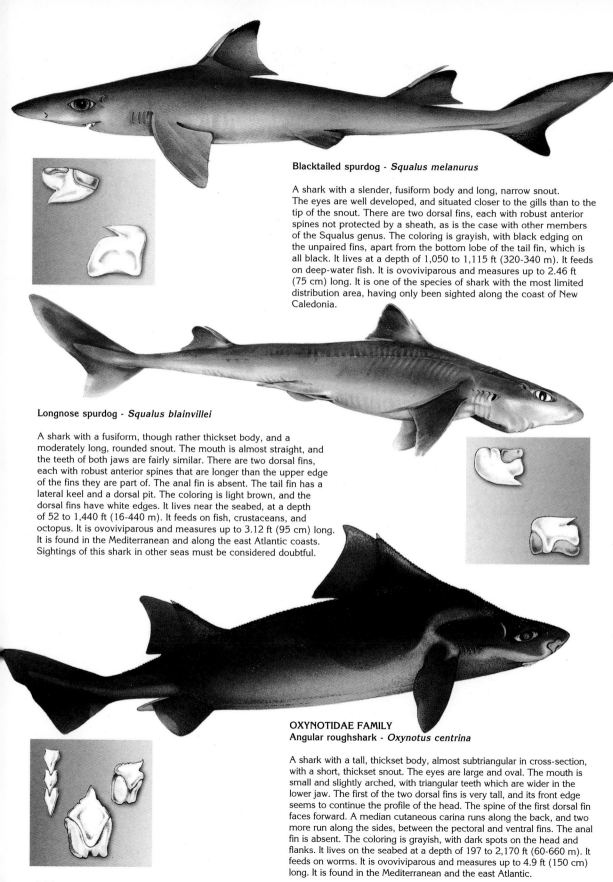

Blacktailed spurdog - *Squalus melanurus*

A shark with a slender, fusiform body and long, narrow snout. The eyes are well developed, and situated closer to the gills than to the tip of the snout. There are two dorsal fins, each with robust anterior spines not protected by a sheath, as is the case with other members of the Squalus genus. The coloring is grayish, with black edging on the unpaired fins, apart from the bottom lobe of the tail fin, which is all black. It lives at a depth of 1,050 to 1,115 ft (320-340 m). It feeds on deep-water fish. It is ovoviviparous and measures up to 2.46 ft (75 cm) long. It is one of the species of shark with the most limited distribution area, having only been sighted along the coast of New Caledonia.

Longnose spurdog - *Squalus blainvillei*

A shark with a fusiform, though rather thickset body, and a moderately long, rounded snout. The mouth is almost straight, and the teeth of both jaws are fairly similar. There are two dorsal fins, each with robust anterior spines that are longer than the upper edge of the fins they are part of. The anal fin is absent. The tail fin has a lateral keel and a dorsal pit. The coloring is light brown, and the dorsal fins have white edges. It lives near the seabed, at a depth of 52 to 1,440 ft (16-440 m). It feeds on fish, crustaceans, and octopus. It is ovoviviparous and measures up to 3.12 ft (95 cm) long. It is found in the Mediterranean and along the east Atlantic coasts. Sightings of this shark in other seas must be considered doubtful.

OXYNOTIDAE FAMILY
Angular roughshark - *Oxynotus centrina*

A shark with a tall, thickset body, almost subtriangular in cross-section, with a short, thickset snout. The eyes are large and oval. The mouth is small and slightly arched, with triangular teeth which are wider in the lower jaw. The first of the two dorsal fins is very tall, and its front edge seems to continue the profile of the head. The spine of the first dorsal fin faces forward. A median cutaneous carina runs along the back, and two more run along the sides, between the pectoral and ventral fins. The anal fin is absent. The coloring is grayish, with dark spots on the head and flanks. It lives on the seabed at a depth of 197 to 2,170 ft (60-660 m). It feeds on worms. It is ovoviviparous and measures up to 4.9 ft (150 cm) long. It is found in the Mediterranean and the east Atlantic.

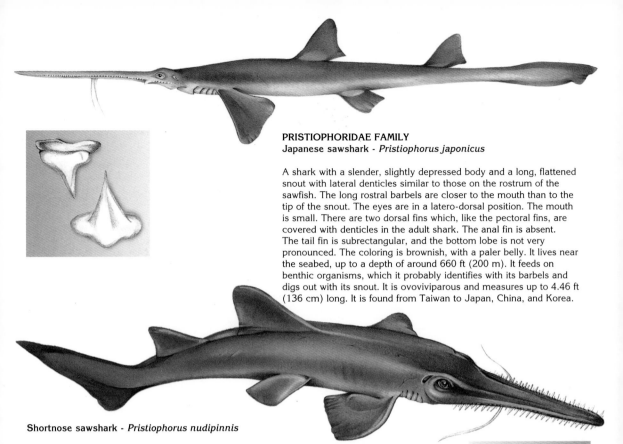

PRISTIOPHORIDAE FAMILY
Japanese sawshark - *Pristiophorus japonicus*

A shark with a slender, slightly depressed body and a long, flattened snout with lateral denticles similar to those on the rostrum of the sawfish. The long rostral barbels are closer to the mouth than to the tip of the snout. The eyes are in a latero-dorsal position. The mouth is small. There are two dorsal fins which, like the pectoral fins, are covered with denticles in the adult shark. The anal fin is absent. The tail fin is subrectangular, and the bottom lobe is not very pronounced. The coloring is brownish, with a paler belly. It lives near the seabed, up to a depth of around 660 ft (200 m). It feeds on benthic organisms, which it probably identifies with its barbels and digs out with its snout. It is ovoviviparous and measures up to 4.46 ft (136 cm) long. It is found from Taiwan to Japan, China, and Korea.

Shortnose sawshark - *Pristiophorus nudipinnis*

A shark with a slender, slightly depressed body and a relatively short, wide snout with pointed lateral denticles. The long rostral barbels are closer to the mouth than to the tip of the snout. The eyes are in a latero-dorsal position. The mouth is small. There are two dorsal fins, not covered with denticles. The anal fin is absent. The tail fin is subrectangular, and the bottom lobe is not very pronounced. The coloring is brownish, with a paler belly. It lives near the seabed, at a depth of 120 to 540 ft (37-165 m). It feeds on benthic organisms, which it probably identifies with its barbels and digs out with its snout. It is ovoviviparous and measures up to 4 ft (122 cm) long. It is found along the southern coast of Australia.

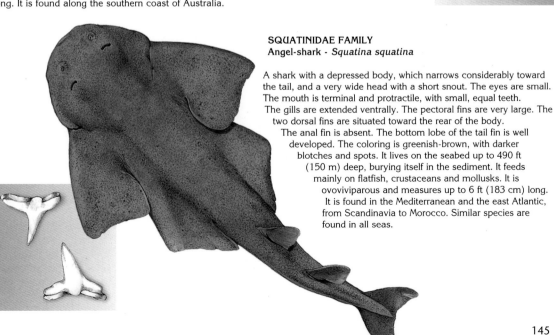

SQUATINIDAE FAMILY
Angel-shark - *Squatina squatina*

A shark with a depressed body, which narrows considerably toward the tail, and a very wide head with a short snout. The eyes are small. The mouth is terminal and protractile, with small, equal teeth. The gills are extended ventrally. The pectoral fins are very large. The two dorsal fins are situated toward the rear of the body. The anal fin is absent. The bottom lobe of the tail fin is well developed. The coloring is greenish-brown, with darker blotches and spots. It lives on the seabed up to 490 ft (150 m) deep, burying itself in the sediment. It feeds mainly on flatfish, crustaceans and mollusks. It is ovoviviparous and measures up to 6 ft (183 cm) long. It is found in the Mediterranean and the east Atlantic, from Scandinavia to Morocco. Similar species are found in all seas.

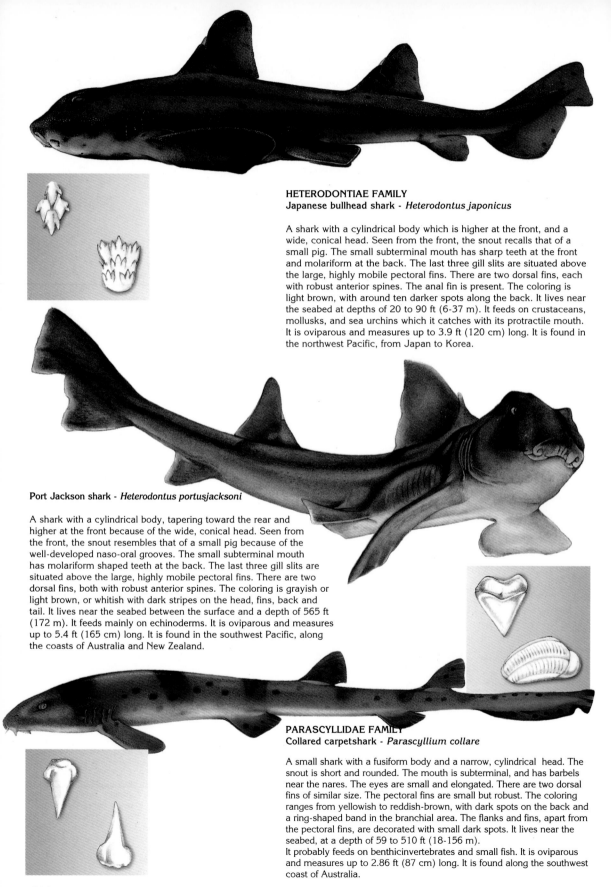

HETERODONTIAE FAMILY
Japanese bullhead shark - *Heterodontus japonicus*

A shark with a cylindrical body which is higher at the front, and a wide, conical head. Seen from the front, the snout recalls that of a small pig. The small subterminal mouth has sharp teeth at the front and molariform at the back. The last three gill slits are situated above the large, highly mobile pectoral fins. There are two dorsal fins, each with robust anterior spines. The anal fin is present. The coloring is light brown, with around ten darker spots along the back. It lives near the seabed at depths of 20 to 90 ft (6-37 m). It feeds on crustaceans, mollusks, and sea urchins which it catches with its protractile mouth. It is oviparous and measures up to 3.9 ft (120 cm) long. It is found in the northwest Pacific, from Japan to Korea.

Port Jackson shark - *Heterodontus portusjacksoni*

A shark with a cylindrical body, tapering toward the rear and higher at the front because of the wide, conical head. Seen from the front, the snout resembles that of a small pig because of the well-developed naso-oral grooves. The small subterminal mouth has molariform shaped teeth at the back. The last three gill slits are situated above the large, highly mobile pectoral fins. There are two dorsal fins, both with robust anterior spines. The coloring is grayish or light brown, or whitish with dark stripes on the head, fins, back and tail. It lives near the seabed between the surface and a depth of 565 ft (172 m). It feeds mainly on echinoderms. It is oviparous and measures up to 5.4 ft (165 cm) long. It is found in the southwest Pacific, along the coasts of Australia and New Zealand.

PARASCYLLIDAE FAMILY
Collared carpetshark - *Parascyllium collare*

A small shark with a fusiform body and a narrow, cylindrical head. The snout is short and rounded. The mouth is subterminal, and has barbels near the nares. The eyes are small and elongated. There are two dorsal fins of similar size. The pectoral fins are small but robust. The coloring ranges from yellowish to reddish-brown, with dark spots on the back and a ring-shaped band in the branchial area. The flanks and fins, apart from the pectoral fins, are decorated with small dark spots. It lives near the seabed, at a depth of 59 to 510 ft (18-156 m).
It probably feeds on benthicinvertebrates and small fish. It is oviparous and measures up to 2.86 ft (87 cm) long. It is found along the southwest coast of Australia.

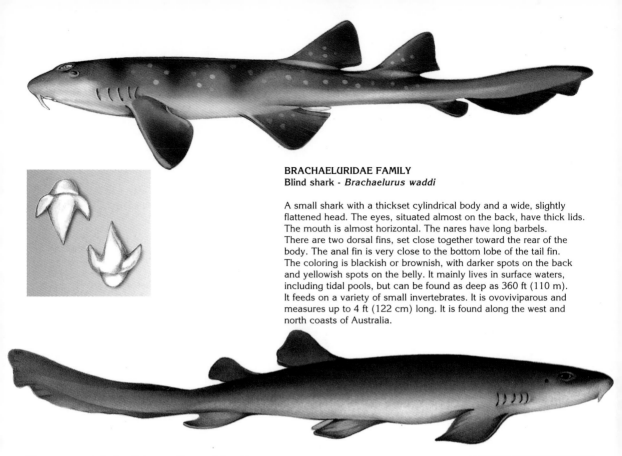

BRACHAELURIDAE FAMILY
Blind shark - *Brachaelurus waddi*

A small shark with a thickset cylindrical body and a wide, slightly flattened head. The eyes, situated almost on the back, have thick lids. The mouth is almost horizontal. The nares have long barbels. There are two dorsal fins, set close together toward the rear of the body. The anal fin is very close to the bottom lobe of the tail fin. The coloring is blackish or brownish, with darker spots on the back and yellowish spots on the belly. It mainly lives in surface waters, including tidal pools, but can be found as deep as 360 ft (110 m). It feeds on a variety of small invertebrates. It is ovoviviparous and measures up to 4 ft (122 cm) long. It is found along the west and north coasts of Australia.

Bluegray carpetshark - *Heteroscyllium colcloughi*

A small shark with a robust subcylindrical body and a rounded snout. The mouth is small, and preceded by well-developed barbels. The first dorsal fin is well developed. The second, smaller dorsal fin is almost opposite the anal fin. The tail fin is fairly long. The dorsal coloring is grayish and the ventral coloring is white. It lives in inshore waters, close to the seabed. It feeds on small benthic invertebrates. It is probably ovoviviparous and measures up to 1.96 ft (60 cm) long. It is found along the Queensland coast of Australia.

ORECTOLOBIDAE FAMILY
Ornate wobbegong - *Orectolobus ornatus*

A shark with a body flattened toward the front, a wide head and a truncated snout. The eyes are situated in a dorso-lateral position. The mouth is wide and almost terminal, and partly covered with ramified nasal barbels. Characteristic dermal lobes are present on either side of the head. The two dorsal fins are situated toward the rear of the body, between the ventral fins and the anal fin, very close to the bottom lobe of the tail fin. The coloring is highly variegated, with numerous irregular dark patches on the back, flecked with pale spots and separated by areas of lighter color. It lives on the seabed in waters close to the surface, and in tidal pools. It feeds on benthicinvertebrates and fish. It is ovoviviparous and measures up to 9.45 ft (288 cm) long. It is found in the west Pacific, from Japan to Australia.

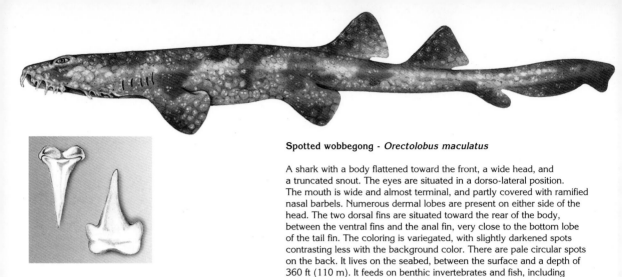

Spotted wobbegong - *Orectolobus maculatus*

A shark with a body flattened toward the front, a wide head, and a truncated snout. The eyes are situated in a dorso-lateral position. The mouth is wide and almost terminal, and partly covered with ramified nasal barbels. Numerous dermal lobes are present on either side of the head. The two dorsal fins are situated toward the rear of the body, between the ventral fins and the anal fin, very close to the bottom lobe of the tail fin. The coloring is variegated, with slightly darkened spots contrasting less with the background color. There are pale circular spots on the back. It lives on the seabed, between the surface and a depth of 360 ft (110 m). It feeds on benthic invertebrates and fish, including crabs, lobsters and octopus. It is ovoviviparous and measures up to 10.5 ft (320 cm) long. It is found in the west Pacific, from Japan to Australia.

HEMYSCYLLIDAE FAMILY
Gray bambooshark - *Chiloscyllium griseum*

A shark with a robust body, a fairly elongated tail and a rounded snout. The eyes are situated in a dorso-lateral position. The nares are subterminal, and supplied with barbels. The dorsal fins are smaller than the ventral fins. The anal fin is almost joined to the tail fin. The coloring is light brown in the adults, while the juveniles have wide dark transverse stripes. It lives in inshore waters, close to the seabed. It mainly feeds on invertebrates. It is oviparous and measures up to 2.42 ft (74 cm) long. It is found in the Indo-Pacific, from the Persian Gulf to Papua New Guinea.

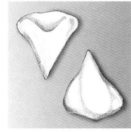

Arabian carpetshark - *Chiloscyllium arabicum*

A shark with a highly fusiform body and tail, and a snout rounded at the front. A lateral carina runs along the abdomen. The mouth is small and almost transverse. The nares are supplied with barbels. The dorsal fins are well developed, and the rear ends are unattached to the body. The coloring is light brown and uniform. It lives on the seabed between 10 and 330 ft (3-100 m) deep. It feeds on benthic fish and invertebrates. It is oviparous and measures up to 2.3 ft (70 cm) long. It is only found in the Persian Gulf.

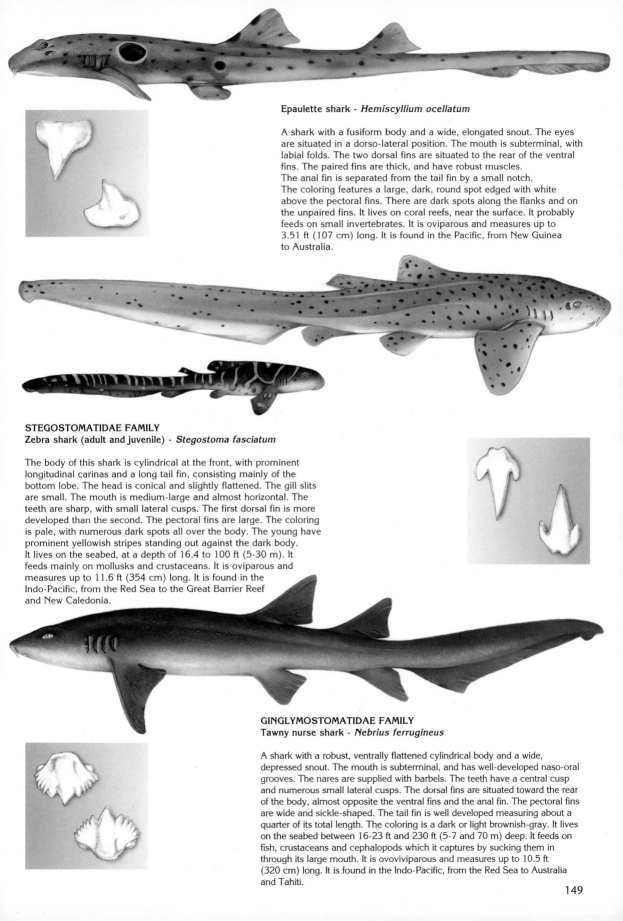

Epaulette shark - *Hemiscyllium ocellatum*

A shark with a fusiform body and a wide, elongated snout. The eyes are situated in a dorso-lateral position. The mouth is subterminal, with labial folds. The two dorsal fins are situated to the rear of the ventral fins. The paired fins are thick, and have robust muscles.
The anal fin is separated from the tail fin by a small notch.
The coloring features a large, dark, round spot edged with white above the pectoral fins. There are dark spots along the flanks and on the unpaired fins. It lives on coral reefs, near the surface. It probably feeds on small invertebrates. It is oviparous and measures up to 3.51 ft (107 cm) long. It is found in the Pacific, from New Guinea to Australia.

STEGOSTOMATIDAE FAMILY
Zebra shark (adult and juvenile) - *Stegostoma fasciatum*

The body of this shark is cylindrical at the front, with prominent longitudinal carinas and a long tail fin, consisting mainly of the bottom lobe. The head is conical and slightly flattened. The gill slits are small. The mouth is medium-large and almost horizontal. The teeth are sharp, with small lateral cusps. The first dorsal fin is more developed than the second. The pectoral fins are large. The coloring is pale, with numerous dark spots all over the body. The young have prominent yellowish stripes standing out against the dark body.
It lives on the seabed, at a depth of 16.4 to 100 ft (5-30 m). It feeds mainly on mollusks and crustaceans. It is oviparous and measures up to 11.6 ft (354 cm) long. It is found in the Indo-Pacific, from the Red Sea to the Great Barrier Reef and New Caledonia.

GINGLYMOSTOMATIDAE FAMILY
Tawny nurse shark - *Nebrius ferrugineus*

A shark with a robust, ventrally flattened cylindrical body and a wide, depressed snout. The mouth is subterminal, and has well-developed naso-oral grooves. The nares are supplied with barbels. The teeth have a central cusp and numerous small lateral cusps. The dorsal fins are situated toward the rear of the body, almost opposite the ventral fins and the anal fin. The pectoral fins are wide and sickle-shaped. The tail fin is well developed measuring about a quarter of its total length. The coloring is a dark or light brownish-gray. It lives on the seabed between 16-23 ft and 230 ft (5-7 and 70 m) deep. It feeds on fish, crustaceans and cephalopods which it captures by sucking them in through its large mouth. It is ovoviviparous and measures up to 10.5 ft (320 cm) long. It is found in the Indo-Pacific, from the Red Sea to Australia and Tahiti.

149

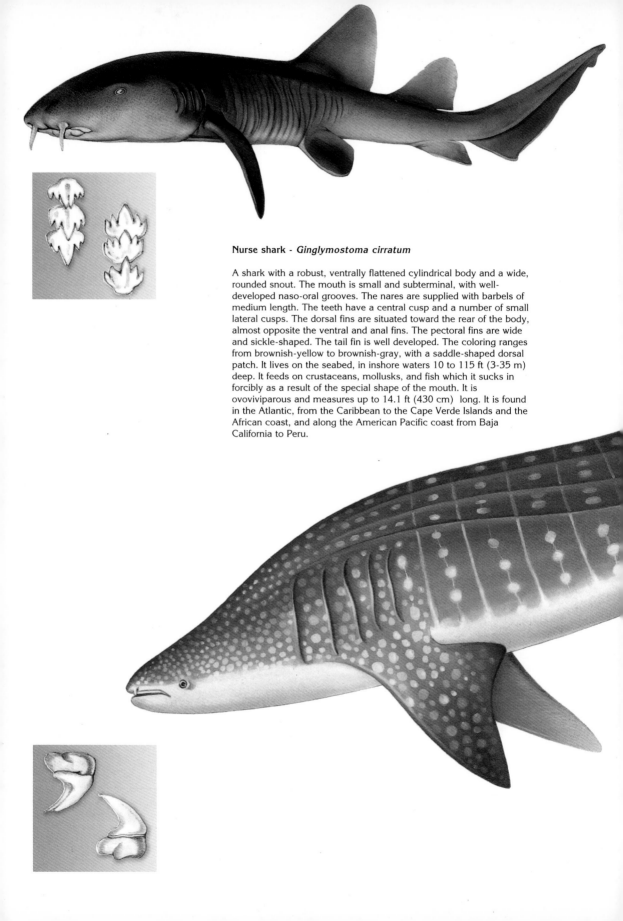

Nurse shark - *Ginglymostoma cirratum*

A shark with a robust, ventrally flattened cylindrical body and a wide, rounded snout. The mouth is small and subterminal, with well-developed naso-oral grooves. The nares are supplied with barbels of medium length. The teeth have a central cusp and a number of small lateral cusps. The dorsal fins are situated toward the rear of the body, almost opposite the ventral and anal fins. The pectoral fins are wide and sickle-shaped. The tail fin is well developed. The coloring ranges from brownish-yellow to brownish-gray, with a saddle-shaped dorsal patch. It lives on the seabed, in inshore waters 10 to 115 ft (3-35 m) deep. It feeds on crustaceans, mollusks, and fish which it sucks in forcibly as a result of the special shape of the mouth. It is ovoviviparous and measures up to 14.1 ft (430 cm) long. It is found in the Atlantic, from the Caribbean to the Cape Verde Islands and the African coast, and along the American Pacific coast from Baja California to Peru.

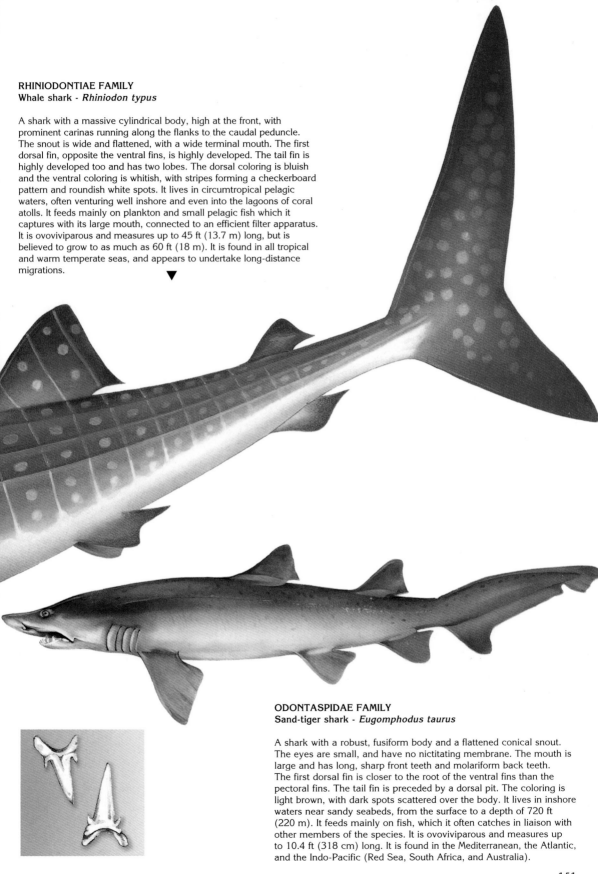

RHINIODONTIAE FAMILY
Whale shark - *Rhiniodon typus*

A shark with a massive cylindrical body, high at the front, with prominent carinas running along the flanks to the caudal peduncle. The snout is wide and flattened, with a wide terminal mouth. The first dorsal fin, opposite the ventral fins, is highly developed. The tail fin is highly developed too and has two lobes. The dorsal coloring is bluish and the ventral coloring is whitish, with stripes forming a checkerboard pattern and roundish white spots. It lives in circumtropical pelagic waters, often venturing well inshore and even into the lagoons of coral atolls. It feeds mainly on plankton and small pelagic fish which it captures with its large mouth, connected to an efficient filter apparatus. It is ovoviviparous and measures up to 45 ft (13.7 m) long, but is believed to grow to as much as 60 ft (18 m). It is found in all tropical and warm temperate seas, and appears to undertake long-distance migrations.

ODONTASPIDAE FAMILY
Sand-tiger shark - *Eugomphodus taurus*

A shark with a robust, fusiform body and a flattened conical snout. The eyes are small, and have no nictitating membrane. The mouth is large and has long, sharp front teeth and molariform back teeth. The first dorsal fin is closer to the root of the ventral fins than the pectoral fins. The tail fin is preceded by a dorsal pit. The coloring is light brown, with dark spots scattered over the body. It lives in inshore waters near sandy seabeds, from the surface to a depth of 720 ft (220 m). It feeds mainly on fish, which it often catches in liaison with other members of the species. It is ovoviviparous and measures up to 10.4 ft (318 cm) long. It is found in the Mediterranean, the Atlantic, and the Indo-Pacific (Red Sea, South Africa, and Australia).

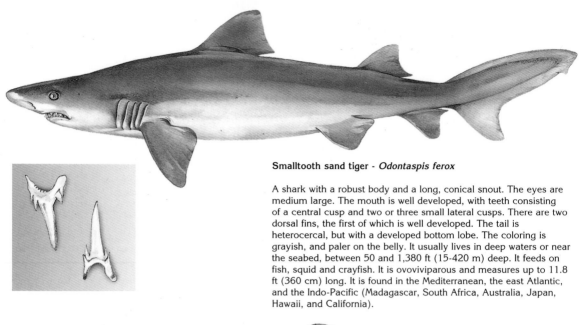

Smalltooth sand tiger - *Odontaspis ferox*

A shark with a robust body and a long, conical snout. The eyes are medium large. The mouth is well developed, with teeth consisting of a central cusp and two or three small lateral cusps. There are two dorsal fins, the first of which is well developed. The tail is heterocercal, but with a developed bottom lobe. The coloring is grayish, and paler on the belly. It usually lives in deep waters or near the seabed, between 50 and 1,380 ft (15-420 m) deep. It feeds on fish, squid and crayfish. It is ovoviviparous and measures up to 11.8 ft (360 cm) long. It is found in the Mediterranean, the east Atlantic, and the Indo-Pacific (Madagascar, South Africa, Australia, Japan, Hawaii, and California).

MITSUKURINIDAE FAMILY
Goblin shark - *Mitsikurina owstoni*

A shark with a flabby, elongated body, easily recognized by the long snout shaped like a flattened blade above a large protractile mouth with long, sharp teeth. The eyes are small. There are two dorsal fins of similar sizes. The tail fin is long, with no bottom lobe. The coloring is whitish-pink. It lives in deep waters, up to a depth of 1,805 ft (550 m). It probably feeds on fish, squid, and crayfish. It is probably ovoviviparous and measures up to 11 ft (335 cm) long. It is found in the Atlantic and the Pacific.

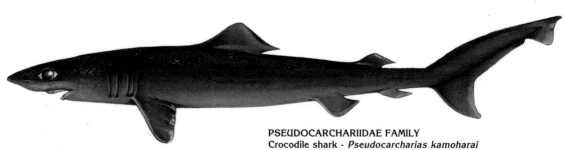

PSEUDOCARCHARIIDAE FAMILY
Crocodile shark - *Pseudocarcharias kamoharai*

A shark with a subcylindrical but fusiform body, with a pointed conical snout. The eyes are quite large. The mouth is large, with pointed front teeth and razor-like back teeth. There are two spineless dorsal fins. The anal fin is present. The caudal peduncle has carinas. The tail fin is asymmetrical, but the ventral lobe is well developed. The coloring is bluish-gray. It lives in ocean waters, between the surface and a depth of 985 ft (300 m). It probably feeds on pelagic deep-water fish, crustaceans, and squid, which it catches with its highly protractile mouth. It is ovoviviparous and is the smallest of the mackerel sharks, measuring up to 3.6 ft (110 cm) long. It is found in the tropical pelagic waters of the Atlantic and the Indo-Pacific, often near islands (Cape Verde, Madagascar, Japan, Hawaii, and the Marquesas).

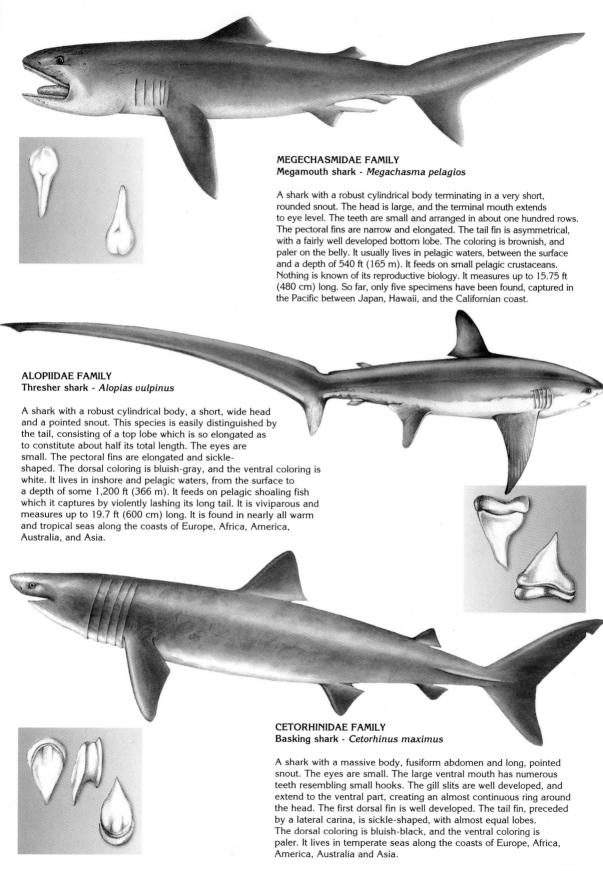

MEGECHASMIDAE FAMILY
Megamouth shark - *Megachasma pelagios*

A shark with a robust cylindrical body terminating in a very short, rounded snout. The head is large, and the terminal mouth extends to eye level. The teeth are small and arranged in about one hundred rows. The pectoral fins are narrow and elongated. The tail fin is asymmetrical, with a fairly well developed bottom lobe. The coloring is brownish, and paler on the belly. It usually lives in pelagic waters, between the surface and a depth of 540 ft (165 m). It feeds on small pelagic crustaceans. Nothing is known of its reproductive biology. It measures up to 15.75 ft (480 cm) long. So far, only five specimens have been found, captured in the Pacific between Japan, Hawaii, and the Californian coast.

ALOPIIDAE FAMILY
Thresher shark - *Alopias vulpinus*

A shark with a robust cylindrical body, a short, wide head and a pointed snout. This species is easily distinguished by the tail, consisting of a top lobe which is so elongated as to constitute about half its total length. The eyes are small. The pectoral fins are elongated and sickle-shaped. The dorsal coloring is bluish-gray, and the ventral coloring is white. It lives in inshore and pelagic waters, from the surface to a depth of some 1,200 ft (366 m). It feeds on pelagic shoaling fish which it captures by violently lashing its long tail. It is viviparous and measures up to 19.7 ft (600 cm) long. It is found in nearly all warm and tropical seas along the coasts of Europe, Africa, America, Australia, and Asia.

CETORHINIDAE FAMILY
Basking shark - *Cetorhinus maximus*

A shark with a massive body, fusiform abdomen and long, pointed snout. The eyes are small. The large ventral mouth has numerous teeth resembling small hooks. The gill slits are well developed, and extend to the ventral part, creating an almost continuous ring around the head. The first dorsal fin is well developed. The tail fin, preceded by a lateral carina, is sickle-shaped, with almost equal lobes. The dorsal coloring is bluish-black, and the ventral coloring is paler. It lives in temperate seas along the coasts of Europe, Africa, America, Australia and Asia.

153

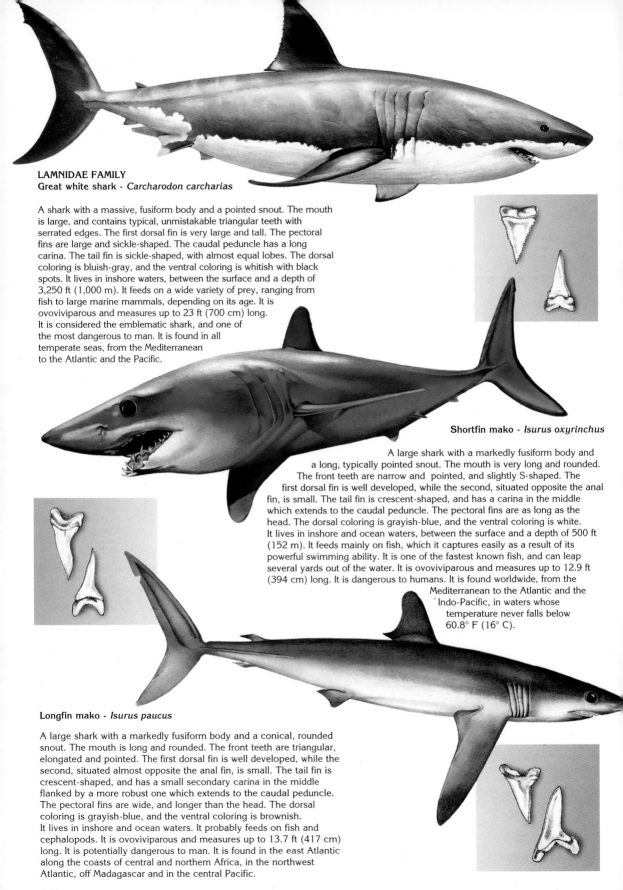

LAMNIDAE FAMILY
Great white shark - *Carcharodon carcharias*

A shark with a massive, fusiform body and a pointed snout. The mouth is large, and contains typical, unmistakable triangular teeth with serrated edges. The first dorsal fin is very large and tall. The pectoral fins are large and sickle-shaped. The caudal peduncle has a long carina. The tail fin is sickle-shaped, with almost equal lobes. The dorsal coloring is bluish-gray, and the ventral coloring is whitish with black spots. It lives in inshore waters, between the surface and a depth of 3,250 ft (1,000 m). It feeds on a wide variety of prey, ranging from fish to large marine mammals, depending on its age. It is ovoviviparous and measures up to 23 ft (700 cm) long. It is considered the emblematic shark, and one of the most dangerous to man. It is found in all temperate seas, from the Mediterranean to the Atlantic and the Pacific.

Shortfin mako - *Isurus oxyrinchus*

A large shark with a markedly fusiform body and a long, typically pointed snout. The mouth is very long and rounded. The front teeth are narrow and pointed, and slightly S-shaped. The first dorsal fin is well developed, while the second, situated opposite the anal fin, is small. The tail fin is crescent-shaped, and has a carina in the middle which extends to the caudal peduncle. The pectoral fins are as long as the head. The dorsal coloring is grayish-blue, and the ventral coloring is white. It lives in inshore and ocean waters, between the surface and a depth of 500 ft (152 m). It feeds mainly on fish, which it captures easily as a result of its powerful swimming ability. It is one of the fastest known fish, and can leap several yards out of the water. It is ovoviviparous and measures up to 12.9 ft (394 cm) long. It is dangerous to humans. It is found worldwide, from the Mediterranean to the Atlantic and the Indo-Pacific, in waters whose temperature never falls below 60.8° F (16° C).

Longfin mako - *Isurus paucus*

A large shark with a markedly fusiform body and a conical, rounded snout. The mouth is long and rounded. The front teeth are triangular, elongated and pointed. The first dorsal fin is well developed, while the second, situated almost opposite the anal fin, is small. The tail fin is crescent-shaped, and has a small secondary carina in the middle flanked by a more robust one which extends to the caudal peduncle. The pectoral fins are wide, and longer than the head. The dorsal coloring is grayish-blue, and the ventral coloring is brownish. It lives in inshore and ocean waters. It probably feeds on fish and cephalopods. It is ovoviviparous and measures up to 13.7 ft (417 cm) long. It is potentially dangerous to man. It is found in the east Atlantic along the coasts of central and northern Africa, in the northwest Atlantic, off Madagascar and in the central Pacific.

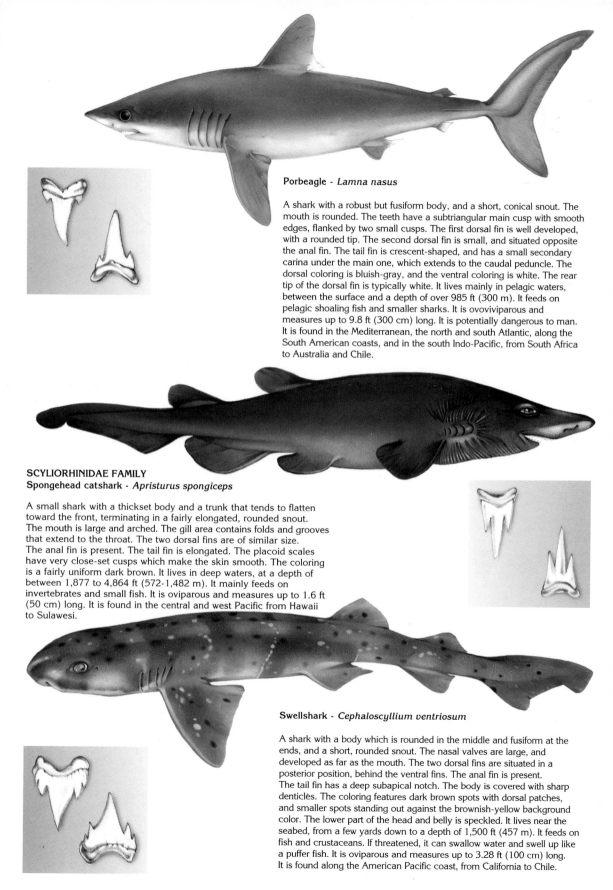

Porbeagle - *Lamna nasus*

A shark with a robust but fusiform body, and a short, conical snout. The mouth is rounded. The teeth have a subtriangular main cusp with smooth edges, flanked by two small cusps. The first dorsal fin is well developed, with a rounded tip. The second dorsal fin is small, and situated opposite the anal fin. The tail fin is crescent-shaped, and has a small secondary carina under the main one, which extends to the caudal peduncle. The dorsal coloring is bluish-gray, and the ventral coloring is white. The rear tip of the dorsal fin is typically white. It lives mainly in pelagic waters, between the surface and a depth of over 985 ft (300 m). It feeds on pelagic shoaling fish and smaller sharks. It is ovoviviparous and measures up to 9.8 ft (300 cm) long. It is potentially dangerous to man. It is found in the Mediterranean, the north and south Atlantic, along the South American coasts, and in the south Indo-Pacific, from South Africa to Australia and Chile.

SCYLIORHINIDAE FAMILY
Spongehead catshark - *Apristurus spongiceps*

A small shark with a thickset body and a trunk that tends to flatten toward the front, terminating in a fairly elongated, rounded snout. The mouth is large and arched. The gill area contains folds and grooves that extend to the throat. The two dorsal fins are of similar size. The anal fin is present. The tail fin is elongated. The placoid scales have very close-set cusps which make the skin smooth. The coloring is a fairly uniform dark brown. It lives in deep waters, at a depth of between 1,877 to 4,864 ft (572-1,482 m). It mainly feeds on invertebrates and small fish. It is oviparous and measures up to 1.6 ft (50 cm) long. It is found in the central and west Pacific from Hawaii to Sulawesi.

Swellshark - *Cephaloscyllium ventriosum*

A shark with a body which is rounded in the middle and fusiform at the ends, and a short, rounded snout. The nasal valves are large, and developed as far as the mouth. The two dorsal fins are situated in a posterior position, behind the ventral fins. The anal fin is present. The tail fin has a deep subapical notch. The body is covered with sharp denticles. The coloring features dark brown spots with dorsal patches, and smaller spots standing out against the brownish-yellow background color. The lower part of the head and belly is speckled. It lives near the seabed, from a few yards down to a depth of 1,500 ft (457 m). It feeds on fish and crustaceans. If threatened, it can swallow water and swell up like a puffer fish. It is oviparous and measures up to 3.28 ft (100 cm) long. It is found along the American Pacific coast, from California to Chile.

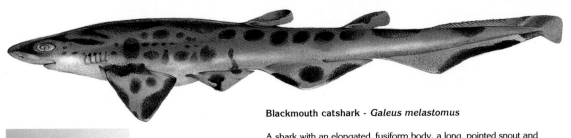

Blackmouth catshark - *Galeus melastomus*

A shark with an elongated, fusiform body, a long, pointed snout and a depressed head. The mouth is medium-large and arched, and the small teeth have a sharp central cusp and small lateral cusps. The dorsal fins are small and subequal. The top lobe of the tail is under-developed, and presents a raised carina consisting of large scales on the dorsal part. The coloring is grayish-brown with irregular dark spots. The rear edge of the dorsal fins and tail fin is white. The mouth is typically black. It lives near the seabed at a depth of 180 to 3,280 ft (55-1,000 m). It feeds on benthic invertebrates and deep-water fish. It is oviparous and measures up to 2.95 ft (90 cm) long. It is found in the Mediterranean and the east Atlantic, from Scandinavia to Senegal.

Small-spotted catshark - *Scyliorhinus canicula*

A shark with a slender body and a pointed snout. The mouth is highly arched, and when closed, the anterior edge is covered by the adjacent nasal valves. The teeth have a median cusp and two smaller lateral cusps. The dorsal fins are set quite a long way apart. The ventral fins are long, narrow and triangular. The apical lobe of the tail fin is well developed. The coloring ranges from reddish-gray to brown, with brown and white patches on the fins as well as the body. It lives on the seabed, from a few yards down to a depth of approximately 1,310 ft (400 m). It feeds on mollusks, crustaceans, and bottom-dwelling fish. It is oviparous and measures up to 3.28 ft (100 cm) long. It is found in the Mediterranean and in the east Atlantic, from Scandinavia to Senegal.

Nursehound - *Scyliorhinus stellaris*

A shark with a more thickset body than the previous species and a wide, slightly flattened head. The mouth is fairly arched; when closed, its anterior edge is not covered by the nasal valves, which are quite distinct. The first dorsal fin is situated immediately behind the ventral fins, while the second dorsal fin is just behind the anal fin. The ventral fins are quadrangular. The coloring is yellowish or grayish-brown, with large purplish-black spots on the fins as well as the body. The belly is whitish. It lives on the seabed, from a few yards down to a depth of approximately 410 ft (125 m). It feeds on mollusks, crustaceans, and bottom-dwelling fish. It is oviparous and measures up to 5.32 ft (162 cm) long. It is found in the Mediterranean and in the east Atlantic, from Scandinavia to Senegal.

PROSCYLLIDAE FAMILY
Pygmy ribbontail shark - *Eridacnis radcliffei*

A shark with a slender, fusiform body and a flattened, rounded snout. The eyes are well developed, and have a nictitating membrane. The mouth is triangular, and the labial folds are almost absent. The two dorsal fins are well developed, unlike the anal fin. The tail fin is practically straight, and almost ribbon-like. The coloring is dark brown, with blackish spots on the dorsal fins and tail fin. It lives on the seabed, at a depth of 230 to 2,515 ft (70-766 m). It feeds on small fish and crustaceans. It is oviparous and measures up to 9.5 in (24 cm) long. It is found in the Indo-Pacific, from the Gulf of Aden to India, the Philippines.

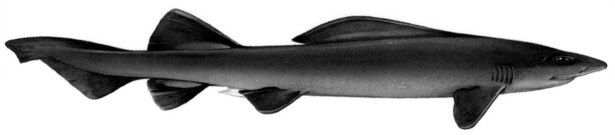

PSEUDOTRIAKIDAE FAMILY
False catshark - *Pseudotriakis microdon*

A shark with a fairly thickset, flabby body and a pointed snout. The eyes are elongated, like a cat's, and have a nictitating membrane. The large, almost triangular mouth contains numerous small but sharp teeth. The first dorsal fin is long, with a carina. The bottom lobe of the tail fin is under-developed. The coloring is grayish-brown, with darker fins. It lives near the seabed, at a depth of 660 to 4,920 ft (200-1,500 m). It feeds on benthic invertebrates and fish. It is ovoviviparous and measures up to 9.69 ft (295 cm) long. It is found in the Atlantic and the Indo-Pacific, with a cluster distribution (Iceland, France, Madeira, the Azores, Cape Verde, Aldabra, Japan, and Hawaii).

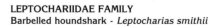

LEPTOCHARIIDAE FAMILY
Barbelled houndshark - *Leptocharias smithii*

A shark with a fusiform body, a short snout and a pointed head. The eyes are oval and have a nictitating membrane. The nares have small barbels. The mouth is long and arched, and the teeth have a central cusp and small lateral points. The dorsal fins are similar; the anal fin is present. The tail fin has an underdeveloped ventral lobe. The coloring is gray or brownish-gray. It lives near the seabed, at a depth of 32 to 250 ft (10-75 m). It feeds on benthic crustaceans and small fish. It is viviparous and measures up to 2.69 ft (82 cm) long. It is found in the Mediterranean and the east Atlantic, from Mauritania to Angola.

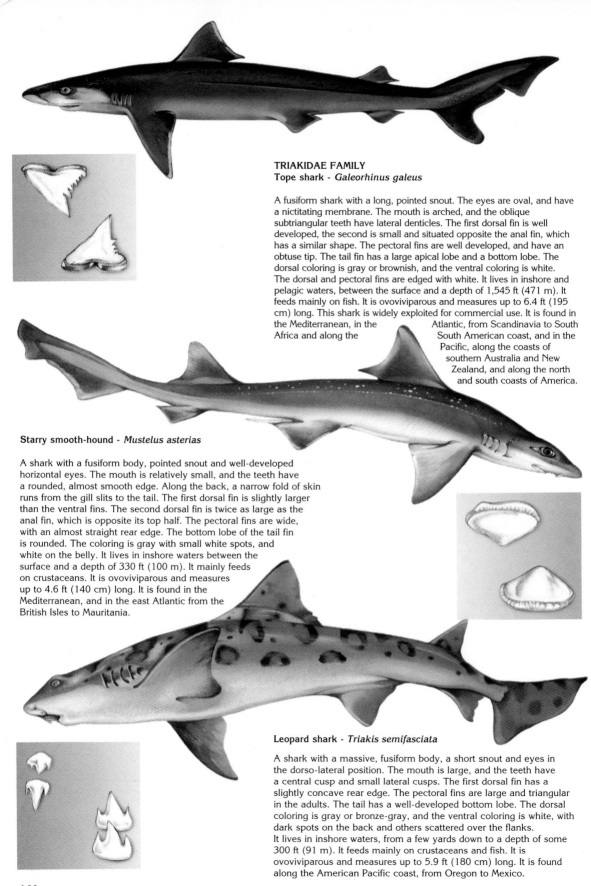

TRIAKIDAE FAMILY
Tope shark - *Galeorhinus galeus*

A fusiform shark with a long, pointed snout. The eyes are oval, and have a nictitating membrane. The mouth is arched, and the oblique subtriangular teeth have lateral denticles. The first dorsal fin is well developed, the second is small and situated opposite the anal fin, which has a similar shape. The pectoral fins are well developed, and have an obtuse tip. The tail fin has a large apical lobe and a bottom lobe. The dorsal coloring is gray or brownish, and the ventral coloring is white. The dorsal and pectoral fins are edged with white. It lives in inshore and pelagic waters, between the surface and a depth of 1,545 ft (471 m). It feeds mainly on fish. It is ovoviviparous and measures up to 6.4 ft (195 cm) long. This shark is widely exploited for commercial use. It is found in the Mediterranean, in the Atlantic, from Scandinavia to South Africa and along the South American coast, and in the Pacific, along the coasts of southern Australia and New Zealand, and along the north and south coasts of America.

Starry smooth-hound - *Mustelus asterias*

A shark with a fusiform body, pointed snout and well-developed horizontal eyes. The mouth is relatively small, and the teeth have a rounded, almost smooth edge. Along the back, a narrow fold of skin runs from the gill slits to the tail. The first dorsal fin is slightly larger than the ventral fins. The second dorsal fin is twice as large as the anal fin, which is opposite its top half. The pectoral fins are wide, with an almost straight rear edge. The bottom lobe of the tail fin is rounded. The coloring is gray with small white spots, and white on the belly. It lives in inshore waters between the surface and a depth of 330 ft (100 m). It mainly feeds on crustaceans. It is ovoviviparous and measures up to 4.6 ft (140 cm) long. It is found in the Mediterranean, and in the east Atlantic from the British Isles to Mauritania.

Leopard shark - *Triakis semifasciata*

A shark with a massive, fusiform body, a short snout and eyes in the dorso-lateral position. The mouth is large, and the teeth have a central cusp and small lateral cusps. The first dorsal fin has a slightly concave rear edge. The pectoral fins are large and triangular in the adults. The tail has a well-developed bottom lobe. The dorsal coloring is gray or bronze-gray, and the ventral coloring is white, with dark spots on the back and others scattered over the flanks. It lives in inshore waters, from a few yards down to a depth of some 300 ft (91 m). It feeds mainly on crustaceans and fish. It is ovoviviparous and measures up to 5.9 ft (180 cm) long. It is found along the American Pacific coast, from Oregon to Mexico.

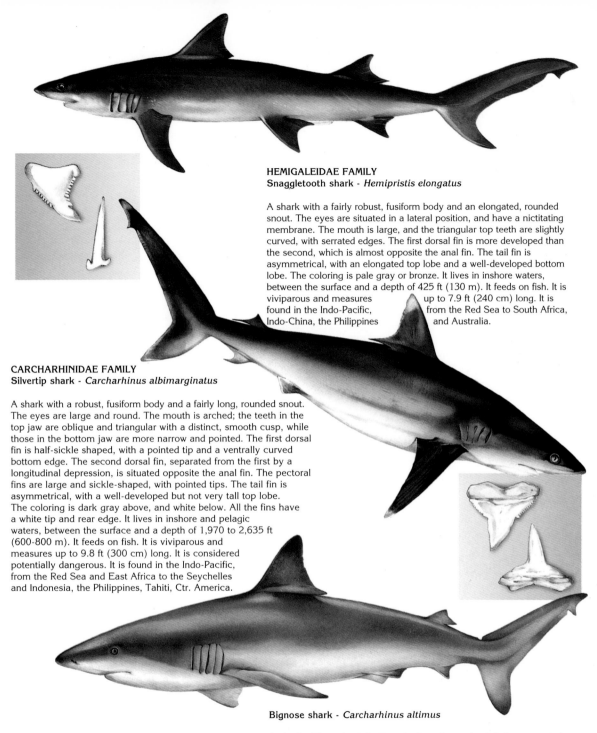

HEMIGALEIDAE FAMILY
Snaggletooth shark - *Hemipristis elongatus*

A shark with a fairly robust, fusiform body and an elongated, rounded snout. The eyes are situated in a lateral position, and have a nictitating membrane. The mouth is large, and the triangular top teeth are slightly curved, with serrated edges. The first dorsal fin is more developed than the second, which is almost opposite the anal fin. The tail fin is asymmetrical, with an elongated top lobe and a well-developed bottom lobe. The coloring is pale gray or bronze. It lives in inshore waters, between the surface and a depth of 425 ft (130 m). It feeds on fish. It is viviparous and measures up to 7.9 ft (240 cm) long. It is found in the Indo-Pacific, from the Red Sea to South Africa, Indo-China, the Philippines and Australia.

CARCHARHINIDAE FAMILY
Silvertip shark - *Carcharhinus albimarginatus*

A shark with a robust, fusiform body and a fairly long, rounded snout. The eyes are large and round. The mouth is arched; the teeth in the top jaw are oblique and triangular with a distinct, smooth cusp, while those in the bottom jaw are more narrow and pointed. The first dorsal fin is half-sickle shaped, with a pointed tip and a ventrally curved bottom edge. The second dorsal fin, separated from the first by a longitudinal depression, is situated opposite the anal fin. The pectoral fins are large and sickle-shaped, with pointed tips. The tail fin is asymmetrical, with a well-developed but not very tall top lobe. The coloring is dark gray above, and white below. All the fins have a white tip and rear edge. It lives in inshore and pelagic waters, between the surface and a depth of 1,970 to 2,635 ft (600-800 m). It feeds on fish. It is viviparous and measures up to 9.8 ft (300 cm) long. It is considered potentially dangerous. It is found in the Indo-Pacific, from the Red Sea and East Africa to the Seychelles and Indonesia, the Philippines, Tahiti, Ctr. America.

Bignose shark - *Carcharhinus altimus*

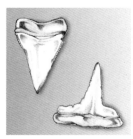

A shark with a robust, fusiform body and a moderately long, rounded snout. The nares have a short lobe. The mouth is arched, with triangular serrated teeth which are narrower and sharper in the lower jaw. The first dorsal fin is fairly tall, sickle-shaped and narrow at the tip. The second dorsal fin is situated opposite the anal fin, and of similar size. The pectoral fins are large and sickle-shaped, with pointed tips. The tail fin is asymmetrical, with a well-developed top lobe. The coloring is bronze-gray above and white below, and the fins have darker tips. It lives near the seabed at a depth of 295 to 1,410 ft (90-430 m). It feeds on fish. It is viviparous and measures up to 9.8 ft (300 cm) long. It is found in warm temperate waters in the Mediterranean, the Atlantic (Central Africa and the Caribbean) and the Indo-Pacific (the Red Sea, Madagascar, India, China, Hawaii, Ctr. America).

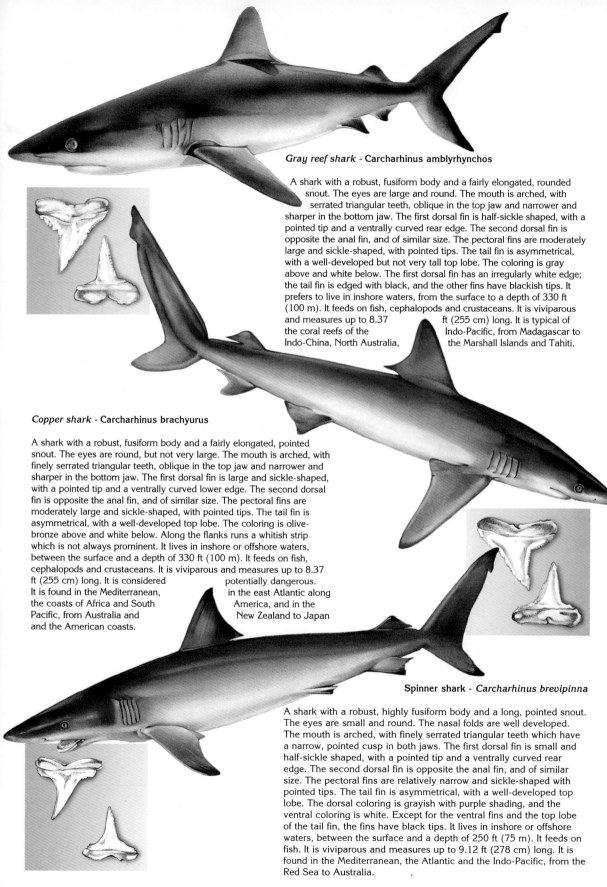

Gray reef shark - Carcharhinus amblyrhynchos

A shark with a robust, fusiform body and a fairly elongated, rounded snout. The eyes are large and round. The mouth is arched, with serrated triangular teeth, oblique in the top jaw and narrower and sharper in the bottom jaw. The first dorsal fin is half-sickle shaped, with a pointed tip and a ventrally curved rear edge. The second dorsal fin is opposite the anal fin, and of similar size. The pectoral fins are moderately large and sickle-shaped, with pointed tips. The tail fin is asymmetrical, with a well-developed but not very tall top lobe. The coloring is gray above and white below. The first dorsal fin has an irregularly white edge; the tail fin is edged with black, and the other fins have blackish tips. It prefers to live in inshore waters, from the surface to a depth of 330 ft (100 m). It feeds on fish, cephalopods and crustaceans. It is viviparous and measures up to 8.37 ft (255 cm) long. It is typical of the coral reefs of the Indo-Pacific, from Madagascar to Indo-China, North Australia, the Marshall Islands and Tahiti.

Copper shark - Carcharhinus brachyurus

A shark with a robust, fusiform body and a fairly elongated, pointed snout. The eyes are round, but not very large. The mouth is arched, with finely serrated triangular teeth, oblique in the top jaw and narrower and sharper in the bottom jaw. The first dorsal fin is large and sickle-shaped, with a pointed tip and a ventrally curved lower edge. The second dorsal fin is opposite the anal fin, and of similar size. The pectoral fins are moderately large and sickle-shaped, with pointed tips. The tail fin is asymmetrical, with a well-developed top lobe. The coloring is olive-bronze above and white below. Along the flanks runs a whitish strip which is not always prominent. It lives in inshore or offshore waters, between the surface and a depth of 330 ft (100 m). It feeds on fish, cephalopods and crustaceans. It is viviparous and measures up to 8.37 ft (255 cm) long. It is considered potentially dangerous. It is found in the Mediterranean, in the east Atlantic along the coasts of Africa and South America, and in the South Pacific, from Australia and New Zealand to Japan and the American coasts.

Spinner shark - Carcharhinus brevipinna

A shark with a robust, highly fusiform body and a long, pointed snout. The eyes are small and round. The nasal folds are well developed. The mouth is arched, with finely serrated triangular teeth which have a narrow, pointed cusp in both jaws. The first dorsal fin is small and half-sickle shaped, with a pointed tip and a ventrally curved rear edge. The second dorsal fin is opposite the anal fin, and of similar size. The pectoral fins are relatively narrow and sickle-shaped with pointed tips. The tail fin is asymmetrical, with a well-developed top lobe. The dorsal coloring is grayish with purple shading, and the ventral coloring is white. Except for the ventral fins and the top lobe of the tail fin, the fins have black tips. It lives in inshore or offshore waters, between the surface and a depth of 250 ft (75 m). It feeds on fish. It is viviparous and measures up to 9.12 ft (278 cm) long. It is found in the Mediterranean, the Atlantic and the Indo-Pacific, from the Red Sea to Australia.

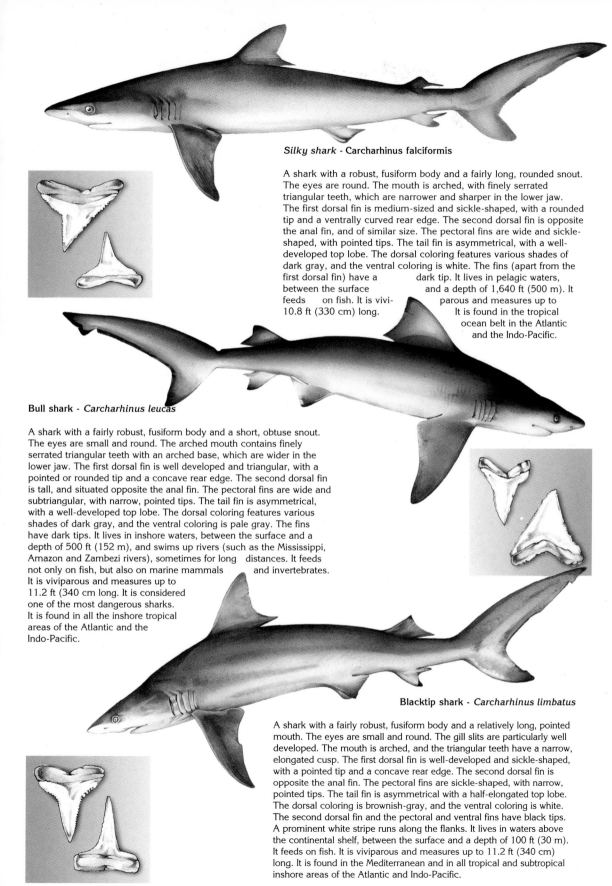

Silky shark - Carcharhinus falciformis

A shark with a robust, fusiform body and a fairly long, rounded snout. The eyes are round. The mouth is arched, with finely serrated triangular teeth, which are narrower and sharper in the lower jaw. The first dorsal fin is medium-sized and sickle-shaped, with a rounded tip and a ventrally curved rear edge. The second dorsal fin is opposite the anal fin, and of similar size. The pectoral fins are wide and sickle-shaped, with pointed tips. The tail fin is asymmetrical, with a well-developed top lobe. The dorsal coloring features various shades of dark gray, and the ventral coloring is white. The fins (apart from the first dorsal fin) have a dark tip. It lives in pelagic waters, between the surface and a depth of 1,640 ft (500 m). It feeds on fish. It is viviparous and measures up to 10.8 ft (330 cm) long. It is found in the tropical ocean belt in the Atlantic and the Indo-Pacific.

Bull shark - *Carcharhinus leucas*

A shark with a fairly robust, fusiform body and a short, obtuse snout. The eyes are small and round. The arched mouth contains finely serrated triangular teeth with an arched base, which are wider in the lower jaw. The first dorsal fin is well developed and triangular, with a pointed or rounded tip and a concave rear edge. The second dorsal fin is tall, and situated opposite the anal fin. The pectoral fins are wide and subtriangular, with narrow, pointed tips. The tail fin is asymmetrical, with a well-developed top lobe. The dorsal coloring features various shades of dark gray, and the ventral coloring is pale gray. The fins have dark tips. It lives in inshore waters, between the surface and a depth of 500 ft (152 m), and swims up rivers (such as the Mississippi, Amazon and Zambezi rivers), sometimes for long distances. It feeds not only on fish, but also on marine mammals and invertebrates. It is viviparous and measures up to 11.2 ft (340 cm long. It is considered one of the most dangerous sharks. It is found in all the inshore tropical areas of the Atlantic and the Indo-Pacific.

Blacktip shark - *Carcharhinus limbatus*

A shark with a fairly robust, fusiform body and a relatively long, pointed mouth. The eyes are small and round. The gill slits are particularly well developed. The mouth is arched, and the triangular teeth have a narrow, elongated cusp. The first dorsal fin is well-developed and sickle-shaped, with a pointed tip and a concave rear edge. The second dorsal fin is opposite the anal fin. The pectoral fins are sickle-shaped, with narrow, pointed tips. The tail fin is asymmetrical with a half-elongated top lobe. The dorsal coloring is brownish-gray, and the ventral coloring is white. The second dorsal fin and the pectoral and ventral fins have black tips. A prominent white stripe runs along the flanks. It lives in waters above the continental shelf, between the surface and a depth of 100 ft (30 m). It feeds on fish. It is viviparous and measures up to 11.2 ft (340 cm) long. It is found in the Mediterranean and in all tropical and subtropical inshore areas of the Atlantic and Indo-Pacific.

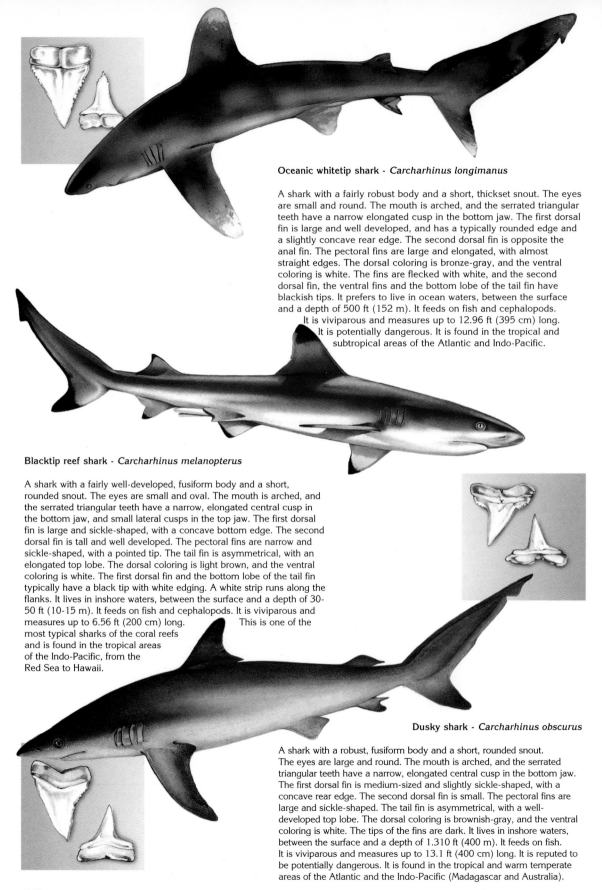

Oceanic whitetip shark - *Carcharhinus longimanus*

A shark with a fairly robust body and a short, thickset snout. The eyes are small and round. The mouth is arched, and the serrated triangular teeth have a narrow elongated cusp in the bottom jaw. The first dorsal fin is large and well developed, and has a typically rounded edge and a slightly concave rear edge. The second dorsal fin is opposite the anal fin. The pectoral fins are large and elongated, with almost straight edges. The dorsal coloring is bronze-gray, and the ventral coloring is white. The fins are flecked with white, and the second dorsal fin, the ventral fins and the bottom lobe of the tail fin have blackish tips. It prefers to live in ocean waters, between the surface and a depth of 500 ft (152 m). It feeds on fish and cephalopods. It is viviparous and measures up to 12.96 ft (395 cm) long. It is potentially dangerous. It is found in the tropical and subtropical areas of the Atlantic and Indo-Pacific.

Blacktip reef shark - *Carcharhinus melanopterus*

A shark with a fairly well-developed, fusiform body and a short, rounded snout. The eyes are small and oval. The mouth is arched, and the serrated triangular teeth have a narrow, elongated central cusp in the bottom jaw, and small lateral cusps in the top jaw. The first dorsal fin is large and sickle-shaped, with a concave bottom edge. The second dorsal fin is tall and well developed. The pectoral fins are narrow and sickle-shaped, with a pointed tip. The tail fin is asymmetrical, with an elongated top lobe. The dorsal coloring is light brown, and the ventral coloring is white. The first dorsal fin and the bottom lobe of the tail fin typically have a black tip with white edging. A white strip runs along the flanks. It lives in inshore waters, between the surface and a depth of 30-50 ft (10-15 m). It feeds on fish and cephalopods. It is viviparous and measures up to 6.56 ft (200 cm) long. This is one of the most typical sharks of the coral reefs and is found in the tropical areas of the Indo-Pacific, from the Red Sea to Hawaii.

Dusky shark - *Carcharhinus obscurus*

A shark with a robust, fusiform body and a short, rounded snout. The eyes are large and round. The mouth is arched, and the serrated triangular teeth have a narrow, elongated central cusp in the bottom jaw. The first dorsal fin is medium-sized and slightly sickle-shaped, with a concave rear edge. The second dorsal fin is small. The pectoral fins are large and sickle-shaped. The tail fin is asymmetrical, with a well-developed top lobe. The dorsal coloring is brownish-gray, and the ventral coloring is white. The tips of the fins are dark. It lives in inshore waters, between the surface and a depth of 1.310 ft (400 m). It feeds on fish. It is viviparous and measures up to 13.1 ft (400 cm) long. It is reputed to be potentially dangerous. It is found in the tropical and warm temperate areas of the Atlantic and the Indo-Pacific (Madagascar and Australia).

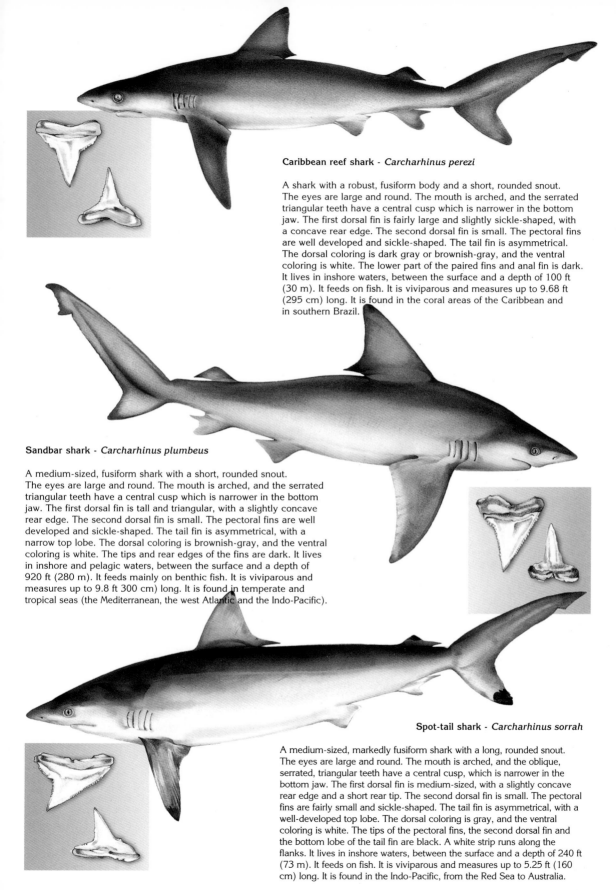

Caribbean reef shark - *Carcharhinus perezi*

A shark with a robust, fusiform body and a short, rounded snout. The eyes are large and round. The mouth is arched, and the serrated triangular teeth have a central cusp which is narrower in the bottom jaw. The first dorsal fin is fairly large and slightly sickle-shaped, with a concave rear edge. The second dorsal fin is small. The pectoral fins are well developed and sickle-shaped. The tail fin is asymmetrical. The dorsal coloring is dark gray or brownish-gray, and the ventral coloring is white. The lower part of the paired fins and anal fin is dark. It lives in inshore waters, between the surface and a depth of 100 ft (30 m). It feeds on fish. It is viviparous and measures up to 9.68 ft (295 cm) long. It is found in the coral areas of the Caribbean and in southern Brazil.

Sandbar shark - *Carcharhinus plumbeus*

A medium-sized, fusiform shark with a short, rounded snout. The eyes are large and round. The mouth is arched, and the serrated triangular teeth have a central cusp which is narrower in the bottom jaw. The first dorsal fin is tall and triangular, with a slightly concave rear edge. The second dorsal fin is small. The pectoral fins are well developed and sickle-shaped. The tail fin is asymmetrical, with a narrow top lobe. The dorsal coloring is brownish-gray, and the ventral coloring is white. The tips and rear edges of the fins are dark. It lives in inshore and pelagic waters, between the surface and a depth of 920 ft (280 m). It feeds mainly on benthic fish. It is viviparous and measures up to 9.8 ft 300 cm) long. It is found in temperate and tropical seas (the Mediterranean, the west Atlantic and the Indo-Pacific).

Spot-tail shark - *Carcharhinus sorrah*

A medium-sized, markedly fusiform shark with a long, rounded snout. The eyes are large and round. The mouth is arched, and the oblique, serrated, triangular teeth have a central cusp, which is narrower in the bottom jaw. The first dorsal fin is medium-sized, with a slightly concave rear edge and a short rear tip. The second dorsal fin is small. The pectoral fins are fairly small and sickle-shaped. The tail fin is asymmetrical, with a well-developed top lobe. The dorsal coloring is gray, and the ventral coloring is white. The tips of the pectoral fins, the second dorsal fin and the bottom lobe of the tail fin are black. A white strip runs along the flanks. It lives in inshore waters, between the surface and a depth of 240 ft (73 m). It feeds on fish. It is viviparous and measures up to 5.25 ft (160 cm) long. It is found in the Indo-Pacific, from the Red Sea to Australia.

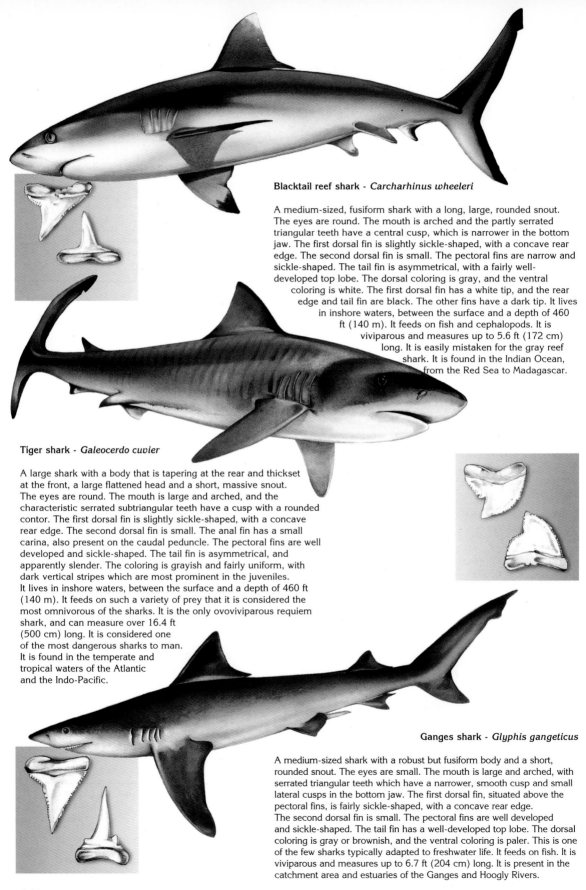

Blacktail reef shark - *Carcharhinus wheeleri*

A medium-sized, fusiform shark with a long, large, rounded snout. The eyes are round. The mouth is arched and the partly serrated triangular teeth have a central cusp, which is narrower in the bottom jaw. The first dorsal fin is slightly sickle-shaped, with a concave rear edge. The second dorsal fin is small. The pectoral fins are narrow and sickle-shaped. The tail fin is asymmetrical, with a fairly well-developed top lobe. The dorsal coloring is gray, and the ventral coloring is white. The first dorsal fin has a white tip, and the rear edge and tail fin are black. The other fins have a dark tip. It lives in inshore waters, between the surface and a depth of 460 ft (140 m). It feeds on fish and cephalopods. It is viviparous and measures up to 5.6 ft (172 cm) long. It is easily mistaken for the gray reef shark. It is found in the Indian Ocean, from the Red Sea to Madagascar.

Tiger shark - *Galeocerdo cuvier*

A large shark with a body that is tapering at the rear and thickset at the front, a large flattened head and a short, massive snout. The eyes are round. The mouth is large and arched, and the characteristic serrated subtriangular teeth have a cusp with a rounded contor. The first dorsal fin is slightly sickle-shaped, with a concave rear edge. The second dorsal fin is small. The anal fin has a small carina, also present on the caudal peduncle. The pectoral fins are well developed and sickle-shaped. The tail fin is asymmetrical, and apparently slender. The coloring is grayish and fairly uniform, with dark vertical stripes which are most prominent in the juveniles. It lives in inshore waters, between the surface and a depth of 460 ft (140 m). It feeds on such a variety of prey that it is considered the most omnivorous of the sharks. It is the only ovoviviparous requiem shark, and can measure over 16.4 ft (500 cm) long. It is considered one of the most dangerous sharks to man. It is found in the temperate and tropical waters of the Atlantic and the Indo-Pacific.

Ganges shark - *Glyphis gangeticus*

A medium-sized shark with a robust but fusiform body and a short, rounded snout. The eyes are small. The mouth is large and arched, with serrated triangular teeth which have a narrower, smooth cusp and small lateral cusps in the bottom jaw. The first dorsal fin, situated above the pectoral fins, is fairly sickle-shaped, with a concave rear edge. The second dorsal fin is small. The pectoral fins are well developed and sickle-shaped. The tail fin has a well-developed top lobe. The dorsal coloring is gray or brownish, and the ventral coloring is paler. This is one of the few sharks typically adapted to freshwater life. It feeds on fish. It is viviparous and measures up to 6.7 ft (204 cm) long. It is present in the catchment area and estuaries of the Ganges and Hoogly Rivers.

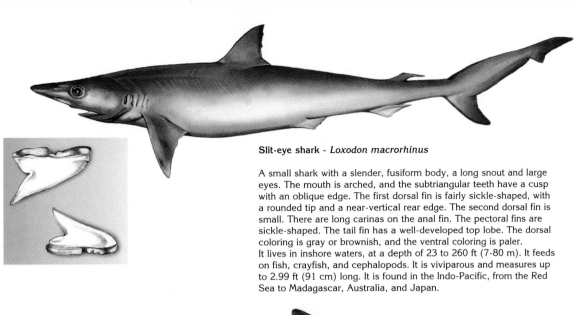

Slit-eye shark - *Loxodon macrorhinus*

A small shark with a slender, fusiform body, a long snout and large eyes. The mouth is arched, and the subtriangular teeth have a cusp with an oblique edge. The first dorsal fin is fairly sickle-shaped, with a rounded tip and a near-vertical rear edge. The second dorsal fin is small. There are long carinas on the anal fin. The pectoral fins are sickle-shaped. The tail fin has a well-developed top lobe. The dorsal coloring is gray or brownish, and the ventral coloring is paler.
It lives in inshore waters, at a depth of 23 to 260 ft (7-80 m). It feeds on fish, crayfish, and cephalopods. It is viviparous and measures up to 2.99 ft (91 cm) long. It is found in the Indo-Pacific, from the Red Sea to Madagascar, Australia, and Japan.

Lemon shark - *Negaprion brevirostris*

A shark with a robust, fusiform body, a wide, flattened head and a short snout. The eyes are small. The mouth is arched, and the subtriangular teeth have a cusp with a smooth, oblique edge. The two dorsal fins are fairly similar and slightly sickle-shaped, with a somewhat concave rear edge. The pectoral fins are subtriangular. The tail fin has a well-developed top lobe with a deep subapical notch. The dorsal coloring is pale brownish-yellow, and the ventral coloring is paler. It lives in inshore waters, between the surface and a depth of 300 ft (92 m), and is sometimes found in river estuaries.
It mainly feeds on fish. It is viviparous and measures up to 11.16 ft (340 cm) long. It is found in the east Atlantic (Senegal and the Ivory Coast), the west Atlantic, from New Jersey to Brazil, and the east Pacific, from California to Ecuador.

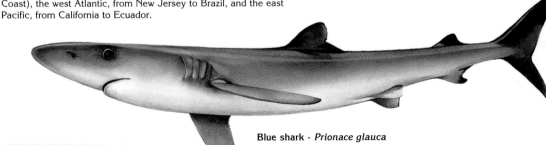

Blue shark - *Prionace glauca*

A shark with a highly fusiform body and a long, sharp snout. The eyes are large, and have a nictitating membrane. The mouth is arched, and the subtriangular teeth are wider and oblique in the top jaw. The first dorsal fin is small, with a rounded tip. The pectoral fins are long and sickle-shaped, but the edges are almost straight. The tail fin is asymmetrical, with acute lobes. The dorsal coloring is greenish-blue, and the ventral coloring is white. It lives in inshore and pelagic waters, between the surface and a depth of 500 ft (152 m). It feeds on fish and benthic invertebrates. It is viviparous and measures up to 12.57 ft (383 cm) long. It is found in temperate and tropical waters, from the Mediterranean to the Atlantic and the Indo-Pacific.

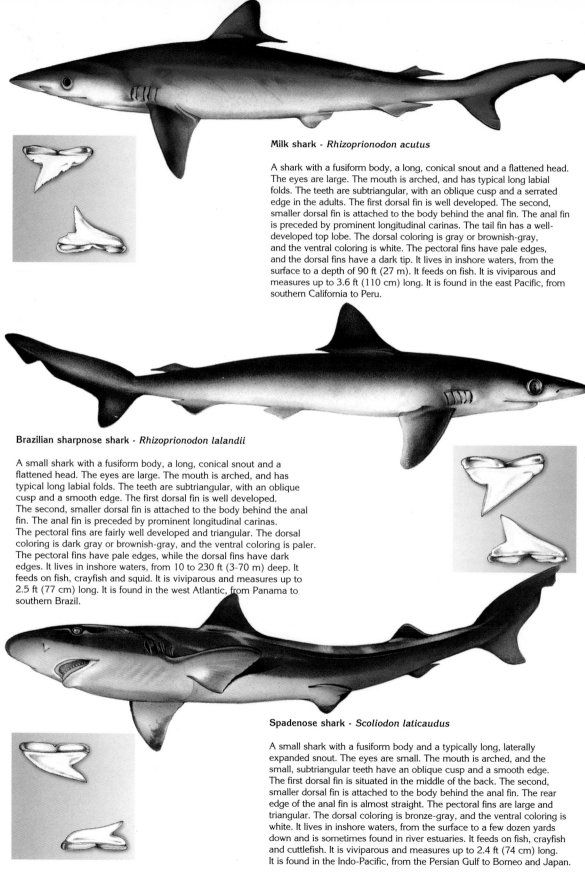

Milk shark - *Rhizoprionodon acutus*

A shark with a fusiform body, a long, conical snout and a flattened head. The eyes are large. The mouth is arched, and has typical long labial folds. The teeth are subtriangular, with an oblique cusp and a serrated edge in the adults. The first dorsal fin is well developed. The second, smaller dorsal fin is attached to the body behind the anal fin. The anal fin is preceded by prominent longitudinal carinas. The tail fin has a well-developed top lobe. The dorsal coloring is gray or brownish-gray, and the ventral coloring is white. The pectoral fins have pale edges, and the dorsal fins have a dark tip. It lives in inshore waters, from the surface to a depth of 90 ft (27 m). It feeds on fish. It is viviparous and measures up to 3.6 ft (110 cm) long. It is found in the east Pacific, from southern California to Peru.

Brazilian sharpnose shark - *Rhizoprionodon lalandii*

A small shark with a fusiform body, a long, conical snout and a flattened head. The eyes are large. The mouth is arched, and has typical long labial folds. The teeth are subtriangular, with an oblique cusp and a smooth edge. The first dorsal fin is well developed. The second, smaller dorsal fin is attached to the body behind the anal fin. The anal fin is preceded by prominent longitudinal carinas. The pectoral fins are fairly well developed and triangular. The dorsal coloring is dark gray or brownish-gray, and the ventral coloring is paler. The pectoral fins have pale edges, while the dorsal fins have dark edges. It lives in inshore waters, from 10 to 230 ft (3-70 m) deep. It feeds on fish, crayfish and squid. It is viviparous and measures up to 2.5 ft (77 cm) long. It is found in the west Atlantic, from Panama to southern Brazil.

Spadenose shark - *Scoliodon laticaudus*

A small shark with a fusiform body and a typically long, laterally expanded snout. The eyes are small. The mouth is arched, and the small, subtriangular teeth have an oblique cusp and a smooth edge. The first dorsal fin is situated in the middle of the back. The second, smaller dorsal fin is attached to the body behind the anal fin. The rear edge of the anal fin is almost straight. The pectoral fins are large and triangular. The dorsal coloring is bronze-gray, and the ventral coloring is white. It lives in inshore waters, from the surface to a few dozen yards down and is sometimes found in river estuaries. It feeds on fish, crayfish and cuttlefish. It is viviparous and measures up to 2.4 ft (74 cm) long. It is found in the Indo-Pacific, from the Persian Gulf to Borneo and Japan.

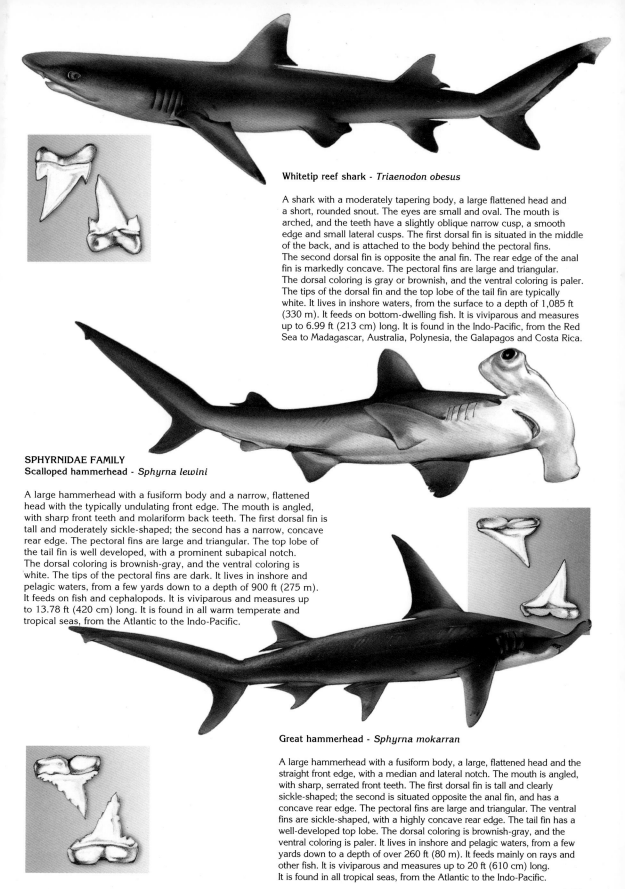

Whitetip reef shark - *Triaenodon obesus*

A shark with a moderately tapering body, a large flattened head and a short, rounded snout. The eyes are small and oval. The mouth is arched, and the teeth have a slightly oblique narrow cusp, a smooth edge and small lateral cusps. The first dorsal fin is situated in the middle of the back, and is attached to the body behind the pectoral fins. The second dorsal fin is opposite the anal fin. The rear edge of the anal fin is markedly concave. The pectoral fins are large and triangular. The dorsal coloring is gray or brownish, and the ventral coloring is paler. The tips of the dorsal fin and the top lobe of the tail fin are typically white. It lives in inshore waters, from the surface to a depth of 1,085 ft (330 m). It feeds on bottom-dwelling fish. It is viviparous and measures up to 6.99 ft (213 cm) long. It is found in the Indo-Pacific, from the Red Sea to Madagascar, Australia, Polynesia, the Galapagos and Costa Rica.

SPHYRNIDAE FAMILY
Scalloped hammerhead - *Sphyrna lewini*

A large hammerhead with a fusiform body and a narrow, flattened head with the typically undulating front edge. The mouth is angled, with sharp front teeth and molariform back teeth. The first dorsal fin is tall and moderately sickle-shaped; the second has a narrow, concave rear edge. The pectoral fins are large and triangular. The top lobe of the tail fin is well developed, with a prominent subapical notch. The dorsal coloring is brownish-gray, and the ventral coloring is white. The tips of the pectoral fins are dark. It lives in inshore and pelagic waters, from a few yards down to a depth of 900 ft (275 m). It feeds on fish and cephalopods. It is viviparous and measures up to 13.78 ft (420 cm) long. It is found in all warm temperate and tropical seas, from the Atlantic to the Indo-Pacific.

Great hammerhead - *Sphyrna mokarran*

A large hammerhead with a fusiform body, a large, flattened head and the straight front edge, with a median and lateral notch. The mouth is angled, with sharp, serrated front teeth. The first dorsal fin is tall and clearly sickle-shaped; the second is situated opposite the anal fin, and has a concave rear edge. The pectoral fins are large and triangular. The ventral fins are sickle-shaped, with a highly concave rear edge. The tail fin has a well-developed top lobe. The dorsal coloring is brownish-gray, and the ventral coloring is paler. It lives in inshore and pelagic waters, from a few yards down to a depth of over 260 ft (80 m). It feeds mainly on rays and other fish. It is viviparous and measures up to 20 ft (610 cm) long. It is found in all tropical seas, from the Atlantic to the Indo-Pacific.

167

168 The grey reef shark (Carcharhinus amblyrhynchos) *is perhaps one of the most typical species* of the coral reefs of the Indopacific, where it has been observed by thousands of divers.

ILLUSTRATION CREDITS